The Mail-Coach Men

The Mail-Coach Men

of the late Eighteenth Century

by

EDMUND VALE

CASSELL · LONDON

CASSELL & COMPANY LTD
35 Red Lion Square · London W C 1
and at
MELBOURNE · SYDNEY · TORONTO · CAPE TOWN
JOHANNESBURG · AUCKLAND

Set in 11 on 12 pt. Bembo type and
printed in Great Britain by
Cox & Wyman Ltd., London, Fakenham and Reading
F.1159

To
RUSSELL AND RICHENDA ACHESON

Then the pace of the Mail was always good. Again, the Mail was not encumbered with huge piles of massive black boxes, fantastically worked with brass nails, belonging to the lady passenger inside; and last, not least, there was a glorious autocratical independence when you felt that every vehicle on the road made way for the Royal Mail.

LORD WILLIAM PITT LENNOX

Contents

		page
I	The Sinews of Glamour	1
II	John Palmer	10
III	The Mail-Coach Concern	39
IV	Letters to the Postmasters-General (1) 1794	60
V	Letters to the Postmasters-General (2) 1795	102
VI	Letters to the Postmasters-General (3) January to June, 1796	148
VII	Letters to Mail-Coach Personnel and others (1) June to August, 1796	160
VIII	Letters to Mail-Coach Personnel and others (2) August to November, 1796	188
IX	Miscellany	208
X	Time-Bills of 1797	221
	List of the Time-Bills	227
XI	Instructions and Circulars, 1792 to 1817	262
XII	Palmer's Last Man	282
	A Short Bibliography	287
	Index	289

List of Illustrations

facing page

The easy way with young post-boys   28

An undated print showing an almost daily occurrence before the
introduction of the mail-coach.

A stage-coach with basket to accommodate passengers as well as
luggage.   From a painting by Cordery   29

The vehicle is in separate units, the body being slung between the
coachman's box and the frame holding the wicker-work basket.
Seven passengers are visible and there are probably two more inside.
The proprietors would not object to as many more as cared to rough
ride among the luggage and parcels in the basket. The basket coach
was introduced fairly early in the 18th century.

The first mail-coach, 1784   44

The first vehicles were ordinary stage-coaches. The guard is seen
sitting beside the driver with his blunderbuss slung over his shoulder
and the paintwork shows a mixture of official and private emblems—
the royal arms over the name of Fromont of the King's Head, Thatcham,
flanked by Wilson's Swan with Two Necks.

An early patent mail-coach   45

It is seen driving through St George's Circus, Southwark. The
drawing of the coach is sadly deficient in detail.

Besant's patent mail-coach   76

The drawing accompanying his patent specification of 1786. It shows
lock-release (A.B.C.) and self-acting band-brake (D.E.F.).

xi

facing page

Mail-coach of post-Vidler design   76

The new standard pattern approved after Vidler's contract had expired in 1836 and hardly varied until the end of the mail-coach era. No brake was fitted.

Sir Francis Freeling, Bart., Secretary to the Post Office 1798–1836. From a painting by G. Jones, engraved by C. Turner and published in 1834   77

John Palmer aged about seventeen. A painting in the Council Chamber at Bath by William Hoare   77

Guard's blunderbuss, pistols, time-piece, pouch and bag (?) for powder-horn and shot   92

An early private bag: the pattern is similar to that of the bye- or strap bag   92

The bag, kindly lent for use as an illustration by Mr Clough Williams-Ellis of Brondanw, Merioneth, has been in his family since first granted by the Post Office to a forebear in the late 18th or early 19th century. Its plate bears the name of the house.

A Coach snow-bound. By James Pollard. Print dated 1825   93

The guard rides off on one of the leading pair with mail-bags and time-piece. Outside passengers help the coachman to take out the wheel horses, while an 'inside' is content to advise on the situation.

The Leeds Mails passing midway. By Charles Cooper Henderson. Print dated 1837   140

The York Mail. The horsekeepers put to a fresh team at the Marquis of Granby Inn   141

The stage-coach, Cheltenham 'Magnet', is forced to give way to the Mail   156

Its driver takes full advantage of the rule to avoid loose stones. The picture by C. B. Newhouse is called suggestively 'A passing remark'. Print dated 1834.

A midnight change. The coachman unhooking the leaders, the guard producing the horsekeeper. By C. B. Newhouse   157

LIST OF ILLUSTRATIONS

facing page

The Poole and Exeter Mails loading at the Gloucester Coffee House with bags brought from the G.P.O. by mail-cart   188

All the West Country Mails started from Piccadilly. The mail-carts were provided and horsed by the contractors. The nearest bears the name 'W. J. Waterhouse, Lad Lane' (successor to Wilson), the next 'Thos. Ince & Co, Bell and Crown, Holborn'. By James Pollard, print dated 1828.

A time-bill of 1797   189

It is made out for the information of Lord Chesterfield with the scheduled times of arrival only, filled in.

The guard insists on the right of the Royal Mail to make all other traffic give way. Lithograph by J. Sturgess   204

Late for the Mail   205

From Fores's *Coaching Incidents*. Print dated 1848.

The illustrations mentioned below are reproduced by courtesy of the persons stated from prints and photographs in their possession, and their assistance is gratefully acknowledged:

The Postmaster-General: pp. 44, 76 (*below*), 92 (*above*), 93, 140, 141, 188, 205.

The Director of the Borough of Tottenham Libraries and Museum: pp. 28, 77 (*left*), 156, 157, 189.

The Committee of the Victoria Art Gallery, Bath: p. 77 (*right*).

The Comptroller-General of the Patent Office: p. 76 (*above*).

Maps

	pages
The mail-coach routes of the 18th century	xvi-xvii
Routes of the Glasgow and Edinburgh Mails	101
Bramham Cross-roads	143
The Scarborough and Whitby Mails	258

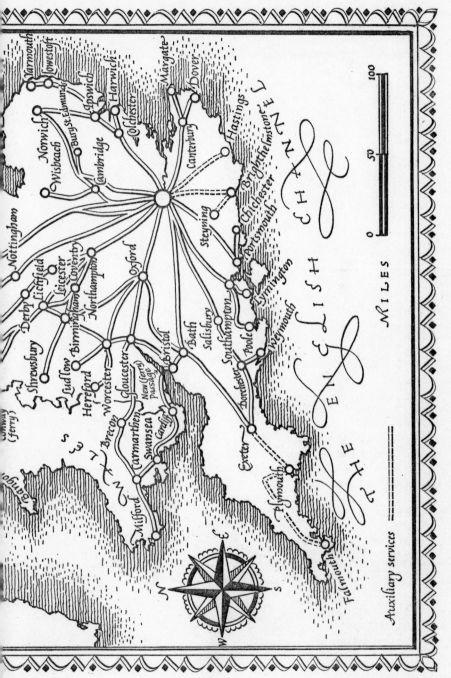

THE ENGLISH CHANNEL

MILES

Auxiliary services

Drawn by Jack Trodd

Returning Thanks

THE opportunity to render in print for the first time the principal letters of the incomparable Thomas Hasker was made possible to me by helpers whose kindness I should like to pay tribute to here. To Mr E. C. Baker, Archivist of the General Post Office, and Mr G. W. P. Devenport, of the Record Room there, who arranged for me to have the relevant documents made available on Post Office premises nearer home. To Mr M. Morgan, Head Postmaster of Bangor and his courteous staff, who gave me a delightful room to work in, overlooking the comings and goings of motorised vehicles still bearing the magic legend 'Royal Mail' and the Sovereign's monogram. To Mr A. W. McClellan, Director of the Libraries and Museum of the Borough of Tottenham, for allowing me to borrow a collection of mail-coach time-bills for the year 1797, and to Mr F. Fenton of Bruce Castle for much help. Also to Mr Emyr Gwynne Jones, Librarian of the University College of North Wales, and Mr W. J. Jones, Librarian of the Bangor City Library, through whose good offices I was able to procure and make use of some valuable works of reference.

E. V.

CHAPTER I

The Sinews of Glamour

IT was the pure glamour of the thing which called forth from De Quincey that extraordinary literary fugue *The English Mail-Coach*. Near the beginning of that essay he takes the reader a little into his confidence and says, by way of explaining the strong reaction which the subject had on his imagination: 'These mail-coaches, as organised by Mr Palmer, are entitled to a circumstantial note from myself, having had so large a share in the anarchies of my subsequent dreams; an agency which they accomplished, first, through velocity, at that time unprecedented—for they first revealed the glory of motion; secondly, through grand effects for the eye between lamp-light and the darkness upon solitary roads; thirdly, through animal beauty and power so often displayed in the class of horses selected for this service; fourthly, through the conscious presence of a central intellect, that, in the midst of vast distances—of storms, of darkness, of danger—over-ruled all obstacles into one steady co-operation to a national result.'

To the passage 'in the midst of vast distances' the author gave a footnote which must not be missed. 'One case was familiar to mail-coach travellers, where two mails in opposite directions, north and south, starting at the same minute from points six hundred miles apart, met almost constantly at a particular bridge which bisected the total distance.'

It was indeed Mr Palmer of Bath who had both conceived and organised the mail-coach system, but De Quincey's memories of it are from his college days and later, that is, from about the year 1803, long after Mr Palmer had been ignominiously dismissed from the Post Office and the carrying on of his scheme had been left to someone else. It was this person, then, and not Mr Palmer that was the 'central intellect' noted by De Quincey whose influence was so pervasive of the

I

system as to strike his imagination as a *conscious presence* overruling all obstacles. But, unlike Mr Palmer, his name has never caught the eye of any of our historians or even the compilers of the *Dictionary of National Biography*. Yet it is a fair guess that if this person had not happened to be just the sort of man he was, the mail-coach organisation would have fallen to pieces before the 18th century was out, which would have been such a set-back to rapid communication, on which our business men were beginning to rely, that the story of our spectacular rise as a great industrial power would have been different.

I was first introduced to this man by paying a chance visit to a second-hand bookstall from which I carried off a copy of Cary's *New Itinerary of the Great Roads of England and Wales* issued in 1802 (the year before De Quincey went up to Oxford and ten after the departure of Mr Palmer from the Post Office). This book, like others of its kind, described both main and cross-roads throughout the country, with distances from place to place. But, unlike others which relied on 'reputed miles', it claimed to be drawn up from 'an Actual Ad-measurement made by Command of His Majesty's Postmaster General for Official purposes; under the Direction and Inspection of Thomas Hasker Esqr., Surveyor and Superintendant of the Mail Coaches'. It was dedicated to the Earls of Chesterfield and Leicester who shared the office of Postmaster-General.

At the end of the volume there was a short report of a lawsuit in which John Cary, who was both author and publisher, sued the publisher of a rival road book for infringement of copyright. There were several road books on the market at that time and they were best sellers. The defendants in the case were the proprietors of the most popular of these works, which had first been issued in 1772 in the name of the Assistant Quartermaster General of H.M. Forces, Daniel Patterson. This book had gone into eleven editions before Cary issued his first, which was not until 1798. In its style and layout Cary was an un-blushing imitation of Patterson in all respects, and the owners of Patterson would have had just grounds of complaint if they had not done an incredibly foolish thing. They rushed out a twelfth edition immediately after Cary's book had appeared, but amended the distances to agree with the new measurements found in Cary and lifted a great deal more information from that work besides. This was proved by a compositor who deposed that a large part of the new edition had been set from Cary's printed text.

In fact, each of these rivals had imitated the other to such an extent it might have been hard to prove which was the more deserving to win the suit for infringement. But Cary had a witness who evidently impressed the jury, when he called the Superintendent of the Mail-Coaches, Thomas Hasker. Mr Hasker showed to what expense the Post Office had been put to secure the services of John Cary in making the survey. The work entailed appointing five district surveyors to cover all the main roads of England and Wales. They appointed reliable men to traverse every inch on foot, from one fixed point in a town or village to another in the next, pushing a wooden wheel called a *perambulator* which recorded every revolution in the manner of a modern cyclometer. This, Hasker emphasised, was not only of use to the Post Office (the new check had enabled it to effect a saving of about one hundred and forty pounds in the past year) but it was a work of national importance. The Post Office had paid Mr Cary ninepence a mile for this survey and that was exactly what he had had to pay his surveyors. But he had been granted sole rights for publishing the figures arrived at, and to rob him of his only chance of making a profit was sheer piracy. Cary won his case.

There was something about the nature and directness of Hasker's answers under cross-examination which (subconsciously), coupled with the sound of his name, suggested to me someone extra brisk, extra competent, and possessed of a personality I would like to know more of. Besides, he must surely be the 'central intellect' mystically surmised by De Quincey, here revealed in the flesh! I fully shared De Quincey's feeling for the glamour enshrined in those words 'the Royal Mail', though what for him had been a four-in-hand coach was for me a steam-driven express train. Some vital link between the two had been preserved so well that the motto on the old mail-coach token, 'Speed, Regularity, and Security', still held as good as ever, and the steam Irish Mail was only the horse-drawn Holyhead Mail in a new shape but of the same spirit.

A well-planned and successful organisation can perpetuate itself like a living organism through the process called 'handing down', and become a *tradition* outlasting the lives of several generations of its human hosts. The Irish Mail (a chief idol of my boyhood, as the Holyhead Mail had been of De Quincey's) was a fair example of this. It was then one of the most famous trains in the world, the direct heir of the best-equipped and fastest long-distance mail-coach in the

British Isles. Part of its reputation was due to its speed, which seemed at that time a wonder, for there were then very few motor-cars on the roads and no aeroplanes at all in the sky. It was also noted for its absolute regularity in point of time. But there was something more about it than could be explained by having these assets—a mystical attribute of romance and glamour that touched the hearts of railway-men and non-railwaymen alike.

The London and North Western Railway, which had grown out of the London and Birmingham, the Grand Junction, and the Chester Holyhead Companies, had inherited the letter-bags, parcels, and passengers of the Holyhead Mail, the Chester Mail, and the Liverpool Mail (all serving packet-stations for Ireland) now, under the name Irish Mail, operated the Post Office contract over the landward portion of the principal link with Dublin. But this great and powerful company, known at that time as the 'Premier Line' of Britain, had not succeeded in getting the contract for the rest of the journey. That remained securely in the hands of the Irish contractors, the City of Dublin Steam Packet Company, who had held it since 1850. Their ships berthed alongside the old stone pier at the entrance to the Inner Harbour, constructed by Telford in 1821 to terminate his great Holyhead Road.

The North-Western Company had used every kind of stratagem and pulled every kind of wire to gain the mail contract for the sea passage each time it was due for renewal. In the intervals they did their utmost at least to despoil the mail-packet of her passengers and thus discourage her owners from competing. They ran their own steamers and constantly improved them. They brought the sea into the railway station so that passengers could step off the train and on to the boat within a few paces, while those on the Irish Mail had to wait for the big engine to be taken off and a small one coupled on, to draw them along a winding and jolting track which followed the old coach road down to Telford's pier, exposed to fearful and quelling gusts in sou-westerly weather. Here rode those destroyer-like craft with raking black funnels, black hulls, and turtle-decked bows which looked almost as if they invited bad weather as a sporting challenge. But they carried the much-envied pennon bearing the words 'Royal Mail'. Grim and purposeful brachets of the chase across the tempestuous Irish Sea! Even in the shelter of the pier they heaved a little, straining at their hawsers. Fine sea-boats, one was told, but given to rolling horribly. But the

4

mail-pennon hung in their fore-rigging, and their captains and mates (who stuck conservatively to an antique style of seaman's peaked cap) always seemed conscious of that. They were reputed to be wonderful hosts to the passenger. Their chief stewards were likened in their manner to country-house butlers.

The North-Western steamers were bigger, faster, and handsomer than anything serving the Continent across the English Channel, creations so pleasing to the eye that nobody but Denny of Dumbarton could have turned them out. Like the mail-boats, they ran a day and night service, but instead of landing their passengers at Kingstown, where they had to be taken on again by train to Dublin, the railway boats went up the Liffey to North Wall in the heart of the city. To beat the night and day Irish Mails, the North-Western ran expresses from Euston at times calculated to suit public convenience rather than the demands of the Post Office and arranged departure times from Dublin also accordingly. As a last touch, the Irish Day Express was timed to do the journey to Holyhead quicker than the Mail.

Yet the Mail continued to be the fuller and more popular train, and all the best people travelled by it. The station-master at Holyhead, when he met the Irish Day Express, turned out in frock-coat and top-hat; but when he met the Mail he wore a buttonhole in addition. Even the directors of the line took a secret pride in this train, which they maintained superbly and with more attention to detail and picked staff than their own.

Such favouritism shown by the uncommitted public and even the committed opposition is a testimony to what tricks tradition will play with man's fancy. What's in a name? Not Shakespeare's answer in this case!

The epic struggle between the English and Irish companies for the cross-sea mail contract ended with the simultaneous disappearance of both as soon as the first German War was over. The London and North-Western vanished in the railway amalgamation. The Directors retired in a body, and with them went their long-established system of working and discipline, handed directly down from the last and greatest days of the mail-coaches. At the same time, the City of Dublin Steam Packet Company, rather than replace their necessary fourth steamer, the *Leinster*, torpedoed during the war, and begin the struggle afresh with new men, took the ample endowment in insurance she had bequeathed them and retired from Holyhead.

The company created by the merger was called the London Midland and Scottish. Its directors were men who came almost entirely from the former Midland Railway and immediately introduced their ideas, colour schemes, and 'Midland working' into their new empire, to the contemptuous disgust of all those railway servants trained in the much more aristocratic tradition of the London and North Western. Links with the past were strained, but not yet broken.

The mail contract was at last in the hands of a single company, whose large new steamers flew the long-coveted pennon and tied up in the station-harbour instead of alongside the remote and draughty mail-pier. But the old glamour still invested the Irish Mail, and I may call to witness its reaction on a group of tolerably hard-headed fellows shortly after the new régime had begun. These had forgathered on a stormy night in the Station Hotel at Holyhead for an impending business conference—a mixed party of directors of a large omnibus company and of the railway, including Ashton Davies, a high official of the line.

We had a sitting-room ready with a nice fire and plenty of sandwiches and drinks. The wind roared away outside, and they were getting warm and comfortable when Ashton Davies looked at his watch. It was time for the mail-boat to arrive.

'Come out and let's see the boat in,' he said, but at first there was some reluctance to leave the fireside. Wreathall (Chairman of the 'bus company) was frankly sceptical.

'My dear man, it won't arrive for hours. Can't you hear the wind? No boat could get in to time on a night like this.'

Ashton Davies jumped up from his chair. 'The mail-boat is never late,' he said, 'and I bet you half a crown she's coming in this very minute. Anybody take me?'

Old Wreathall stirred from his place by the fire.

'All right then,' he replied, 'we'll go and see.'

The rest of us naturally had to follow. We got our coats and turned up our collars before going out on to the quay which is only twenty yards from the hotel door. Sure enough, there she was, just closing in to the side with the mooring ropes already fast. Wreathall felt in his pocket for the half-crown and handed it over in silence.[1]

[1] *The Sowing and the Harvest* by W. J. Crosland-Taylor, 1948.

In the eye of imagination, glamour is a thing of beauty in lith and limb. Nevertheless, these lineaments are supported by what may be likened to bone and sinew, usually of very material derivation, referable to creators in the past that were human beings and not either gods or fairies. Such was John Palmer, the author of the mail-coach system which revolutionised the letter post in Great Britain. His name is well remembered in all encyclopaedic works. He devised the plan and began to carry it out, but in the first flush of its success, he was deprived of its control. At that stage the elaborate organisation, hastily contrived and legally unsecured at vital points by proper attestation, depending only on word-of-mouth promises and gentlemen's agreements, would most likely have dropped to pieces if the right man had not been in the right place to prevent it. His was the name I have already mentioned, Thomas Hasker.

It was some time before my latent curiosity about this man with a brisk name and sharp answers, whom I had met in the addendum to Cary's road book, roused me sufficiently to go to the obvious place, the General Post Office at St Martin's-le-Grand. Here I was kindly received by the archivist who said that there were indeed some Hasker relics still preserved in the Muniment Room, which was really quite miraculous in view of the fearful and indiscriminate depredations which had been made by pulp-hunters during the paper shortages of the last two wars. I called again the next day and found four largish volumes awaiting me on a table in the Record Room. Three were in modern bindings, the fourth in its original vellum with the royal arms impressed on the front cover, and on the spine, in large gilt letters, the significant word 'Hasker'.

Of these volumes two were letter-books covering a period from April the 11th, 1794, to November the 17th, 1796. The other two contained collections of printed circulars and handbills, instructions to guards and directions to contractors and postmasters—all relating to the mail-coach organisation during the time when Hasker was in charge, that is, 1792 to 1817.

As soon as I opened the books I found my guess amply confirmed about the sort of person T.H. was—a single-minded man of boundless energy and resource, absolutely devoted to the cause of consolidating Palmer's plan and seeing it through to success in the face of immense difficulties. With a small and ill-paid staff and no office telephone, he managed to keep his finger on everything that went on over the great distances which his mail-coaches travelled, knew everyone concerned in the business personally, and had their characters summed up to a nicety.

Even on that first dip into the books I quickly gained the impression that Thomas Hasker was a strict but not a rigid disciplinarian. He was just, he was even kind-hearted; he had a sense of humour. His understanding of matters relating to the whole complex system was masterly, down to the last detail—not only about men but horses, harness, construction and repair of vehicles, the then much varying state of every road, when to drive hard bargains and when to give way, and (a speciality) the eternal problem of managing that wily, opinionated, shifty person, the mail-coach contractor, without whose cooperation no mail-coach wheel could revolve. Nor have those first impressions changed since the opportunity came to make a fuller study of Hasker's works. Everything he wrote, in letter or circular, bore the stamp of individuality. It was not only direct and lucid, but so original in composition as to make entertaining reading even when fact was reduced to figures in his argument. Always deferential to 'their Lordships the Postmaster-General' (properly so styled like royalty in reverse) he stuck firmly to his own views and ideas and would not, for instance, pass a man for service as mail-guard whom he had not personally seen and tested, though backed by their Lordships and a third and more influential peer (p. 118). Even in an age when 'birth and worth' were regarded as almost divine rights, T.H. would allow no social convention to impair efficiency.

The mail-coach system was not a normal step-up in the evolution of rapid communication. It came about through the accident of one man's persistence and was forced on an unwilling and even hostile Post Office only through the personal intervention of the Prime Minister. Yet this was a time when a rapid exchange of correspondence was more urgent than it had ever been before. We were in the throes of that sudden new expansion of manufactures that has since been labelled the Industrial Revolution. It had a sad and seamy side but it was, in fact, the impulse which led to our commercial supremacy and, with it, our leadership in world affairs—the long *Pax Britannica* of Victoria and Edward VII. It is interesting to speculate what would have happened to the Industrial Revolution if the Post Office had been left to its old time-honoured devices and no reply could be expected to a provincial business man's letter in less than a week, more

8

often a fortnight. Within a year of the mail-coaches coming on the road a London merchant could write to a Birmingham manufacturer and expect to get a reply by what we still call 'return of post', that is, the day after tomorrow.

Only for eight years was Palmer allowed to direct the course of his plan. By then it had become so popular, and was believed on all hands to be so essential, that the Post Office would have been bound to continue it if there had been no Hasker. But, reading the letters of this able successor, it must seem inevitable that it would not have been at all the same thing that he made it. De Quincey, I am quite sure, would never have been able to write that footnote about the two long-distance coaches passing at a particular bridge *dead on time*. There would have been lacking that strong emulation of the Mail which first prompted all other stage-coaches to bid against it in speed, comfort, and smartness, which then compelled the Turnpike Trusts to improve the more rotten stretches of their indifferent roads, and finally moved the State, itself, to employ Thomas Telford to make mail-coach highways reckoned to be the best in the world.

CHAPTER II

John Palmer

THE story of the mail-coach episode would have provided the perfect theme for Shakespeare's genius to have worked on. It was stagy from beginning to end; and not only were the human reactions highly dramatic, but the principal characters were those of a theatre proprietor and a tragedian actor.

There were two John Palmers, father and son. The elder, a citizen of Bath, was a brewer and maltster. He also had many other commercial interests, including the part ownership of a new theatre in the town. In the early 18th century, players and their playhouses had not recovered from the kill-joy régime of the Commonwealth Government. They still had no protection from the law except under licence, and there were then only three licensed premises—all in London, the Theatres Royal at Drury Lane and Covent Garden, and the Haymarket. Not a single provincial theatre had this privilege, nor could it be gained except by Act of Parliament. It was in pursuance of this end that young Palmer first showed his capacity for getting things done. When still in his early twenties, his father sent him to London to organise the necessary petition. It was not by any means an easy assignment, but he carried it through successfully, and in 1768 the patent was granted. The Orchard Street Theatre then became the Theatre Royal, Bath, the first to be licensed in the provinces.

It was a remarkable thing that John Palmer, senior, should have believed his son capable of carrying out such a difficult and important mission, for there had been very strained relations between the two. The boy, who had set his heart on a commission in the Army, had been thwarted, whilst he, in turn, had refused to adopt the career marked out for him which was just the opposite, namely the Church.

The pictures we have of him in early, middle, and late life, all reflect complete self-confidence heightened by the sort of arrogance which sustains a man in upholding his own convictions.

To the management of the theatre at Bath was added that of another at Bristol, for which, also, a royal patent was successfully procured, and all the famous players of the day, including Sarah Siddons and the Kembles, appeared on the boards of one or both the Palmer theatres. A thing in connection with this dual management should be mentioned here as possibly having a bearing on the future activities of John Palmer. It was the problem of getting a quick exchange of actors and properties between the two places separated by twelve miles. He solved it by organising a service of rapid travelling post-chaises.

Far more important than that must have been the presence of a living fellow-citizen who had effected one of the most important reforms in the long history of the Post Office and had thereby become not only greatly honoured but also fabulously rich—rewards seldom met with by reformers. This was Ralph Allen, whose enormous mansion, Prior Park, was being completed about the year of John's birth. Allen was the son of an innkeeper in the middle of Cornwall. He was sent when eleven years old to his grandmother who had just been made postmistress of the small office at St Columb on the new post road, opened in 1704, between Launceston and Falmouth. He seems to have been put in charge of records immediately for, shortly afterwards, a visiting Post Office surveyor took note of his methodical accounting, written in a beautiful copperplate hand, and presently got him a clerkship in the office at Bath, where he went in 1710. The story that, while so employed, he uncovered a Jacobite plot and gave a timely warning to that distinguished soldier and road-maker General Wade, there seems no good reason to doubt—for spying into suspected correspondence was regularly done at the G.P.O. in London and doubtless elsewhere. At any rate he made a complete conquest of the General, who not only got him appointed Postmaster of Bath when the vacancy occurred but went on to give him his natural daughter in marriage with a large dowry. This took place in 1718 when Allen must have been twenty-five years old. It was in the year following this stroke of luck that he went up to London to confront the heads of the Post Office with a remarkable proposal.

Before saying what that was it should be explained that letters were distributed under four heads—London letters, country letters, bye-letters, and cross-post letters. In the first group were letters going only to London: country letters were those which went to London up one road and were then forwarded to their destination down another; bye-letters were those going between two places on the way to or from London, but not passing through the G.P.O. The cross-post was a mail which neither started nor finished in London, but travelled across country between two provincial towns. At the time in question there were only two cross-posts. The older had been established as early as 1696 from Exeter to Bristol, and had later been extended through Worcester up to Chester. The other was between Bath and Oxford. Allen's proposal was to undertake the 'farm' of the bye- and cross-post letters, by which was meant that on payment of a fixed sum for a number of years he would manage these two branches of the post and be entitled to the money they brought in.

It was estimated by the Post Office that the annual value of the bye- and cross-posts was round about £4,000. Allen offered to pay £6,000 a year for seven years. It was an astonishing bid to make for a young man of twenty-six who does not appear to have had any money except the small salary as postmaster and his wife's dowry. Another wonder is that the cautious heads of the Department, who must have known his circumstances, should agree to a deal of this magnitude. But they did; and in the following year, 1720, the lease was signed and sealed for a term of seven years.

Allen certainly undertook this contract with his eyes open as, during his term as Postmaster of Bath, it had been his duty to supervise the Exeter cross-post and deal with all the bye-letters exchanged along that route. He knew that under its traditional organisation there were exceedingly bad leaks in the revenue. Many letters were carried by the post-boys to their own advantage and never went into an official bag. Many which did get so far were not recorded by the postmaster who received them.

When it is borne in mind that there was no prepayment of letters in those days and that they were only charged for on delivery it will be easily seen how bye-letters could pass between postmasters who 'understood' each other without being accounted for. Allen's plan was to devise a series of checks and cross-checks on all letters sent and delivered by a system of vouchers returned to him in Bath from all post-offices. These he personally scrutinised closely for discrepancy which, if detected, was quickly followed up by one of his travelling surveyors. The success of such a complex operation of remote control over subordinates determined to outwit him, required unremitting vigilance and endless patience, and these qualities Allen possessed in an unusual degree. Undeterred by making a loss in his first septennial term, he was allowed to renew the contract and to continue to do so to the end of his life. When he had mastered the situation completely and was making a large profit out of his farm he began to introduce a number of new cross-posts, to his own increased advantage and that of the country.

This was not the only outlet for Allen's industry. He had become owner of a large amount of land, beneath whose surface lay that excellent building-stone, Bath oolite. His rise to fortune coincided with the re-planning of the medieval city and its enlargement into a great residential spa under the aegis of John Wood. Allen, responding to the new demand for local stone, opened old and new quarries on his land, working them with the latest equipment, including a metal tramway. This business he carried on as profitably and with the same thoroughness as his Post Office reform. Becoming Mayor of Bath, he dominated the Council, which was portrayed in a famous caricature as the One-Headed Corporation.

Ralph Allen died in 1764, famous alike for his wealth, his works, and his eminent friends in the arts, the Church, and politics. John Palmer was then in his twenty-second year and must have been duly impressed by what a man could achieve by finding a weak spot in Post Office organisation and having sufficient gumption and drive to set it to rights against all odds. The other weak spot which Palmer saw had, indeed, been obvious to the public at large for some time, namely, the method of carrying the mail. This was done by an old-established relay system, dating back at least as far as the 15th century, which no one had made any serious attempt to alter or expedite. Horses were kept in readiness at post-houses placed at more-or-less convenient intervals along the six Great Roads leading from the capital to the extremities of the island, and the mail was carried from one to another by a post-boy who might be of any age from his early teens upwards.

These post-houses were in charge of postmasters whose functions were twofold. They received and forwarded the mail, delivering letters which arrived for their own area, and they also hired out horses and guides for travellers to proceed along the same relay system (the travelling-post). The fees for the latter went into their own pockets, which were by no means well-lined by what they could make out of the letter-post. Both the letter- and the travelling-post had, from the beginning, been royal monopolies which gave postmasters the advantage of being the only people legally entitled to provide horses for travellers. They enjoyed this privilege down to the year 1780, after which the letting of horses was thrown open to the public and any innkeeper could call his establishment a 'posting-house'. This did not apply to the state monopoly of the letter-post which is still jealously guarded from private enterprise.

No test of education or reliability was imposed on the post-boys and probably few of them could read for themselves the ominous injunction printed at the foot of the way-bill they carried, which ran:

> This Mail must be conveyed at the Rate of Six Miles in the Hour at least. . . . And if any Post-Boy or Rider[1] conveying this Mail is found loitering on the Road, he will be committed to the House of Correction, and confined to hard Labour for one Month.

That over-all speed of six miles an hour was an improvement of a mile an hour over the earlier rate. Even this modest advance had only been made possible by the industry of Allen, and it was made the rule under the Post Office Act of 1765, a year after his death. But 'Haste, Post, haste!' was only a wishful thought on the part of the sender of a letter. When Allen's influence was removed, the motto seems to have been 'Go as you please', and the General Convention of the Royal Boroughs of Scotland complained to the Postmasters-General that 'every common traveller passes the King's mail on the first road in the kingdom'. They meant the Great North Road. It had been earliest to receive the attention of the Turnpike Trusts in matters of repair and maintenance, but in 1782, the year in which Palmer made his proposal, it was not in so good a shape as the Bristol Road. Yet, along that highway, at that time, the mail was taking thirty-eight hours to go from Bath to London. A letter posted on Monday would not be delivered in the capital until late on Wednesday afternoon and no reply could be expected before Saturday, at the earliest.

---

[1] 'Or rider' suggests the employment of the opposite sex. At least one instance can be cited. An entry in the *Torrington Diaries* for July the 29th, 1793, says 'the *mail-girl* . . . outrode me' near Corwen, North Wales.

Besides being dreadfully slow the mail was also exceedingly insecure. Anyone armed with a pistol or fowling-piece could make quite certain of intercepting and overpowering a young post-boy and carrying off his bags. Courage was of little avail. Tales going the round of every parish hearth told how often resistance was countered by murder. In fact, robberies were so frequent and counter-measures so futile that the Post Office was driven to the humiliating resort of officially advising the public to cut bank-notes in half, posting one portion only, then waiting to hear of its safe arrival before sending the other.

In public communications, everything except the post was being speeded up to meet the growing demands of industry. New Turnpike Acts were constantly being passed to improve more stretches of the six Great Roads and branches off them, the huge network of canals had been started, and traffic was mounting and moving faster everywhere. The stage-coach was keeping pace with the times and proprietors were beginning to combine in companies and arrange through connections one with the other. Among these new ventures was a coach which ran from Bristol via Bath to London in seventeen hours, less than half the time taken by the Royal Mail. It carried parcels as well as passengers. Though it was against the law to send letters by any means except the post or a private messenger there was nothing to stop you disguising your letter as a parcel, when it would be delivered in London the next morning. This diversion of revenue from the public purse which was, in fact, going on all over the country where stage-coach services had been improved was an open secret. It failed to rouse the Post Office, but not Palmer. He had his plan ready by the above-named date of 1782.

It happened that two years before, a man of great influence in political circles had become Member for Bath. This was John Jeffreys Pratt, Baron Camden, heir to the earldom of that name. Palmer had convinced him of the value of his scheme to carry the mail in a fast coach guarded by an armed man instead of the slow and defenceless post-boy. An approach to the Government on the subject was expedited by a political crisis. Death had carried off the head of the Rockingham administration after it had been in power only a few months. Lord Shelburne became Prime Minister. He had been leader of the great party under William Pitt the elder and he now took his old chief's son into his cabinet and made him Chancellor of the Exchequer, although he had only celebrated his twenty-third birthday two months earlier. Camden had also been chosen and was at the Admiralty. He put Palmer's plan before Pitt who grasped its importance at a glance.

Palmer now determined to devote himself entirely to the furtherance of his idea. He parted with his interests in the theatres and went up to London to take up matters personally with the authorities, as Allen had done earlier. To have won a friend in that impregnable citadel, the Treasury, was a tactical gain even more important than to have secured one in the Post Office as that department, no matter how willing to try something new, could not do it without money. So half the battle was over through a single lucky shot. The second half was immediately begun by placing the mail-coach scheme before the Postmasters-General—the Lords Tankerville and Carteret. They passed it on to the District Surveyors who supervised the working of the horse-mail in the four quarters. In passing it back to the author after nearly a year's study, they, to use Palmer's own words, 'furnished three volumes of objections'. Perhaps the most notable of these was that to carry an armed guard would be to invite resistance if the coach were attacked by highwaymen, and involve the Post Office in charges of murder. The report wound up with a declaration that the present arrangements of the post could not possibly be improved.

Palmer returned a detailed reply to all the points raised. But the Shelburne administration lasted only till the beginning of 1783 and was replaced by the infamous coalition of Fox and North. Under this régime of place-hunters nothing further could be expected by another appeal to the Post Office. Yet the Treasury remained sympathetic to Palmer[1] and, while biding his time, he took the opportunity of making a practical investigation into the coaching system as worked by private enterprise. For this he travelled all the roads in England and Wales where stage-coaches ran, checking their fares, examining their arrangements for changing horses, and timing their speed from point to point.

King George, who detested his new ministry, managed by quite unconstitutional means to get it turned out after only a year in office, when he named young Pitt as his chief minister. The disgruntled opposition threw out every bill Pitt presented. Almost immediately he went to the country and, in the election of March 1784, was returned

[1] A friendly kindred spirit, R. B. Sheridan, the dramatist, was at that time Secretary to the Treasury.

with an overwhelming majority. This was a most remarkable stroke of good luck for Palmer. His friend in need was now firmly in the saddle and in a far stronger position than when he had first seen virtue in the mail-coach proposal. Calling a conference of all concerned in June of the same year, Pitt, having listened to a recitation of all those objections on the part of the Post Office, used his authority to overrule them. The plan, he said, must be given a period of trial during which it would be seen whether or not it could succeed. The trial was to take place on the Bristol and Bath road and to be undertaken at Palmer's expense.

The experiment was scheduled to begin on Monday, the 2nd of August. Palmer had said that he would beat the stage-coach (which was doing the journey in seventeen hours) by an hour. This was laughed at. Arrangements were only completed on the 31st of July (a Saturday) and agreements signed. Five innkeepers were to provide horses at fairly short intervals along the road at 3d. per mile, which was the same as was hitherto paid to the postmasters for their mounted boys. It can't have been at all easy to find and settle with contractors for the work; the principal innkeepers either owned or horsed stage-coaches with which the Mail was now to run in competition. But as Palmer could not trust the old-established post-houses whose masters he had stigmatised, he had to settle on new stages and new men where there was good stabling and smart horsekeepers to make the changes as rapidly as possible. These five contractors were located in London, Thatcham, Marlborough, and Bath (two). Wilson of London, proprietor of the Swan with Two Necks in Lad Lane, was the most important of them. He became a permanent institution and had Hasker's full confidence. We shall hear of him constantly. Fromont of the King's Head, Thatcham, also stayed the course and is the subject of many of Hasker's letters but mainly those couched in abusive terms.

On the Monday (only two days after the signing) the first mail-coach ran from Bristol at 4 P.M. It carried the guard, sitting on the box by the coachman, the mail, and four passengers—the full complement, for no 'outsides' were then allowed. It travelled through the night without a hitch and reached the G.P.O. in London at 8 in the morning, exactly on schedule time and, as predicted, an hour short of that taken by the stage-coach. The service was then made two-way, the down mail left London at 8 P.M., reaching Bath at 10 the next morning, and Bristol at 12.

Before the trial had run its allotted time it was plain that, in the eyes of the public, at any rate, the plan was a huge success and there was no more talk of taking the mail-coach off the road again. But within the Post Office there was no rejoicing. High officials retained their inveterate hostility and in the lower ranks there was real ground for complaint of a kind likely to be much aggravated if the scheme were to be extended. The speed of the new mail dislocated the established organisation for bye- and cross-country posts and postmasters who had for long enjoyed unbroken nights—for the horse-post went mainly in daylight hours only—must get out of bed twice to receive, sort, and dispatch bags by mails going either way.

Pitt and the Treasury had good reason to be satisfied that things were going well. Besides the proved efficiency and safety from robbers of the mail-coach Palmer had saved for them another situation. The national finances were at a very low ebb when Pitt took office and in June he introduced a budget in which a tax on coal at 2s. a ton was proposed. This provoked a violent storm from the ironmasters who, at long last, had found a method of smelting by coal instead of charcoal which cheapened the cost of production (for they raised it from their own pits at their own door). A solid phalanx of opposition was organised, one of its leaders stating the case simply and truthfully in a letter to Earl Gower, President of the Council: 'The only chance we have of making iron as cheap as it can be imported from Russia, is the low price of our fuel . . . coal and ironstone have no value in their natural state, produce nothing until they are consumed or manufactured; and a tax upon coal which as I said is the only article that in any degree compensates for the high price of labour &c. . . . would entirely ruin this very populous county (Shropshire).'[1]

Palmer, himself, claims to have put the thought into Pitt's mind that he could avoid this unpopular measure by raising the rate of postage. New revenue from the expected large increase in correspondence due to the mail-coach service, when it should be fully extended, would answer as well and could be excused on grounds of additional expenditure. The hint was taken, an enabling Act introduced, and postage went up just a month after mail-coaches started running. It was a fearful risk to take, as the public were bound to blame the new drawback on the cost of running the new facility, and refuse to take

[1] Letter of Richard Reynolds quoted from *Dynasty of Ironfounders* by Arthur Raistrick.

the looked-for advantage of writing more letters. This, however, did not happen, and Pitt saved his face; though we do not hear of the ironmasters returning thanks to Palmer. But, though the Post Office tried to prevent it, he was ordered to extend his range. This he immediately did with the most astonishing speed and vigour.

In March of the following year (1785) the Norwich mail-coach was started, in May, the Bristol and Portsmouth (the first of the cross-posts to be converted). During the summer, mail-coaches began to run from London to Dover, Portsmouth, Exeter, Leeds, Manchester, Liverpool, Birmingham and Shrewsbury, Chester and Holyhead, Worcester, and to the heart of South Wales and its western extremity to Milford Haven (p. 73).

This was an immense programme, and the achievement is all the more remarkable when it is remembered that Palmer was carrying it out at his own expense, paying even for the mail-guards which had not as yet been enrolled as Post Office servants. But the Great North Road (which had rightly been called 'the first road in the kingdom') had not yet been given a mail-coach owing to delaying tactics within the Post Office organised by the Secretary, Anthony Todd, and enthusiastically seconded by Philip Allen, nephew of Ralph the reformer, who had stepped into his uncle's shoes as Controller of the Bye- and Cross-Posts. One might have expected Philip to have been sympathetic to the new crusader; but it was more human that he should resent a second prophet coming out of the same country as his notable relative, and attempting to emulate him in fame and power. His influence in the Office was great and he used it to Palmer's disadvantage, backing up Todd whole-heartedly.

The conspirators proceeded to develop a plan for Palmer's downfall which was as ludicrous as it was remarkable and wrong-headed. Though the mail-coach was a novelty, the one-horse mail-cart was not. It was only rare, compared with the riding-post. Hasker's letters show that one was actually in use between Marlborough and Bristol before Palmer's plan was adopted and its driver had the honour of becoming the first mail-guard and took charge of the inaugural journey (p. 69). A trotting horse between shafts can make better time than a mounted man with a heavy load of mail on his back, even if his load is distributed on that of a led pack-horse. Todd and Allen now began to extol the virtues of the mail-cart for both speed and safety and put a number of new ones on the road. They even had one constructed entirely of iron, but this vehicle had the misfortune to be held up by highwaymen and robbed, the driver not being armed.

These methods of open competition were indulged in in spite of explicit orders from Pitt to co-operate with Palmer in every way. They had, however, been obliged to submit to his instructions with regard to times of dispatch and delivery in London. Formerly, the G.P.O. had remained open till midnight, or later. Now it had to close at 7 P.M. so that the mail-coaches could leave punctually at 8 o'clock. This caused some inconvenience to the great merchant houses of the City which had been accustomed to keep their clerks late at work and then send in their letters. But that was offset by a regular early delivery in the morning, replacing the old custom of waiting till all the mails had arrived, which meant that the letters were seldom sent out before the early or late afternoon. However, the merchants began a series of protests, mainly based on the early closing of the G.P.O.—and it would be hard to believe that they were not inspired. In February, 1786, they held a grand conclave at the London Tavern, with one of the Sheriffs of London in the chair, calling for the removal of 'the inconveniences which had hitherto been experienced from the establishment of mail-coaches'. Pitt duly received a copy of the resolution. His attention was also called to the general discontent now being felt throughout the country. All along the new routes travelled by the mail-coaches, the same confusion was taking place which had made itself felt along the Bristol road when the first mail-coach began running, though much aggravated by the widely extended scale of operations. Bye- and cross-post letters were thrown into disorder by the speed of the coach and the fact that it made no detours from the main roads, as the riding-post had done. Those who should have made proper allowances for the change had, of course, not done so. Deputy postmasters were in a thoroughly rebellious mood; contractors were discontented with their bargains and offering to resign.

The claim for safety of the mail, however, had been amply justified. Not a single attempt at robbery had been made on the coaches. But the unofficial mail-guards, many of them old soldiers 'accustomed to the Discharge of Fire Arms', had been so bored at the lack of a foe that they had been taking pot-shots with their blunderbusses at poultry and game and the tempting hams of retreating pigs. Another thing was that, while the safety of the mail had been assured, the same thing could not be said about the coaches themselves. They had not stood the

racket of furious driving over roads which had more stretches of
bad than good surface, and those which had not already dropped to
pieces were getting in a deplorable state. Meanwhile, Secretary Todd
had been collecting adverse evidence and comment of all kinds and
had embodied it in an official report which, on March the 1st, the
Post Office Board presented to the Treasury, in which the mail-coach
was utterly damned but the mail-cart recommended.

Palmer was now nearly at the end of his financial resources. The
trial of his plan, instead of lasting only a week or two on one road, had
been expanding on a national scale for nearly two years. With a very
few exceptions, such as those already mentioned, it had met with great
success and, in spite of the unfortunate rise in postal charges, correspondence was already on the increase—the best unsolicited testimonial.
Still there was no sign of its adoption, and now came this official
rebuff which the promoters hoped would be a knock-out blow.

But Pitt remained convinced of the advantages of the plan, and his
steadfastness here is a fine sidelight on the high qualities of his mind
and spirit that were later to guide England through the most dangerous
tide of its history since the Norman Conquest. Now, he not only dis-
regarded for a second time what the Post Office had to say about the
plan, he stopped the machinery which had been carefully organised
within that department to prevent its complete success, by getting
Palmer installed in the heart of the citadel in a new key post created
for the purpose, not on the existing establishment of the Post Office.
The Treasury warrant was issued on the 5th of August, 1786. Under
it, Palmer became Surveyor and Comptroller General of the Post
Office with a salary of £1,500 a year and (after some further delay)
a bonus of 2½ per cent on all revenue above £300,000 per annum, a
sum which was estimated to be the value of the posts at the time when
the mail-coach was introduced. He also had part of his expenses re-
funded.

These arrangements, however, fell short of what he had hoped for.
He had expected, and Pitt had promised him, an appointment under
the Treasury, independent of the Post Office Board. But a legal hitch
was discovered which prevented this. Under the Post Office Act of
1711 no appointment connected with the posts could be held except
under the direct authority and control of the Postmasters-General.
This clause was, in fact, one of the things which had considerably
hampered Ralph Allen in his work and initiative. Even the officers he

chose, employed, and paid to make his routine inspections could not be appointed, or their salaries fixed, without the concurrence of the Postmasters-General, nor could any instructions be issued to them without first being approved in writing. But Allen's dogged perseverance was matched by his patience, which remained unruffled under the greatest provocation. Palmer was only endowed in like measure with the former. He was now forced to accept the conditions which offered the only means of carrying out his plan and recovering his losses, but he continued to insist that he must be given an entirely free hand.

Thus, with this personal reservation and protest, he entered the sacred pale of the Post Office as a rather uncivil servant with a salary (on paper) better by £1,300 than that of the Secretary, though the latter, through perquisites and other arrangements, undisclosed in the printed list of establishment, was probably worth twice as much. In his new high command of the whole Office he was able to abolish those restrictive practices which had worked against him and make the slow branch posts agree in timing with his fast mails. The next important step was to make Post Office officials of the men he had trained to supervise the organisation already built up. He managed to arrange this soon after his own affairs were settled. Among those men were Charles Bonnor, appointed Deputy Comptroller General, Francis Freeling, who was given the vacant post of Resident Surveyor —he was destined to become one of the most famous Secretaries of the Post Office and earn a baronetcy—and finally Thomas Hasker, made Superintendent of Mail-Coaches with two Deputies, W. Woolmer and S. Wilkins.

Of these, only one was a link with Palmer's old life of the theatre, his chosen second-in-command, Bonnor, an actor who had appeared on his boards at Bath and Bristol and had later made some reputation on the London stage. In all his nominees except this man Palmer's choice was proved by subsequent events to be thoroughly sound. Bonnor seems to have been selected for the most important and responsible post in Palmer's gift almost entirely on grounds of friendship. The only other claim he could have put forward would have been that he was once apprenticed to a firm of coach-builders; but he could hardly be regarded as an expert adviser on the subject, as he had broken his indentures before his time was served in favour of the more attractive and Bohemian life of the footlights. That he was an extravagant fellow Palmer must have known, as he seems to have rescued him from his creditors more than once. But Bonnor's talent of acting doubtless served him as well off the stage as on it, and he could play the ingratiating part of hero-worshipper well enough. Hard-headed men have their weaknesses, and Palmer was very hard-headed.

The custom had grown up of appointing two noblemen to the headship of the Post Office, a duality singularly expressed in official address as 'their Lordships the Postmaster-General'. At the time when Palmer entered the citadel Lords Carteret and Clarendon ruled. But Clarendon died at the end of the year and his place was not filled until July, 1787. During that interval Carteret presided over the Department alone and was content to leave Palmer to his own devices. Being now in control of the Inland Office his sphere of action was very much wider than the management of the mail-coaches, though the perfecting of that system remained his first great object. It was now he took the opportunity of putting to rights what had proved to be the weakest point of the plan—the frailty of the coaches themselves. These, like the rest of the equipage, had been supplied by contractors who had an eye to cheapness and wanted to make as much profit as they could out of their hard-driven bargains. The vehicles had not stood up to the work at all well and were constantly getting into trouble. In that year, it happened that John Besant, a coach-builder with a more inventive turn of mind than the rest, took out a patent for an 'improved wheel carriage' which, though nothing was said about it in the specification, was clearly intended to be a mail-coach, for the drawing which accompanied it showed the royal arms emblazoned on the doors. This was brought to Palmer's notice and he wished to give it a trial on the road. But just then he was on the eve of departure for France to confer with Baron D'Orgny, who was Minister of Posts in the last days of the old monarchy. When he returned, he found that his Deputy had clinched a bargain with Besant and committed the Post Office to an initial contract for these patent coaches.

In July the second P.M.G. was at last appointed. He was Thomas de Grey, 2nd Baron Walsingham, the son of an eminent lawyer who had been ennobled on account of his great professional skill and industry. The son inherited the latter quality in a form so extreme as to be disconcerting. His application to business was unflagging and he had a microscopic eye for the scrutiny of detail. On coming to the

Post Office in the middle of 1787 it was likely that he would have great scope for exercising these gifts, as a Royal Commission was about to make a round of enquiries into abuses and irregularities in Government Departments, beginning with the Post Office. A hundred years had rolled by since such a dangerous process had taken place. They began sitting in December, 1787. This gave Walsingham the perfect excuse (if he needed one) of making a thorough investigation of the practices and finances of the Post Office on his own account, with a view to stopping leaks and effecting economies. His method of working was to issue countless minutes, and he had the irritating habit of minutely annotating every document which came to his hands. He did not immediately interfere with Palmer's large-scale operations and the Commission even took occasion to applaud them and give them their official blessing.

The Comptroller General spent little time in his office these days, leaving the routine work there to be supervised by Bonnor. He was continually travelling along his established lines of communication, consolidating, making new contacts, breaking fresh ground. There was a sense of great adventure about the enterprise, and one may fancy that the rhythmic trample of the horses going at a long trot or full canter, the resounding rumble of the wheels, the clarion blast of the guard's horn warning the next turnpike man to throw his gate open at the approach of the Mail, and the excitement of change after change of teams, recalled in him a natural devotion to the muse he had formerly served. But this drama was real and he its author as well as its promoter!

No such romantic glow enlightened the part the late actor, Charles Bonnor, had to play. The drudgery of office routine irked him and, though he now had to handle large sums of money, he was deficient in knowledge of accountancy. In his present post he had what was then a very substantial income of £500 a year but he does not seem to have been able to live within it. In January, 1788, a cleaner going her rounds discovered his office to be on fire. The flames were extinguished before great damage was done though many papers were charred. The incendiary was never found. A little later, a robbery took place in the same premises when he was absent. His desk was found broken open and a dispatch-box missing. One or two unfortunate clerks came under suspicion but nothing could be proved. In the light of subsequent events, these two incidents may perhaps be

388   V23

C. l

regarded as precautionary measures on the part of the Deputy Comptroller against a day of reckoning.

But Walsingham had not yet got round to Bonnor's affairs; he had been occupied intensively with irregularities in the service of the Post Office sailing packets and with adjustments in staff salaries. But he had already had his first clash with Palmer. It was a childish affair quite unworthy of both men, but a very revealing spark.

In the early summer, the King had the first warnings of an illness which recurred later on in a much more severe form and rendered him temporarily insane. The doctors, who were puzzled by the symptoms and quite unable to prescribe treatment, suggested a visit to the mineral spring at Cheltenham which had recently been discovered. A plan for the whole Court to move there for a stay of six weeks was at once adopted and put into effect on July the 12th. It occurred to Walsingham that it would be a great convenience to the King and Court, and do credit to the Post Office, that a special mail-coach should be put on to run between London and Cheltenham during the time of the royal visit. It happened that Palmer was then away in Ireland and Hasker in Scotland, and one is tempted to think that these absences had something to do with the proposal. Walsingham was not by any means opposed to the mail-coach system, whose improvement over the older methods of transmission he fully recognised, but he had noted Palmer's contempt of control by their Lordships. He was known to have carried out important alterations without consulting them, and Walsingham's perpetual stream of minutes addressed to him were seldom acknowledged. Here was an opportunity to show who was master in Lombard Street. He now ordered Bonnor to produce the special coach and, for once, casting aside his natural guardedness and parsimony, made it understood that the turn-out was to be a smart one and no expense spared.

Bonnor put this urgent commission entirely in the hands of Wilson, proprietor of the Swan with Two Necks in Lad Lane, the most important and reliable of the London contractors, who personally arranged with sub-contractors for teams to horse the coach at all stages along the road, ordering new harness, and freshly painted vehicles. New uniforms were found for coachmen as well as guards and also for men specially stationed at the post office at Benson (p. 63) and the small receiving office at Cheltenham.

Palmer took great offence when he heard what had been done.

He regarded it as a clear act of aggression in what he still deemed to be entirely his own province. But he waited for the bill, which was not long in coming and amounted to a matter of a thousand pounds. He forwarded it to Lord Walsingham with the comment that it was preposterous and he would refuse to certify it. There was an exchange of letters on the subject, in the course of which Palmer insinuated the moral that people who interfered with what was not their business were apt to get badly stung. He hoped to shame Walsingham into an admission of folly, when he believed he would foot the bill without further remonstrance. But the P.M.G. took an unexpected line. He said the Post Office would contest the bill in open court. That was not at all what Palmer wanted, and he now argued strongly for settlement. The coach had only been meant as a nice compliment to the King, but what would the public and the press make of the cost of that attention? They would see what a monstrous indiscretion had been committed! His Lordship would be subpoenaed and made to look ridiculous by counsel. This had the desired effect on the lawyer's son and the matter was settled by compromise for £857 5s. 6d.

Unfortunately for our respect for Palmer, this was all a put-up job, the inner history of which is told in a letter to Bonnor which he was indiscreet enough to write, and Bonnor clever enough to keep. The relevant portion runs thus:

> The lesson I would have given Wilson is this: that it is impossible for me, or anyone the most ignorant, not to be sensible of the shameful Conduct of the Business, or the Charges of his Bills, and not officially to condemn it; at the same Time, I have recommended Lord W. to pay it, and shall continue to do so; as having made the Charge, if he recedes from it, it will be proclaiming himself a Rascal. I think Lord W. saw Wilson himself, and gave him Orders to spare no Expence &c., if so, that should be the Point most pressed by Wilson.
>
> I shall advise him to see Wilson, who must be damned firm with him; insist on every Article being just; that he has charged nothing for his Trouble; that £200 could not pay his loss in his other Business, by attending to this, which made him very ill:—the first time his Character was called in Question, to be suspected and treated in this Manner, after all he has done for the Office, the World will cry Shame on it. [He then refers to the cut price for the regular mail

services to contractors.] That to get down the Price for carrying the Mail . . . they understood they should always have 3d. a Mile, the first Price; that in obeying my Orders, and assisting to get it down to a Penny, he got the ill-will of all his Partners and Friends; that he saw they would not do it much longer, if they had not their old Price, and what they deserved, for they lost God knows what by it; but if he was to be treated in this shabby Way, he knew what he had to do, and should take Care of himself &c. &c. &c. This is a private Hint and Advice from your Friendship to him; that you know I shall not object to his taking any Merit to himself, to get out of his present Scrape.

The matter should be quietly to throw this Load upon his Lordship; let him be bullied, perplexed, and frightened, and made apprehensive that his foolish Interference may even occasion a rising of the Mail Prices at £20,000 per Annum Difference to the Office. Think of all this, for he must not escape this Bout. The fun would be to get Wilson to a Board, and let him bamboozle his Lordship with his Slouch and his Slang, and his Blackguard. Wilson must be well lessoned; tell him Lord W's Declaration to me in his Letter about the Bill, but that I shall still advise Payment.

After this hullabaloo it might be thought that the King's holiday mail-coach would never be heard of again. But it reappeared the very next year when the royal vacation was spent at Weymouth instead of Cheltenham and became an annual feature and one (as will be seen) on which Hasker bestowed his maximum effort to achieve perfection.

In 1789 relations between the principals did not improve. They remained in a watchful state of armed neutrality. During the following year Palmer, having succeeded in getting his intended reforms in the English Post Office carried out, sent the able Freeling to Scotland to put matters into a better shape there. At that time the headquarters of the Scottish post were in Edinburgh and its affairs conducted by a Deputy Postmaster-General who took orders from London. This man, Robert Oliphant, does not seem to have offered the slightest objection to Palmer's ambassador, and probably welcomed him, for he was both more tactful and more truly business-like than his master. His efforts were rewarded by a personal letter from Lord Ashburnham congratulating him on the improvement of the post to Scotland. This tribute, which he believed to be as much due to Palmer's enterprise as his own work, he innocently let Walsingham see. But the P.M.G. had not been told of the mission to Scotland, much less consulted before it had been undertaken. Oliphant was written to at once and ordered to suspend all new arrangements until proper authority was forthcoming from London (copy to Mr Palmer). Freeling was merely snubbed.

Carteret had now retired and Walsingham's new colleague was Philip Stanhope, fifth Earl of Chesterfield. He was a distant cousin and godson of the fourth earl who had written the famous *Letters to his Son*. On the sad death of this heir there had come *Letters to his Godson*. The object of these last was an easy-going person who had lately been Ambassador to the Court of Madrid, an appointment he had held for three years without troubling to visit Spain. Perhaps that was the safer course for our diplomacy, if Fanny Burney's brief description of the man gives a true picture. 'How would that quintessence of high *ton*, the late Lord Chesterfield, blush to behold his successor! who, with much share of humour, and of good humour also, has as little good breeding as any man I ever met with.'[1] A fair sense of humour (which his formidable partner entirely lacked) he does seem to have had, and is said to have been greatly amused by the state of affairs he found at the Post Office. He called Palmer 'our Dictator'.

If Walsingham had not been deficient in that saving grace he would have seen that in his next quarrel with Palmer he was creating an absurd situation. Early in 1791 the contractors for the mail-coach running between Dumfries and Portpatrick, which was a Post Office packet-station for the Irish crossing to Donaghadee, had complained that they could not possibly carry on at the basic rate of 1d. a mile. Their profits, drawn from passengers and parcels, which were both scarce on this rough, unfrequented route through wild Galloway, did not cover costs. Palmer, like Allen before him, had made himself personally acquainted with every part of the country through which his plan operated. He realised the fairness of their claim and agreed that the Gallovidians should have 2d. a mile. He passed on their warrant to the P.M.G. for signature in the usual way, but Walsingham refused to pay without additional authority from the Treasury. This had never had to be sought in previous arrangements made with contractors and was quite unnecessary. But it was now held that 1d. had become the basic rate nearly everywhere and exceptions mustn't be made. The strictest economy must be observed! This exactly

[1] *Diary*, February, 1790.

*The easy way with
young post-boys*

reversed the positions which the two disputants had taken up over the royal Cheltenham Special.

Palmer rightly saw in this obstructive move just another blow to his authority. He reacted violently. If this were P.M.G. logic, he would draw a logical conclusion. There were still a few coaches bound by earlier agreements whose proprietors and contractors had not yet been ground down to the minimum rate. Four of them were on routes of first-rate importance for the circulation of the inland and foreign mail—to Bristol, Portsmouth, Plymouth, and Falmouth. These four coaches Palmer cancelled simultaneously with a stroke of the pen. He pointed the moral by telling Walsingham that he feared if these coaches continued to run at the higher price the penny-a-milers would soon be demanding more. Walsingham had to give way, but he now determined to get rid of the fellow at whatever cost to the efficiency of the public service.

In spite of this unfortunate antagonism everything was going well with the mail-coach plan, correspondence was increasing and revenue rising beyond the highest hopes and expectations. Freeling, Hasker, and their subordinates were all working harmoniously with a will, stimulated subconsciously, like their chief, by the lure of the rolling wheel and the urgency of far-flung destinations to be reached on time. If Palmer had only to hit back at the noble lords when they attempted to frustrate him, he must have reflected that they came and went (three had gone in his short time), whereas Pitt had assured him that his appointment would be for life. He had, however, begun to have a sickening feeling that all was not right within his own domain. Bonnor was not turning out at all well. Walsingham was now probing the finances over which he had control and the result was not satisfactory. Besides, Bonnor had let him down over Besant's patent coach and committed the Post Office to a long contract for supplying it before it had been given a proper trial. That was contrary to Palmer's instructions. He knew, moreover, that this was not a mere indiscretion. Part of the deal had been that Bonnor should become a partner in the firm which had thus gained the monopoly for the manufacture of mail-coaches.

By the middle of 1791 Bonnor was unable to conceal any longer deficiencies in the accounts which had been accumulating—sums partly due to the Post Office and partly to Palmer. They amounted to a matter of £2,000 or more. As Palmer had liquidated his debts in days

gone by he now appealed to him again. But his old friend and patron
was no longer so ready to help. He would clear part of the debt only,
and withdrew his favour so far from his protégé as to seek means for
getting rid of him out of the office. An unexpected way presented
itself on the sudden death of John Besant in the following December.
Before this happened, the inventor had given up his own business and
joined forces with John Vidler of the larger coach-building manufactory at Millbank in Westminster, to whom the monopoly for
supplying the patent coach was transferred. Palmer now made use of
a lever which his Deputy had unwittingly furnished—the mail-coach
contract, which Vidler would by no means be anxious to lose. He had
discovered that a secret agreement existed whereby, in the event of
Besant's death, Bonnor should succeed him as manager of the works
whose sole proprietor was now John Vidler. Palmer now hastened to
assure the coach-builder that he would not stand in the way of Bonnor's
leaving the Post Office to take up once more the trade to which he had
been apprenticed.

As Vidler showed no enthusiasm for this plan, Palmer, at the risk of
making a confession that must humiliate him, took the plunge and told
the Postmasters-General about the partnership. After a short interval
Lord Walsingham issued the following minute:

The P.M.G^l have shown to Mr Pitt the letter from the C^r G^l
respecting Mr Bonner's being concerned as a partner or sharer in
the late Mr Besant's coaches.

The P.M.G^l think it their duty to observe that the Dep^y C^r G^l
should have communicated to the P.M.G^l and the C^r G^l his original
intention of being a Partner in the business previous to undertaking
any such Engagement—so should he have made this communication
as soon as he had actually undertaken it, and the C^r G^l should have
done the same, the moment it first came to his knowledge.

It is a principle universally admitted that no Officer ought to be
interested in a business over which he has an Official control, and it
has been peculiarly the object of every Parliamentary Commission
of Account or Commissioners of Enquiry to enforce it.

The Report now before the King in Council peremptorily
recommends that no Person connected with the Office shall have
any concern or Interest in the Packets [i.e. the Post Office sailing
packets for Ireland and overseas], therefore it would be the highest

degree of inconsistency to admit the principle as far as it respects the Packets, and reject it as far as it respects the Mail Coaches.

For these reasons the D^y C^r G^l must make his option between the two situations, of D^y C^r G^l or that of continuing to be interested in the Mail Coach Business, as an Owner or Partner in that Concern, by himself or any other Person directly or indirectly, in any respect whatsoever. The P.M.G^l are under the necessity of giving full notice, upon this occasion, that they shall be obliged to dismiss any of their Officers whom their Lordships may in future discover to have a pecuniary interest in any business which is connected with their Official Appointments.

Palmer must have hoped confidently that, having risked the disclosure of his own concealment of the discreditable affair, the final clause in Walsingham's minute would have been implemented forthwith. The mere warning of dismissal left him in a weaker position than before. But it would seem that it was Bonnor who next held a consultation with the coach-builder. Vidler must have known better than anyone else the nature and extent of Bonnor's secret levies on outside parties engaged in running the mail-coach service, including the late John Besant, and, while fearing for the loss of what promised to be his most important contract with the Government, had no wish to receive such a rascal into his own works. The upshot of the conference was that Bonnor was bought off by Vidler for £6,000 and remained firmly seated at his old desk.

The house in Lombard Street was now doubly divided against itself, with the Principals contending against each other and Bonnor scheming to score off both. The prejudice against 'theatricals' and the folly of admitting them to key positions in an august department of the Civil Service remained alive. Such persons were, in law, still classed as 'strolling players' and liable, on the least pretext, to be haled before any Justice of the Peace and sentenced to be 'grievously whipped'. The situation, while it deeply concerned Walsingham, was causing Chesterfield much amusement. He had written to his colleague, 'Bonnor likes to make pantomime upon times of anarchy and confusion. I shall not be surprised to see the Post Office upon the stage and Todd or you or I acting Harlequin.'

With a few exceptions, Postmasters-General had not thought it necessary to exert themselves in the execution of their duties. The appointment was regarded as almost a sinecure, a 'place' worth £2,000 a year, usually given to a peer friendly to the Government in power, who might be marking time between other appointments or going into political retirement, something of a consolation prize. The extraordinary backwardness of the Post Office and its supine attitude towards any suggested improvement in the system, as revealed by the 'three volumes of objections' to the mail-coach plan in 1782, were due to this means of nominating its chiefs. The pity was that when the Office was fortunate enough to have a man like Walsingham, industrious, scrupulous, prepared to give all his time and energy to putting the service on to a sound footing, and, at the same time, to have in its midst a reformer whose drive and genius for organisation were exceptional (though admittedly not scrupulous), they could not have combined to work for the common weal. But Walsingham, if just, according to his lights, was not very generous. Joyce tells a story about him which gives a clue to his limitations.[1] Daniel Braithwaite, the Clerk to the Postmasters-General, was an exceedingly docile and humble-minded man whom Walsingham, a stickler for forms, had actually twitted 'on the number of "Lordships" he would introduce into a single letter'. Braithwaite had given a junior one of Walsingham's drafts to fair copy. The great man's fist was notoriously difficult to read—Chesterfield had complained 'if you must write legs, let them be cockchafers' and not flies''. Having attempted the transcription of a date, the junior felt sure it could not be right and amended it to what he believed to be correct. Walsingham spotted the erasure and alteration and immediately ordered Braithwaite to suspend the young man.

Braithwaite, in spite of his humility and official deference, was a man of parts, a Fellow of the Royal Society. His sense of common decency rebelled at this instruction and he refused to obey it. For this unheard-of breach of discipline he was called before his chief and severely reprimanded. On hearing his defence, Walsingham asked him if he had never read Breccaria on Crimes and Punishments, to which he replied, 'No, I have not read Breccaria on Crimes and Punishments. But Breccaria, say what he may, will never convince me that it can be right to punish a mistake as though it were a crime.' An answer which prevailed and also gained him the name of Honest Braithwaite.

With Palmer, to disregard instructions, take actions, and make new contracts without any reference to the P.M.G. had become almost a

[1] *The History of the Post Office*, 1893.

routine matter. His motives were indeed partly malicious, Walsingham having now become relentless, but they chiefly sprang from his
determination to assert that independence of control which he had, in
the first instance, been promised and would certainly have been granted
but for that unfortunate clause in Queen Anne's Post Office Act of
1711. He felt that Pitt having given his word on this matter at the
outset, and before he was driven into a corner by having spent his
large fortune on the long drawn-out experiment, the injustice should
have been put right by the only means, and one within the Prime
Minister's power—the passing of a special Act of Parliament. Repeated
personal applications having failed to get this done, public indignation,
if roused on his behalf, might succeed.

The climax came early in 1792. Before the system of prepayment
of letters to which we are accustomed was in use, the pricing of them,
according to distance carried, for payment on delivery, was complex.
It seems to have been evident to all concerned that leaks were occurring
which ought to be stopped. Walsingham proposed to introduce
routine checks in the London office on the pricing of letters which
passed through it against the letter-bills of the deputy postmasters.
Palmer, for once, raised no objection to this, though it was a measure
which was bound to cause a little delay to the delivery of the mail in
London. No complaint would have been made about that, but deliveries began to grow later and later until serious inconvenience was felt
by the business houses of the City.

A grand remonstrance was prepared. Once more the merchants
would forgather at the London Tavern to voice their new grievance.
The meeting was advertised for February the 15th and was duly held
under the presidency of an alderman of the City who was also a
Member of Parliament. The late delivery was then roundly condemned and deputations appointed to wait on the Postmasters-
General and the Comptroller General to enquire into the cause and
have it put right. This was what Palmer wanted. He wished to blame
the delay on the check introduced by Walsingham and bring to public
notice how the efficiency of his scheme was constantly impaired by
restraints imposed from above.

Whatever benefit Palmer might have gained from this important
public demonstration was neutralised within a few days after the
meeting. On the morning of the 18th a London printer issued a
lengthy pamphlet of 32 pages entitled *Facts relating to a Meeting held on*

Wednesday last respecting the Late Delivery of Letters and an Explanation of some Circumstances that have led to a Difference between the Comptroller-General and his Deputy. The author did not attempt to conceal his name. It was Charles Bonnor.

This manifesto was an open accusation of Palmer. It naturally caused a tremendous stir both in the Post Office and the City. Joyce says that the Postmasters-General were 'overwhelmed with astonishment' and believed the document to be a forgery. We may think it more likely that they had already seen and passed the printer's proof. Even before the meeting was held Palmer had broken with Bonnor, who had already gone over to the enemy, and, on the same day that the pamphlet was published, Palmer sent him word that he must no longer regard himself as his Deputy and locked his office, pocketing the key.

During the rest of the month terse notes were exchanged between the P.M.G. and Palmer, the latter disdainfully refusing to give a reason for his suspension of Bonnor and, on March the 6th, he was told that the suspension had been 'taken off'. On the strength of that, Bonnor put in an appearance and demanded the key of his office. This was refused and he was told that if he attempted to come again the constables would be sent for to see him off. This he immediately reported to his new masters who, on the same day, notified Palmer that 'for such disobedience' he, himself, was 'suspended from exercising the duties and enjoying the privileges of Surveyor and Comptroller General'. During the period of this suspension Bonnor was to act in his place.

Palmer was thus rusticated, but probably not discouraged. He believed that when the final tug came he would go back to complete and perfect his plan with the shackles which had for so long galled him struck off. The last word, of course, depended on Pitt. Their mutual friend, Baron Camden, was again active in his advocacy of Palmer's cause. Yet Pitt hardly needed prompting. He still had full faith in the mail-coach plan and other reforms within the Post Office, introduced since Palmer's appointment, and believed that he was the only man to carry out these works to a finish. He was deeply engrossed in the affairs of the moment, for the revolution in Paris was threatening the whole political structure of Europe. He was sick to death of the Postmasters-General and their endless petty complaints. Now they were pressing to see him most urgently. He staved off the interview till the 2nd of May.

For this meeting the two Lords had wound themselves up to a high pitch of righteous fortitude. Much as they both valued the prestige and the fruits of their joint throne they agreed to face the young premier hand in hand with a threat of simultaneous resignation if Palmer's suspension were not converted to dismissal. But when the day came Chesterfield was disabled with gout at Bath (an odd irony) and Walsingham had to wait on the Prime Minister alone, supported only by a long letter from the invalid to Pitt, and one to himself, the gist of which was 'if you find him wavering in the least you know our *Ultimatum* which nothing can make us change'. Pitt, however, did little more than listen, except to say that he must have fuller proof of malpractice before he could decide whether or not it was proper for him to interfere.

In this deadlock there was one person only who had the power to break it, and to do so without any doubt of failure. That was Charles Bonnor. He had never destroyed any of the confidential letters which Palmer had written when he believed he had a friend devoted to himself and his interests in the furtherance of his reforms (by whatever means). They were boisterous, exuberant letters, and terribly indiscreet. The traitor's shame would mark him indelibly if he showed them. Everyone would get to know about it. A more dangerous risk was that they largely incriminated him as an accomplice in some of those actions taken by Palmer to frustrate his superiors. On the other hand, the value of what he held was so high—just at the present moment, when Walsingham was flummoxed by Pitt's coolness—that it could buy a much-needed indulgence towards sins in the past, present, and future. His mind was easily made up. He put the letters together, selected six most likely to hurt and, together with some official papers likely to be damaging, handed them to Walsingham under a covering letter in whose style the former melodramatic tragedian and the present toad-eater were self-evident.

The contents of one of those letters has already been given (p. 26) relating to the King's special coach. It discloses an act of treachery which no one could whitewash. Another contained an admission that the delay in the London deliveries which provoked the London Tavern meeting was deliberately planned. 'We should by Degrees get an hour or two later in the Delivery in a Week or Two; I think it might be quietly and cautiously managed. . . . The Coaches must be kept to their Duty, as they have not been interfered with.' In others

35

their Lordships were made fun of as blockheads or snivellers—'Did Bartlett mention to you they have been telling their story to the King. Pretty Masters! so they complain to Domine of the great Boy.' The Postmistress of Bagshot, who had resented some official reprimand, had made use of an opprobrious expression, common enough, as Fielding says, 'among the lower orders of the English gentry', but which was thought so remarkable as addressed by a lady in her situation to one of her exalted chiefs that it had been quoted *verbatim* in the newspapers. Palmer reflects on this with obvious gusto, 'As to the good woman of Bagshot, she seems a Friend of mine, and to have given the Peer a Dressing for interfering in her Department.... I hope the old woman may be spunk and refuse to apologise, and bid them kiss her B., for the Office is not worth holding.' And there was a somewhat thankless reference to Lord Camden's long and patient advocacy of the writer, 'I have the pleasure to tell you I have had a long conversation with Lord C. this morning, and a gentle and friendly Jobation for basting the Peers. He will see Mr Pitt himself... but this must not be mentioned, nor his Name.'[1]

The said peers were naturally overjoyed to be in possession of these documents. Chesterfield wrote: 'I should like to see Camden's phizz when he (Pitt) communicates them to him.' He took it for granted that the enemy would now be driven ignominiously off the field and trusted that Pitt 'if he acts right will not give Palmer a farthing pension', but he warned, 'Hasker means fairly, but beware of him, of Freeling, and of Johnson. I have some doubts about them, but they must I trust be cunning if they over-reach us.'

The six letters did indeed do what was fully expected of them. Palmer was dismissed. But Pitt, who fully realised the greatness of his achievement and the part it was playing in the growing commercial prosperity of the realm, allowed him a pension of £3,000 a year. He also arranged that he should not suffer the indignity of an official sacking. A new Post Office establishment was prepared and in this list of personnel the appointment of Surveyor and Comptroller General was missing. Bonnor did indeed walk into Palmer's office, but not under the same title. It had been modified to Surveyor and Comptroller of the Inland Office, with a salary of £700 a year. Hasker, who was now quite indispensable, if still suspect, was promoted from

[1] The full contents of the letters are given in *John Palmer* by C. R. Clear (The Blandford Press, 1955).

Superintendent of Mail Coaches to Surveyor and Superintendent of the Mail Coaches (the introduction of the little word 'the' is quite significant as showing that this service was now accepted as part and parcel of the postal system) and drew the same salary as Bonnor.

Though Palmer's candlestick was removed from the Post Office he by no means went into outer darkness. He was widely acclaimed as a public benefactor. Glasgow presented him with a magnificent silver loving-cup. He was given the freedom of eighteen cities and towns. Even in his own country of Bath he was received with as much honour as the prophet Allen had been before him. They struck half-penny tokens showing a mail-coach on the obverse side while the reverse was inscribed 'To J. Palmer Esq, as a token of GRATITUDE for benefits received from the establishment of MAIL COACHES'. They made him Mayor. They elected him to represent them in four successive Parliaments. In 1813 the House awarded him £50,000 in compensation for that 2½ per cent bonus on the increase in postal revenue due to his plan, promised for life at the outset but cancelled on his dismissal. In 1818, full of years, riches, and honour, he departed this life.

Bonnor did not enjoy his new kingdom very long. He outstayed Lord Walsingham who, in 1794, was promoted to the Chairmanship of the Committees in the House of Lords. With him, he lost one who must have felt bound to shield him in all circumstances. His stock fell rapidly, and the next year he was forced to retire with a pension of £460 a year, when he started another campaign of vilification, this time against Freeling, whose star was already in the ascendant. It failed. More pamphlets!—then he disappeared from public life. In 1800, at the copyright trial of Cary v. Patterson, already mentioned, when Hasker was the plaintiff's chief witness, Bonnor was also produced. He deposed that he had given the instructions to Cary to carry out the measurements of the roads for the Post Office and, as a reward, granted him the exclusive right to publish those figures in his new Road Book, in addition to the fee paid by the Post Office (p. 67). We may well guess that this privilege (which ought to have been granted to the long-established Patterson and not the upstart Cary) was not given without a 'consideration'. A paragraph in *The Times* of June the 20th, of the following year, informs us of his London address while attending the trial. It refers to—

a remark in our paper (a day or two before) respecting persons throwing themselves into the King's Bench Prison and there living in affluence on their property to the injury of their creditors. The fact we alluded to is the instance of Mr C. Bonnor formerly of the Post Office from whence he receives an annuity of £400 a year for services during the early appointment of the Mail Coaches. Mr Bonnor at first consented to pay a portion of this sum to his creditors, but since the first half year of his confinement he has set them at defiance, and receives his whole salary.

He is believed to have outlived Palmer by eleven years.

CHAPTER III

The Mail-Coach Concern

PALMER'S last official act had been performed on March the 8th, 1792, when he handed over the key of Bonnor's room (which he had confiscated) to the Solicitor of the Post Office. Thomas Hasker then stood alone to carry on and carry out the 'plan' under the newly constituted establishment. The position cannot have been an enviable one. Although his promotion gave him sole charge of the mail-coaches, which were now in a department of their own, and he was answerable directly to the P.M.G. and not to the Comptroller of the Inland Office (Bonnor's new style), he must have missed the support of that strong dynamic spirit, under whom he had served from the beginning of the enterprise, and sadly deplored the circumstances in which they had been forced to part company. The general atmosphere of mistrust which now pervaded the Office, and the daily sight of the usurper trying to brazen out the part he had played, though now deeply hated and despised by his colleagues and subordinates, must have depressed even such a tough and resilient *ego* as Hasker's. But that was only the least difficulty he had to contend with.

Palmer, in his anxiety to get things done quickly, but without reference to his superiors, had avoided, as far as possible, the signing of new contracts (which would need endorsement by the P.M.G.). Many bargains had been made based only on promises. Hasker now had the sole responsibility of managing a Government service whose working, from day to day, depended on a number of vehicles, running to specified times from point to point all over the United Kingdom by night as by day, in all weathers, without fail. The organisation was a close interlock of fast coach, mounted post-boy, and foot-runner. A complete failure of any one link would cause serious disruption.

Yet some of these vital links were being supplied by proprietors who were under no legal obligation to do so. The man who had made them promises had suddenly lost his power to fulfil them.

The organisation, itself, suffered from the same two weaknesses— haste in the build-up and a make-shift policy due to Palmer's reluctance to admit dependence on a higher power, and his fear of being thwarted if he did. That this fear was not groundless was clearly shown by Walsingham's action, already reported, in which Freeling's good work was deliberately thrown away, to the great detriment of the public service. The result was a half-baked 'plan' that was workable, but basically uneconomic. The fact that the mail-coach was more than paying its way, at the same time that an official economy drive was the fashion, prevented anyone asking for the large outlay of funds which should have been forthcoming to place it on a proper foundation. This weakness remained until the end of the coaching era and was a source of endless trouble to Hasker.

The patent coach had been made to supersede the cheap rattle-traps at first provided by the contractors, and now the contractors were bound (where agreements were signed) to use them and no others. If their performance was, indeed, found to be so satisfactory, the Government should have acquired the patent rights, put their manufacture out to tender and become owners of the vehicles. But, at the outset, the deal over the patent coach had not been a square one. What happened has partly been told; it is more fully disclosed (if we may take the writer's word for it—which I think we may) in the undated draft of a letter in Palmer's handwriting.

This confidence which he [Bonnor] is very sensible he has been losing these four or five years past, from my finding at my return from France as far back as 1787 that during my absence he had, contrary to my directions, been endeavouring to force the patent coaches suddenly on most of the roads, threatening the contractors if they did not comply to turn them out, disgusting them and hazarding a plan scarce yet worked out into regularity; when the real advantage of these coaches was not even yet ascertained—instead of their being introduced by degrees and with the goodwill of the contractors. After my being at the trouble of calling these people together and satisfying them that nothing was intended to their injury, and their again going on well, after speaking to him in the most serious manner never to repeat such conduct, within a few months he again resumes it, and in my absence even turned out the contractors on the Gloucester Road for refusing to adopt these coaches, endeavouring at the same time suddenly to betray me into the signing a contract under a heavy penalty and binding the Office to use them on all routes for a term of years.

From all these circumstances I expressed my suspicions that he had some interest or concern in those coaches yet, after the most solemn disavowal of it on his part, in a few days after, I discovered he was an actual partner in the concern . . . After his confession of this, begging my forgiveness for having acted in this clandestine manner, and solemnly pledging that he would never again resume it, I, a considerable time after, found out that at the very time he had so pledged, he had got a person not only to hold this share for him, but bound the partnership that he should succeed to the actual management of the business in case of Bezant's death.

The sequel we already know. Even then, Mr Vidler might have been bought out if their Lordships had had the clear sight of William Pitt and shared his confidence. In the event, the Postmasters-General remained the prisoners of the coach-builder of Millbank till 1836. The arrangement throughout that time was as follows. The patent coach was to be supplied only to mail-coach contractors. While in use, they were to be regarded as joint-owners with Besant & Vidler and to pay a rental based on mileage at the rate of 2½d. per 'double mile', that is, a mile either way in the double journey which all the coaches made. Vidler was to service the coaches regularly and keep them in repair for an additional fee, also chargeable to the contractors. When the coach ceased to be used it was to be returned to the coach-builder and reverted to him as his sole property.

The contractors then had to find horses to draw the coach over their particular beat (called *ground*) as well as harness and coachmen, at their own expense. They also had to pay a proportion of the bill for oil for the lamps.

The Post Office supplied only the guard, his firearms—a blunderbuss and two horse-pistols, with ammunition—his horn and time-piece. For all this, after much badgering and browbeating, the rate of pay for the privilege of carrying the mail had been got down, in most cases, to 1d. a mile, that is, 2d. a double mile.

The only possible advantages for a contractor were that he took all fares for the passengers and charges for parcels. But then, in early days, only inside passengers were carried, and these were limited to four. This was based on security reasons. A little later, one 'outside' was allowed on the box seat, next the coachman. This number was increased to three, a double seat being added behind the coachman. Only in the very last days (and then only on two day mail-coaches) was anyone allowed at the hind end near the guard. For parcels, too, the room was limited to the fore-boot, under the coachman. A similar space was situated at the back under the guard's feet. But this was occupied by his locked mail-box and, for him, it was a crime of the first order to allow anything but the mail-bags to be placed therein. All this was in strong contrast to the usage of the competitor stage-coach where the number of passengers (often as many as fifteen), and also of luggage and parcels, was unlimited. Moreover, the Stamp Office soon saw a way of diminishing the profits of the mail-coach contractor (as well as the stage-coach proprietor) by imposing a duty on the passenger seating. But the toll-gate money along the turnpike roads was a heavy burden on the stage-coach, whereas the Mail paid no toll. And then there was the not inconsiderable item of prestige. Most of the contractors were innkeepers, some of them combining this trade with the ancient and honourable office of Deputy Postmaster, and it could generally be arranged that a stop for change of horses should be made at your door, and in a few instances, a halt for a full meal. In either case it was advantageous for your house to be known in your district as the place where the Royal Mail regularly deigned to stop. There was more in this than could be made out of drinks and snacks served during a quick change of teams, made in five minutes or less, for people would often use the Mail only for part of a journey, then put up at an inn and go on by post-chaise. It was cheaper than posting all the way and, for the part-time public vehicle, the company of 'insides' could be guaranteed as more select.

THE PATENT COACH

In those far simpler days when an ordinary stake-weir for trapping fish could be called a 'fixed engine' it was common parlance to speak of a coach as a *machine*. Enterprising innkeepers advertised their public road-carriages as Flying Machines or (with improved windowing) as Glass Machines. But Besant's patent coach had indeed some pretension to being mechanical (in the modern sense). It comprised three novel features, a lock-release, a rudimentary band-brake, and a safety axle-box. The ordinary lock had a fixed radius, so that when the vehicle was turned the front wheels were kept well clear of grinding against the body-work. But, if the turn was made too sharply, the effect of exceeding the radius of the lock was to overturn the coach. The patent release was therefore something to be used only in an emergency. It was worked by a small pedal near the coachman's right foot in a similar position to that which operates the clutch in a motor-car.

The second was a mechanism much in advance of its time, for there were no brakes of any kind in use then, either on carriages or coaches and, when they did begin to come in, some forty years later, they were made to work on the tyre of the wheel and were not band-brakes. On moderate hills the wheel-horses were trained to hold back the weight of the coach on their collars; but on steeper descents the drastic and primitive remedy was to stop one wheel from revolving by means of an iron shoe or skid which the guard had to jump down and fix (often in pitch darkness and drenching rain).

The patent band-brake was a singularly ineffective piece of wishful thinking. The coach was built in two parts, with the fore-boot for luggage and parcels, under the driver's seat, mounted over the front axle, but detached from the body of the vehicle, which was suspended from iron braces designed to act as springs. Fastened to the back of the fore-boot was a strap which passed under the body of the coach to a grooved rim attached to the nave (hub) of one of the hind wheels. Here the strap ended in a band round the grooved rim designed to produce friction when the body of the coach lurched forward going down hill and so causing the strap to tighten. Or, in the inventor's own words, 'when the carriage is going down hill, the tendency of the body forward strains the strap "D", and causes the gripe to impede the motion of the wheel in proportion to the descent of the hill.'[1]

A very common accident to the stage-coach was caused by a wheel coming off in mid career and it was to prevent this happening that Besant provided the third of his new devices. The time-honoured method of fitting the wheel was by a linchpin which passed through a hole at the end of the axle with a large washer as face-plate. Against this, the wheel revolved, and even with constant attention and applications of grease, the pin was apt to sheer at an awkward moment and

[1] The Specification, Patent No. 1574. A.D.1796.

the wheel to spin off, either completely oversetting the coach or spilling the outside passengers and crew into the ditch. Besant's improvement was to have a collar formed on the arm of the axle and a plate made to bolt on to the inner side of the nave of the wheel. Unless that plate wore completely through it was impossible for the wheel to escape. Furthermore, by means of a cup and groove along the upper part of the axle-arm he enabled oil to be supplied both to the bearing of the axle and to the surfaces of the plate and collar.

This last, known right down to the end of the coaching era as the 'mail-wheel', was by far the most important contribution of John Besant to his patent coach. It was, of course, during the life of the patent, confined to mail-coaches, but was flattered by more than one imitation which evaded the law. One of these, incidentally, was an early roller-bearing which seems to have met with little success, perhaps because tough steel was not yet in production, but more likely because of the conservative and wholly unscientific outlook of coach-builders. A closer imitation, produced by one Collinge in 1792, was more popular and was destined to share with the mail-wheel a lasting fame whilst coaches, drags, and the larger horse-carriages were still being built.[1]

In the Hasker papers almost every detail of the patent coach construction is mentioned in one connection or another but nothing is said either of the lock-release or the band-brake. They were obviously impracticable gadgets more likely to give trouble than help under those rigorous conditions of 'the Duty', the stony and pot-holed roads, squelching up lashings of mud one day on all fixed and moving parts, raising clouds of dust on another. They must have been conveniently suppressed though perhaps vestiges were allowed to remain to preserve patent rights and give the public confidence, for it must have been these things (or the report of their existence) which earned Besant's machine such a damning criticism in 1798 from a prominent engineer.

Matthew Boulton, the proprietor of the famous metal-working establishment at Soho, near Birmingham, made a journey on the Exeter Mail in 1798 and wrote thus to a friend. 'I had the most disagreeable journey I ever experienced the night after I left you, owing to the new improved patent coach, a vehicle loaded with iron trappings and the greatest complication of unmechanical contrivances jumbled

---

[1] Axle-arms being made in 1914 'They are of two kinds, the "mail" . . . and the "collinge"'—*Encyclopædia Brittanica*, 13th ed.

The first mail-coach, 1784

An early patent mail-coach

together I ever witnessed. The coach swings sideways, with a sickly sway, without any vertical spring; the point of suspense bearing upon an arch called a spring, though it is nothing of the sort.' In fact, the jolting and motion upset him so much that he broke his journey at Axminster, going on by post-chaise to Exeter the next day. But he was destined to be amply avenged on the Mail and every other coach for, with his partner, James Watt, his firm was already manufacturing the first steam engines.

This 'improved' patent coach was probably the type called 'new' by Hasker in 1795 (pp. 123–33). But, from Boulton's description, it must still have been of the two-piece design shown in Besant's diagram, with the coachman's box fixed rigidly over the fore-axle and the body (with the guard's seat and mail-box) detached and in a state of suspension in the manner described by the inventor. This method of supporting the body which Boulton mocked at and found physically nauseating was devised not only 'to give an easy motion fore and aft, as well as sideways' but to make the coach self-righting. Besant claims in his specification that 'the overturning of the carriage will only set the body down on its bottom between the fore and hind wheels when they lay flat on the ground'. It isn't easy to see from the drawing how this safety device could work effectively, and there is nothing in the Hasker letters to suggest that it ever did when a spill took place.

Coaches, like the great pachyderms in their resistance to change, retained in their construction one feature of the primitive wheeled carriage in all stages of their evolution. This was the *perch*, a kind of backbone which bore the same relation to the vehicle as the keel does to a ship and may well have been copied from the shipwright. It was a stout beam of timber in one piece, or spliced to allow it a little give-and-take, which coupled the axle-trees of the fore and hind wheels and provided a firm foundation for the upper-works. These in the earlier coach (including Besant's) were, as already explained, in two parts. The coachman's box and boot was fixed rigidly over the fore wheels, while the body of the coach was slung independently from supports in the form of 'C' springs or otherwise. Besant devised that particular mode of suspension criticised by Boulton. He also used a compound perch of original design, which, he claimed, gave 'elasticity' and, by some means, not so easy to understand, admitted of 'the axletrees pressing against the fore part of the boxes of the wheels, whereby the body of the carriage assists the horses'.

This coach allowed for no outside seats except those for the guard and coachman, with a possible place for one passenger beside the latter. At the next stage of evolution, which occurred near the end of the 18th century, the body and coachman's box were united and framed into a single unit. This allowed a seat for two to be made behind the coachman and also gave him the advantage of sharing what springing there was with the passengers. Whether Vidler was the first to make this improvement or some other builder of stage-coaches I don't know, but it is certain that he began to modify Besant's model early on and simplify or wholly abandon the 'unmechanical contrivances jumbled together'. But, with the older type of springing, the unified body-and-box could hardly have been built. Its design depended on the use of the semi-elliptical laminated spring, called the Telegraph spring, an entirely new departure said to have been first invented for a stage-coach called the *Telegraph*.[1] It was a device which came to stay and is still with us in the motor-car. Probably the same inventor could also claim the honour of the one-piece coach, for which the spring was specially adapted—a pioneer earlier than Besant, but no patentee.

With all Vidler's extensive modifications, the coaches he continued to supply the Post Office with were still called patent coaches, for the long contract engineered by Bonnor remained good,[2] if the patent didn't. But the *livery*—using this term to mean what it still does on the railways, the paintwork of the vehicle—never altered, and on that account, when you look at an old picture, you can see at a glance whether the object is a stage-coach or a Mail. It was exceedingly sober and dignified as well as distinctive. The door and lower panels were maroon, the upper, black, the wheels, 'Post Office red'. On the doors were the royal arms, on the upper panels of the body, the stars of the four principal orders of knighthood, the Garter, the Bath, the Thistle, and St Patrick. On the fore-boot was the cipher of the reigning monarch, and on the hind-boot, the number of the coach. The only lettering was the names of the two places at either end of the journey and the words 'Royal Mail'. The stage-coach was much gayer and gaudier and, to quote De Quincey again, 'had as much writing and painting on its sprawling flanks as would have puzzled

[1] Named after the visual, not the electric, telegraph. A visual telegraph was operated between the Admiralty in London and Portsmouth in the middle of the 18th century, the signals being transmitted from hill-top to hill-top. The name suggests speed.

[2] It was renewed in 1809 and 1813.

a decipherer from the tombs of Luxor'. It also bore an individual pet name.

Apart from Bonnor's obviously interested motive, the idea of having the mail-coaches all of one design and uniform in their parts and fittings was a good one and was probably not his in the first instance, but Palmer's. It was also good to have them properly serviced by one firm. Every coach which set out from, and returned to, London was immediately drawn by one horse from its terminal stables to the works at Millbank, cleaned, greased, overhauled, and sent back in time to go down to the country again. The servicing of the many coaches which did not end their journeys in London was also attended to under special arrangements.

The patent coach was not one of Hasker's problems, only how to keep it going and running on time or, to use his own constantly repeated phrase, 'to keep the Duty regular'. Such regularity was essential to maintain and enhance the success of the 'plan' and also to increase the prestige of the service. There was no scruple about competing with commercial interests then. If competition with the stage-coaches were not keen and effective, the Mail would get neither passengers nor parcels, in which case, the contractors (always grumbling) would make a dead loss and quickly resign or have to be heavily subsidised. This would be followed by the dethronement of Hasker and, what I believe he feared far worse than that, the total collapse of the mail-coach system.

Such regularity could only be achieved if the coaches ran punctually to a given time-table. This was one of the essential features of Palmer's plan, from the very first. But he was at once confronted with an impediment quite unknown in our day. There was no universal Greenwich Mean Time !—there could not be, until the invention of the electric telegraph, which only came near the middle of the last century. Everybody went by local time, which was only to be had when the sun chose to shine on the local sundial. The parish church was generally furnished with one, either on the building or mounted on a pillar in the churchyard. Its clock, and those of the parishioners, was kept corrected from this source. But in the far west the sundial would be as much as twenty minutes slow of London time whilst on the east coast, ten to fifteen minutes fast of it.

The answer which Palmer found to this riddle was for the coach to carry a 'time-piece' which could be easily regulated to gain or lose as required during the given time of a long journey. This time-piece was in a strong case fitted with a lock and placed in a pouch worn over the shoulders of the guard. On long journeys it had to be handed in to the postmaster at certain points to be checked or exchanged for another. At these places the postmasters had keys to unlock the case to wind or regulate the time-piece. At every check-point the instrument had to be signed for and its number entered on the time-bill.

These silent monitors were exceedingly unpopular with the guards as the time they told was entered, not only at every check-point but at every stage, by the local postmaster and showed when and by how much the Mail was running late. Many were the tricks the guards tried to play with these clocks to put them out of action or try to prove they were inaccurate (p. 137). This was the beginning of running 'to schedule time', an important and far-reaching innovation for which Palmer provided the foundation stones, though it was Hasker who laid them well and truly, but only through ceaseless and unremitting effort to inculcate the idea. In Victorian times punctuality had become a moral ethic. The strict observance of it was one of the main forces in the great drive of British industry. By that time it was taken for granted as a typical English characteristic. But I believe the Royal Mail first set the example, and its ubiquity propagated it.

The time-sheets were not mere records to be filed away. They had to be returned to the Office by the next up Mail. As soon as received, they were closely scrutinised for any unaccounted-for delays and the contractor on whose ground it occurred, or the guard (if thought responsible), or both, got a wigging by the next post out of London. The speed with which these blows were delivered, following default, must have added greatly to their effect. For the very long journeys, when the full time-bill could not be got back to London for several days, Hasker devised the 'short bill'. This covered the first and most vital part of the journey from London made during the hours of darkness. Thus short bills for the Holyhead and the two Scotch Mails were posted at Northampton and reached the Office on the morning of the second day after those coaches had started for the North, the completed documents following four days later.

Before this part of the mail-coach intelligence system could be worked properly, and the contractors be kept up to scratch by threats and reprimands, they had, I must repeat, to be secured by signed agreements, still missing in many cases, when Palmer left. When we come to the Hasker letters, beginning in April, 1794, all that had been settled. It remained for the organisation, such as it was, to be consolidated and improved within its imperfect framework as *cheaply* as possible. The chief interest of the Hasker letters is that they give ample clues of how the system was worked up towards the goal of efficiency during those three vital years '94, '95, '96, by the sheer force of a single dominant personality.

ALL CONCERNED

The letters begin just when the Earl of Walsingham was about to take up his Chairmanship in the Lords. He was succeeded by George Townshend, the second Marquis of that name, to which honour the earldom of Leicester had recently been added (the seventh time this ancient title had changed families). His father was a distinguished soldier who had fought at Culloden and commanded the left wing in the attack on the Heights of Abraham where, after Wolfe's death, he succeeded him in command of the army. On those laurels his son rested. The new joint-Postmaster-General was, in contrast to the energetic and industrious Walsingham, a nonentity, who seems to have been happy to practise perpetual concurrence with Lord Chesterfield, now the senior partner. Their brief and tepid endorsements of Hasker's measures, expressed in the least possible number of words, seem more calculated to chill the marrow of the loyal enthusiast than to lend support to his endeavours.

In the new establishment, which omitted the name of Palmer, Hasker had been allowed two Deputy Superintendents, Woolmer and Wilkins. They were badly and unequally paid. His efforts to get some improvements were turned down flat (p. 105). He was also allowed two clerks, Nicholas and White, whom he had to overwork to a degree that would now be thought outrageous. They, too, were shockingly underpaid. He made two applications on their behalf, with no better result (pp. 138, 154). The second refusal was downright ungracious.

In the next list, from which Bonnor's name was also dropped, Hasker was allowed three more Deputies, Charlton, Lawless, and Murrell. They were all stationed at strategic points with roughly defined districts. Woolmer was at Carlisle, Wilkins at Northampton, Lawless at Norwich, Murrell at Manchester, and Charlton at Bristol.

Of all Hasker's staff, the key-men were the mail-guards. Everything depended on their integrity, their loyalty, their tireless zeal in the discharge of their very arduous duties, their hardihood of body as well as of mind. He loved his guards as a great commander loves his soldiers, but he acted on the proverb, 'Chasten thy son while there is hope, and let not thy soul spare for his crying.' His chastisements were fines and suspensions from duty (entailing loss of pay); only in the last resort, dismissal. The pay was 10s. 6d. a week; in addition, there were regular tips, seldom withheld by the public and not discouraged by the Post Office. There was provision for sick-benefit and retirement pension and a contribution of two guineas towards the funeral expenses of a guard (p. 126).

The guard's first duty was to attend to the safety of the mail. The bags were deposited in a locked box under his feet, and this had to be kept locked not only in transit but during halts. When stops were made in places where the post office was off the main road he had, personally, to convey the bags there (p. 219), locking the box meanwhile. It sounds a simple precaution, but on a bitter night when fingers were numbed it might be troublesome to fit the key and unlock the box, and the prospect of having to repeat the operation in a couple of minutes' time when the coach was already late and the coachman clamouring for help if shorthanded in 'putting to' the fresh team, would irk. Even in broad daylight, in fair weather, it would seem 'just another thing' and the guard would 'chance it'. At any rate, it was an omission which proved to be incurable. There were more instructions and warnings issued about this sin than any other and long after Hasker's time they were still being promulgated. I find the familiar fulmination repeated in 1841 when only one or two coaches were still surviving the invasion of the railways. The rule was written into the Sheet of Instructions issued to every guard on his engagement. That proving insufficient, a printed circular was sent out, of which the following is an early example signed by Hasker just after Palmer had left.

After this Notice, if ever you suffer your Mail-Box, when the Mail is therein, to remain unlocked, you will be forfeited a Week's Salary;—and if repeated, be dismissed from the Service. G.P.O. Aug 29, 1792.

More will be found on the subject in Chapters VII and VIII. But the guards were not only responsible for the mails. They were held to be representatives of His Majesty. Although the coach, its horses, and their driver were properties of the contractors and not the Post Office, the guard was in sole charge of all. He was responsible for giving the word to go, for the maintenance of speed, the conduct and sobriety of the coachman, and for taking action when breakdowns and other mishaps occurred. If the journey was brought to a full-stop by these, or snow, or floods, the guard had then to abandon all other considerations to 'get the mail forward'. If the coach had foundered in snow or flood he was to take one or both leading horses and go on with them and the mail-bags. Under more favourable circumstances, and if there were only two passengers (but no more), he was authorised to hire a post-chaise. There are cases on record when neither of these facilities was available and the plucky fellow had made his way on foot through a raging blizzard and deep drifts, shouldering a heavy mail.

In addition, he had to write reports on all failures to 'keep the Duty regular'—loss of time due to the contractors failing to provide strong enough horses and reliable harness, to bad driving by the coachman, or other misdemeanours on his part, notably drunkenness, or—

> When any accident happens, write what it was on the time-bill at the next Stage, and the next Day give a more particular description of it by Letter to me, how it happened, the cause, what was broke, and what Damage was done—mind, and do not neglect this.

It was part of his training to go through the shops of the factory at Millbank and he carried a considerable kit of tools and spares to effect roadside repairs (p. 208). In other respects the King's representative had to exert himself manually. The coach having no brake except the iron shoe skid which locked one wheel, he had to jump down and apply it at the top of every hill too steep for the horses to hold back, and then jump down again to detach it and hang it up on its hook, a feat neither pleasant nor free from danger on frozen roads. All mail-coaches leaving London had to face a night journey at the start. As they drew down into the country, they would find sleep gaining power over all healthy and hard-working countrymen. Where the Mail changed horses it was the bounden duty of the contractors to have the fresh team already harnessed and standing out in the road in readiness, their heads held by the two horse-keepers. How often was the presence of those fellows only made known by the sound of their snoring! Then the guard had to buckle-to with the coachman, fetch out both grooms and fresh horses, turn loose the old team, harness up and put-to the new; darkness prevailing, often thickened by rain, snow, or fog. The horse-keepers thus rudely roused might or might not provide lanthorns (ignited from a hit-or-miss tinder-box), otherwise there was only the wan beam shed by the coach lamps, augmented by the small portable lantern carried by the guard to see the labels on his bags—all burning sperm oil.

For readers who may only be acquainted with automobile transmission gear a few words may be said about that of a four-in-hand. The *perch* has already been described and likened to the backbone of the under-carriage. Its forward end was pivoted on the front axle which steered the coach, the steering being operated by the horses instead of a hand-wheel. The steering-gear was a frame in which the *sway-bar* controlled the radius and limit of turning and the *splinter-bar* to which the horses were attached. Attachment was by four large studs called *roller-bolts*. Projecting from the middle of the frame was a long pole with a large hook at its end and two *pole-chains*, each with a small hook at their ends.

The wheel horses were backed on either side of the pole and secured to the coach by *traces* made of stout double strips of leather, extending from the roller-bolts on the splinter-bar to fastenings about half-way down their collars, passing through the sides of the *saddle-pads* which, like riding saddles, the horses wore on their backs with girths to keep them in place. The traces were also secured at these points by *tugs*. The pole-chains were hooked in to the lowest points of their collars.

The leading horses were then put-to. The traces of each were hooked into a small wooden bar (the *leading-bar*) which had an eye on its far side to hook into a longer one of the same kind called the *main-* or *long-bar*. This had a similar eye for attachment to the large pole-hook. The outer reins wielded by the coachmen were passed on to the leaders through eyelets (*terrets*) in the saddle-pads of the wheelers and on through more terrets on the upper part of the bridles they wore on their heads, then through terrets on the saddle-pads of the leaders to the operational ends at their bits. There were *coupling-reins* between each pair of horses. All having been fixed, coupled, hooked-up, and buckled, the coachman had to run through an over-all check to make sure nothing had been omitted, or there was sure to be trouble, perhaps serious, before the next stage was reached.

In the last days of coaching, under good normal conditions, when everyone was highly trained and knew the drill perfectly, it was reckoned that the change could be done in a minute-and-a-half. Hasker allowed five. Every time-bill issued had printed in bold italic at its foot:

> The Time for working each Stage is to be reckoned from the Coach's arrival. Five Minutes for changing four Horses is as much as is necessary and as the Time, whether more or less, is to be fetched up in the Course of the Stage, it is the Coachman's Duty to be as expeditious as possible and to report the Horse-Keepers if they are not always ready when the Coach arrives, and active in getting it off.

The trials and temptations to which a mail-guard was exposed must have tested both his physical and moral courage to the utmost. Taking the trials first, we may try to imagine what some of them were. He sat all alone at the back of the coach with nothing to do between places where the teams were changed or intermediate stops (if there were any) for post-office duty except in hilly country where the wheel needed skidding. On the other hand, the coachman was very actively employed at every second and nearly always had someone beside him on the box to talk to. Even in fair weather it was a lonesome business and not a little frightening in the dark. Folks suffered much more from the jim-jams then than now. Heavy bumps from loose stones and pot-holes, and dangerous lurches would threaten an 'overturn', which was by no means an infrequent occurrence, especially in the early days. The guard had indeed the solace of music which he could indulge in at the approach to every turnpike gate and stopping place. In foul weather his condition was much aggravated. He had little more protection than the coachman against driving rain and sleet but, unlike the other, he was not heavily clad in a coat of many capes. He did indeed have a skin rug and a truss of straw about his feet, but the iron lid of the mail-box must have given him fearful chilblains and made the pulling on and off of his leather top-boots exceedingly painful.

A mail-guard would travel his ground for forty to sixty miles and perhaps get little sleep before he had to return with the opposite coach.

The passengers had little enough time for meals and then often at very unusual hours. During those breaks the guard was occupied with 'Office Business' at the local post office. He might snatch a warming drink, but when could he eat except while travelling ?

Perhaps an even sorer trial than these might be his relationship with the coachman, whom he was supposed to report for every fault which did not 'keep the Duty regular'. If he should neglect to do so, a passenger would often do it for him, and he would be severely told off by Mr Hasker or punished. If he did give his mate away, the coachman would most likely get it back on him. One of the greatest ills with which the newly constituted régime was ridden came from coachmen who had been born and bred to the stage-coach service. There had not been time to train new men, and the old-stagers had nearly all got the habit of hard drinking, naturally promoted by their exposure to the merciless English weather. If they did not actually get drunk they found it hard to forbear passing friendly doors where they used to stop in the less exacting service and, as the power of the machine was entirely in their hands, it was difficult to stop them doing so without rousing their bitter resentment. Then time would be lost and the guard blamed.

Of temptations, there were two in particular. The same conditions of cold and wet would induce the craving for 'something hot and strong' whenever possible, from which the coachman suffered, and innkeepers were much inclined to placate the guards, in whose power it lay to do them many small favours. But from Hasker's letters one gathers that, on the whole, they resisted this temptation with remarkable fortitude, though the sad story is revealed of the decline and fall through drink of one who should have been the most honoured and respected in the service, poor John Carter, the man picked for the distinction of guarding the first mail-coach that ever ran (p. 69).

The other snare was more subtle, for it must have been regarded as a 'wangle' rather than a sin, a breach of the rules for which you would be made to suffer if caught out, but you would not be conscious of any moral stigma. The contractors depended almost as much on parcels as passengers for making a profit out of carrying the mail. All proceeds from both sources were theirs. Except in London, there was no parcel post until 1883. All the stage-coaches carried parcels, but they did not keep such good and regular time as the Mails. The accommodation on the latter was limited by the amount of luggage carried by passengers and the rule of roof-loading. But this reliable express service offered wonderful opportunities for the transport of perishables—fresh sea fish brought overnight from Bristol to Birmingham in the heart of the Midlands, game from country estates carried overnight to London.

An illicit traffic in such parcels, especially of the kind just mentioned, would add to the guard's slender income. Contractors complained of leaks in their revenue. Landowners complained that along the mail-coach routes poaching was far worse than elsewhere. Not that the guards were accused of this offence, especially heinous in the 18th century. They had 'contacts'. Under cover of darkness, at a lonely spot, an agreed signal would be exchanged, the pace of the Mail reduced, and a sack deftly transferred, to be dropped off somewhere in London before the G.P.O. was reached.

The fore-boot might be fully packed with luggage and properly authorised parcels, overflowing to the loading limit on the roof, but there might still be room in the mail-box in the hind-boot. This was not only locked but had the strict immunity from search of a diplomatic bag. Things got so bad that contractors were given authority to have the sacred receptacle opened and to make a personal search of its contents. This must have been a grievous concession for Hasker to make, and probably it wasn't either the poaching or a little defrauding of the contractors which he minded so much as the interference to efficiency which such goings-on entailed. It meant that for success in either of these private enterprises there must be collusion between guard and coachman, compromising discipline and the rigid authority of His Majesty's representative in lonely outposts of the P.O. empire. An acquiescent coachman could hardly be reported for faults when he had such a ready remedy of revenge. The letters give clues to the extent of these 'wangles', but I think it doubtful if they were ever effectually put a stop to, for stories still linger in the countryside (or did until lately) about 'presents' from the old mail-guards (pp. 213 to 216). In his secret and well-masked humanity, Hasker seems to have dealt leniently with the red-handed, caught out in the parcel and poached game racket, though, of course, he could not do so in the case of smuggling, which also went on—that was official dishonesty and in quite a different moral category.

For all that anybody could know or imagine at that time, the mail-coach system was an institution destined to last for all ages and

Hasker looked beyond his own reign and was determined to build up for the future a *corps d'élite* of mail-guards. For long he insisted on interviewing every candidate for the post himself, though by 1796 he was so busy he allowed his deputies to make choice. He always reserved to himself the full right to accept or reject a man even if the Postmasters-General were the proposers or any other influential person whatsoever. He makes this clear in two typical letters (pp. 118, 182). If anyone should imagine from the somewhat obsequious letters addressed to his chiefs that Hasker was a time-server, or anything approaching it, those two letters would refute the charge.

The candidate for a guard's place having passed muster with the Superintendent (who would doubtless test him on his education in the 'three R's') and able to prove that he was under thirty years of age, was put on the waiting-list, generally a long one, or in special circumstances he could be made, *pro tem*, an extra guard—not a substantive rank. When his turn came to be fully engaged he had to deposit £20, caution money, find two approved sureties, take an oath of fidelity, sign the latest edition of Hasker's Sheet of Instructions, and pay the legal fees in connection with the initiation. He was then sent off to Vidler's coach-building establishment for a fortnight's instruction in the parts and functions of a patent coach and how to make roadside repairs in case of breakdown (the guard and not the coachman being the responsible mechanic). The terms of enlistment are explained in letters on p. 216. His future deviations from the Duty would be duly recorded in the Black Book (p. 95), which would now make very entertaining reading had it been preserved. Unfortunately it has gone the way of the more celebrated one kept by the Vicar-General of Henry VIII to blacken the unhappy monks.

In spite of its hardships and the sound ratings so often received per return of post, the long waiting-list, steadily maintained, amply confirms that the place was a much coveted one. The attractions were partly material, for the post of guard on a 'good ground' (where the coach was well filled and the passengers well-to-do and open-handed) offered a good living, worth several times the weekly 10s. 6d. It was also partly psychological. It was a royal service, a point which Hasker never failed to emphasise, for he wished to enhance its *prestige*. It may be noted here that the word 'royal', which is seen in so many connections without having any truly regal significance, is still not meaningless as applied to the postal services. These were, in the beginning, a wholly royal monopoly. That has long been given up and the royal interest has gradually been merged into the administration of a great Government Department. But it is not 'just another' Government Department. Something of substance as well as glamour remains—the crown and royal cipher which appear on the motor mail-van, the railway travelling post office, and the street letter-box are not ornaments without significance. To quote the words of Joyce, the historian of the Post Office, when mentioning the Act of 1870, 'To Her Majesty alone the law still leaves the supreme controls over the posts.'

In Hasker's time, the outward and visible sign of the superiority of the Royal Mail above mere civilian traffic was shown in two ways. At the turnpike gates the Mail passed free of toll, and the pikeman was ordered to be ready—no matter what time of the day or night—to fling the gate open at the approach warning of the guard's horn so that the coach could go through at top speed. Furthermore, at the same commanding blast, every vehicle must draw to one side and give way to the Mail. If this summons were not obeyed the driver or owner was liable to a legal penalty. However, a much more effective deterrent than bringing a man before the magistrates was devised. Had the usual legal process been followed, news of the misdemeanour and its punishment would reach only a minute section of the population. Prosecutions, with their attendant expenses, would surely be interminable. How much better to let him off, provided he would sign a public apology! This could be printed and go post free all over the kingdom, to be put up in the window of every post office. The result would be widespread publicity with only a trifle to pay the printer. This is a fair sample:

Whereas on the fifth day of October instant, I, THOMAS WARREN, being on the road between Bridgwater and Taunton, with my Cart, did not make way for His Majesty's Mail Coach, but did obstruct it, for which offence the Postmaster-General have ordered a prosecution against me, but have consented to withdraw the same, on my making this public apology, and promising to be more careful in future; now I do hereby return my thanks to the Postmaster-General for the great lenity shown me; and hope this will be a caution to all other drivers, not to offend in like manner.

Witness my hand,

THOMAS WARREN, Taunton.

How deeply this priority became impressed on the guards themselves, is shown by an incident which must have taken place late in
the mail-coach era when the two day Mails to Brighton and Dover
were permitted to carry passengers at the back, beside the guard. It
is related by an eyewitness and vouched for by the author of the
account.

'I saw a great lark at Chatham. The soldiers were marching down
the military road which crossed the main road. Traffic always stopped
for the soldiers; the Mail could not get through, and Elwin, the guard,
with whom I was sitting behind, insisted on the Queen's right. "Damn
the soldiers! Drive through them, Watson!" he cried to the coachman. So the coachman went for them, and the soldiers had to give
way, amidst a fair amount of bad language from the officers which
was freely and smartly returned by the guard and one or two passengers,
especially as the officer had a glass in his eye.'[1]

Guards were issued with a uniform, including a hat, once a year.
The tunic, scarlet, of a military cut, frogged in gold lace (befitting one
accustomed to 'the Discharge of Fire Arms'), gave support to morale
and was highly prized, as is seen in the odd case of the porter at the
Gloucester Coffee House, who was prepared to give free services in
exchange for a uniform (pp. 68, 79).

Extra guards have been mentioned. They were not all recruits
pending full enlistment. Some were old hands taken on for light
duties who could fill a guard's place in an emergency. They were
paid 12s. 6d. a week. The reason for this extra 2s. above the ordinary
wage was because they were not in the way of receiving the usual
vails (tips), and shows that that system was winked at, if not officially
countenanced by the Post Office. They stood by at the G.P.O. and
important centres and were expected to do any odd jobs. Hasker
mentions that they were put to clean his office and complains that they
did so very indifferently (p. 92).

A nice snapshot of the guard of the Shrewsbury Mail of 1793
(Hasker's second year as Surveyor and Superintendent) has been
preserved to us by John Byng, who was staying at the Lion Hotel,
Shrewsbury, then owned by Robert Lawrence, a contractor to whose
public spirit was owed the establishment 'of the first Mail Coach to this
town'.[2]

[1] *The Coaching Age* by Stanley Harris, 1885 (*see* illustration facing p. 204).

[2] His memorial in St Julian's Church, Shrewsbury.

'The guard of the mail coach is one of the grandest and most swaggering fellows I ever beheld, dressed in ruffles and nankeen breeches, and white stockings; and is here named the Prince of Wales.'[1]

Such were the conditions with which Hasker had to contend in what he aptly called the 'Mail Coach Concern' when the surviving letter-books open in the spring of 1794. He had to manage a great sprawling organisation run at desperately cut prices by outsiders whom he could never wholly trust. Most of them had competitive interests in the opposition concern of the stage-coaches and, while bent on getting the most out of the mail contract, were not over-anxious to help the Government beat them at their own game. His staff of clerks and deputies was miserably small, overworked, and underpaid. There were no office amenities at all in the shape of tele-phones, typewriters, filing-cabinets, or even a simple duplicating apparatus. All communications must be by letter—each one written twice over with self-cut quills and much of the time by candle-light. His main dealings were with the wily, horsy tough, 'with his Slouch and his Slang and his Blackguard' (a vanished race), and his methods may be thought crude and over-seasoned with bluff, but they proved eminently successful for, when he handed over in 1817, a household saying was being coined (still often heard in my boyhood), 'Right as the Mail'.

[1] *The Torrington Diaries* by the Hon. John Byng, vol. iii, p. 236.

CHAPTER IV

Letters to the Postmasters-General (1) 1794

THIS year ended the first decade of the mail-coach era. Services along all those roads established by Palmer were being made as regular as possible. Thomas Hasker was still intent on consolidating the loose framework while spending as little money as possible. He was most unwilling to deviate from routes then being worked, much less to break new ground. The following selection of his letters, in full and in brief, is intended to show how he set about this task in the light shed by those two books of his correspondence which survive. It is only a half-light as, in either case, the complementary volumes are missing. The first, containing letters to the P.M.G., are, for the most part, in Hasker's own handwriting and seem to be drafts, as some amendments have been made, but a few have replies appended to them which appear to bear the actual initials of Lords Chesterfield and Leicester—'Ch' and 'Lei'.

Many of the letters relate to others, addressed to Hasker and enclosed for perusal. As these have vanished we could not have known their contents if it had not been Hasker's almost invariable custom to summarise or give the gist of them in his own plain language. He seems to have been determined (after his late experiences) to give no excuse for their Lordships to say 'We were never told' or 'We were never consulted', though it is clear that he often acted first and consulted afterwards. Luckily for our own information, he treated the P.M.G.s as though they could not be expected to keep in mind even the broad lines on which his department was run and had to be constantly instructed in its detail and even its aims. After the Palmer explosion they evidently intended to assume very distant relations with their Superintendent and believed that an attitude of reserve and non-intervention would save them unnecessary fatigue and vexation.

The letters have been transcribed as left by the hands which penned them, with only a few abbreviations enlarged and some punctuation added. With a few exceptions, the spelling is almost up-to-date. Hasker writes 'honor' without a 'u', as the Americans still do, though his younger clerks put it in. He had a curious foible in misspelling proper nouns. For instance, he always puts two 'l's' in Wilson, in spite of his close contact with that important contractor and the daily scrutiny of time-bills where his name appears correctly in print. He likes, too, to spell Waddell, the pushful proprietor of the Castle Hotel, Birmingham, 'Waddle'. Perhaps in this case his cussedness gave him a little secret fun.

The word 'route' is spelt 'rout', as it is still so pronounced both on the railways and in the army—one's ticket is 'routed via—', and one goes on a 'rout-march'.

The words 'proprietor' and 'contractor' do not seem to be used in a precise sense. They are sometimes coupled together as though of differing significance, at others, used interchangeably. With stage-coaches the proprietor was the absolute owner of the coach which went from one end of a long journey to the other, being horsed on the way by various contractors. These men might all be formed into one company and own the coach between them, in which case they would be the proprietors. But all concerned with running a mail-coach, whether singly or in companies, were contractors. Where Hasker distinguishes a proprietor from a contractor he may mean a contractor who was also the owner of one or more stage-coaches.

The word 'ground' has already been explained as the *beat* or distance covered by one contractor; it is also used for the distance travelled by either the guard or the coachman. As contracts for providing the horse-power were sub-let by the bigger men, or shared between the members of an association, the coachman belonging to the allied group might drive for any distance his masters chose to fix, though it did not always suit Hasker's ideas. But he could not interfere, and sometimes his most persuasive arguments failed to get him his own way (p. 185). The guard's ground, however, was a Post Office matter and was held to be a reasonable distance by the standards of toil at that time. It was certainly favourable compared with what was expected of a guard[1] on the private stage-coach who might have to travel as much as a hundred miles at a stretch.

The metropolis being regarded as the high place of the kingdom, the grounds adjacent to it were called the 'upper grounds', those at the other extremity the 'lower grounds', the remainder the 'middle grounds', whence arose the terms *up* to London and *down* to the country, as still preserved on the railways. The best place for the guard was on either of the terminal grounds, where the coach was most likely to be full of passengers in a good frame of mind at the end of the first part of their journey. And the most coveted place was the lower ground of the Bristol Mail. To be demoted from a good to a poor ground was one of the more severe penalties which Hasker could inflict. The guards were paid by deputy postmasters on the grounds where they worked on receipt of vouchers from Hasker, who was able by this means to impose fines by deducting them from the weekly wage.

After the elimination of the two Comptrollers, the functions of the Secretary, Todd, who had put in more than fifty years of service, were gradually taken over by Francis Freeling, though he was not officially made Joint Secretary until 1797, and full Secretary in the following year, on Todd's death. He held the appointment until his own demise in 1836, having been made a baronet eight years earlier. At the time of the Letters, the deputy postmasters came directly under Freeling, who was also, nominally, at least, in charge of the Mail-coach Department, over Hasker. The two always had been, and remained, excellent friends and worked together perfectly. Freeling had been as loyal to Palmer and as much devoted to his plan as the other, and it fell to his lot in the very last year of his life and tenure of office to save the 'plan' when the worst blow of all threatened it, as will be duly recorded in the last chapter.

This selection of the letters is given in chronological order; but readers who wish to follow up immediately any subject which is spread over several letters will find page references, both forward and backward, in every case, which will enable them to do so. It seemed better to choose this method (interspersed with comment) than to bunch letters of one subject together, disregarding time sequence. It

---

[1] 'Guard' is a mail-coach term (implying an armed man). Stage-coaches adopted the name for the footman (also called 'cad' or 'caddie') whose chief employment was to skid the wheel on hills (p. 223).

does mean a little distraction in skipping one or more pages at a time, but the modern magazine has surely got us into the way of doing that even more disruptively—sometimes in the middle of a paragraph, if not a sentence.

The first letter shows how another turn of the screw is being applied to the contractors in the time-honoured semblance of a voluntary contribution:

G.P.O. April 11/94

My Lords

I have talked with Mr Willson respecting the letter he sent your Lordships respecting the Solicitor's charge for a moiety of the Contracts and, as he conceives it is your Lordships' pleasure that he should pay it, he has consented which I hope will induce the other Contractors to make no further objection.

All which

T. Hasker

At least one contractor rebelled against this, as T.H. has occasion to note a year hence (p. 119). The Solicitor to the Post Office was Anthony Parkin, who was paid £300 a year, which, in view of the extra charges he seems to have made, should perhaps be regarded as a retaining fee rather than salary. The headings and endings of these draft letters are rendered as per copy, and it may be mentioned that the full form of the latter is 'All which is humbly submitted'.

On the same day there is a letter which recalls a tale already told, how the cautious Walsingham was tempted into a ridiculous extravagance in a bid to assert his powers when both Palmer and Hasker were away and ordered Bonnor to put a special coach into service for the King on his visit to Cheltenham (p. 25). It was a discreditable affair to all concerned, but the contractor, Wilson, must have made a handsome profit out of it, in spite of the reduction in his artificially inflated bill. While his account had been discharged shortly after the event, that of Mr Shrubles the postmaster of the little village of Benson, on the road from Windsor to Oxford, had remained unpaid during the lapse of six years. Deputy postmasters were being paid badly enough—Derby, Carlisle, and Gloucester at forty pounds a year, Southampton, only twenty. How much can a *sub*-deputy at a place like Benson have got for his pains? Yet, it will be noticed that his account was for money advanced by himself on behalf of the Post Office and the contractor.

G.P.O. Apl 11/94

My Lords

I beg leave to enclose your Lordships a letter from Mr Shrubles the Sub Deputy of Benson, by which you will see he claims the Sum of £4:16:6 he paid to a Person stationed at that place while His Majesty was at Cheltenham to see the duty of the Royal Mail Coach properly done there.

I was in Scotland when this Coach started and of course know but little of it. Mr Bonnor had the direction of it and I believe there was a similar person stationed at Cheltenham. They both had uniforms to make their appearance the more authoritative. If this person is considered a Guard he belongs to the Office. He did all the duty necessary at that place I find both for the Contractor (Mr Willson) and the Office, as Guards or Officers of the Post Office are obliged to do on similar occasions—but as he had a uniform I submit to yr Lordships if he should not be considered a servant of the Office & receive his salary from it.

I have spoken to Mr Willson about it who says he was not employed by him.

All which &c.

T. Hasker

It can at least be said for T.H. that he pointed out an official authority for discharging part of the obligation. The result of his enquiry into the case is given in a further letter on page 67.

*   *   *   *

The following is typical of the Haskerian method of gingering up the flagging contractor. It indicates that in spite of cut prices these men were making a good thing out of the Mail, and the Superintendent was confident that he could carry out his threat if necessary (though this he very rarely did) and quickly replace the defaulter.

Genl Post Office
April 14th 1794

My Lords

I have the honor to enclose your Lordships Mr Weeks's letter which I would not have troubled your Lordships with but that he desired it. I wrote to him and to several others who had done their [work] very ill and given a great deal of trouble during the winter, to the purport that it was your Lordships intention to have dismissed them, but in hopes that they would see their errors and reform you had altered your resolution to see what lenity would do another year.

All which is &c
T. Hasker.

Mr Weeks was the Salisbury contractor who horsed one of the two Exeter Mails and also the 'Royal Weymouth', when it ran. The word 'lenity' has been displaced in favour of 'lenience' and 'leniency'. It was much more used in the 18th century (by Fielding, for instance) and had the rather more special meaning of 'mercy'. Through this lenity T.H. (who was the real dispenser of it and not the P.M.G.) got badly let down by Mr Weeks in the following summer (p. 87).

* * * *

I mentioned at the beginning that I owed my introduction to the writer of these letters to John Cary, the map-maker and publisher of a particular road book, who had been commissioned to measure all the roads over which the mail coaches travelled. He organised this extensive work under five surveyors. Every section of each road was traversed on foot by a man pushing a perambulator (a word not yet captured by the nursemaids), which was a wooden wheel whose revolutions were recorded on a dial. This was exactly the same machine used by John Ogilby, who carried out an equally large survey of the roads for Charles II and published the result in 1675. His measurements were wonderfully exact and subsequent editions were issued.

It is one of the most curious comments on official blindness, that within half a century of the issue of Ogilby's map the Post Office so far ignored its existence as to have established another standard of reckoning at variance with the statute mile. During the time Ralph Allen was carrying out his reforms it was called the Post Office mile.

In Post Office miles the distance from London to Berwick-upon-Tweed was given as 262. We know today, by our A.A. Road Book, that it is 339 miles. That is, in fact, the very same figure which Ogilby gives in his map. Perhaps he was more disbelieved than neglected, for a superstition arose that there must be two kinds of mile, and early road books have two columns with 'C.M.' (computed or reputed miles) and 'M.M.' (measured miles). The doubt had been started by the makers of the turnpike roads. Along the stretches which they took over, they erected milestones based accurately on the statute mile. They multiplied on no given plan and large, unchecked intervals remained. But they greatly embarrassed upholders of the Post Office mile and, of course, the Office itself.

But then, again, what was a *stage*? Rates of postage had always been based on the number of stages a letter was carried, and a stage was understood to mean the interval ridden by a post-boy between two post-houses. Thus, in the table of postage rates, the older (1765) began 'Not exceeding one post stage, 1d'. In the newer, which was authorised in 1784, the year in which the mail-coaches started running, 2d. was charged. But when Palmer, who required to change his horses at shorter intervals to maintain a higher rate of speed, shortened the stages, thus raising their number, this automatically increased the charges for postage. It brought great and justifiable complaints, and it became obvious that the basis of postage should be miles and not stages. But, first of all, it was necessary to establish a new Post Office mile that should be reputable rather than reputed. Probably it was Walsingham who issued the necessary decree for a new measurement of the roads in statute miles to be carried out, though I suspect Bonnor of having steered the commission towards Cary instead of Messrs Longman, who held the rights of the old-established road book bearing the name of its founder, Patterson. At any rate, by 1797, the Post Office had the necessary figures when, under a new Act, the old formula for the table of postages was changed and began 'Not exceeding 15 miles, 3d'. The first edition of Cary, containing 'Admeasurement to upwards of nine thousand miles' (with accuracy that had been guaranteed on oath) was published the following year.

Cary had been paid at the rate of 9d. per mile for this work and granted sole copyright in publishing his findings. He puts in an account to Hasker before the work is completed and T.H., before forwarding it, produces an analysis to show that the work has had another value besides settling an academic question.

G.P.O. April 18th/94

My Lords

I have the honor to enclose your Lordships Mr Cary's bill for measuring the Mail Coach roads—and some two or three others that appeared to me necessary as that there was a probability of their becoming Mail Coach roads.

On some few of the roads the Mail Coach mileage is paid short of the real distance, on others they are overpaid. On the whole measured there will be a saving of 17 miles to the Revenue— fifteen of them at one penny per mile each way or £3:0:10 per mile per Ann., £45:12:6; and two miles on the Glasgow and Carlisle road at 2d per mile, each way £6:1:8 per mile per Annum £12:3:4 (this last figure added to £45:12:6 makes) £57:15:10.

There is about 400 miles more of Mail Coach roads to measure from which I have not a doubt but there will be a further saving of 4 or 5 miles—this summer will complete it; but as Mr Cary is desirous to be paid his bill for the duty done I humbly submit it to your Lordships.

The next Quarter's mileage will bear the alteration according to this admeasurement.

All of which &c

T. Hasker

On the figures above quoted, Hasker's evidence at the trial of Cary *v*. Longman in 1800 may sound rather dressed up in the interest of the plaintiff but another thousand had been added by that time (for a new edition) and at Cary's own expense.

LORD KENYON: Mr Hasker, has there been any Saving to the Post Office, in consequence of Mr Cary's Survey?

MR HASKER: There has, my Lord: the Saving last Year was about One Hundred and Forty Pounds.

*   *   *   *

We return to the sub-postmaster of Benson (previously mentioned p. 64)—

G.P.O. 30 Apr 94

My Lords

Enclosed is the Sub Deputy of Benson's bill. I have enquired of Mr White who fixed Wm. Sargeant there by Mr Bonnor's direction, what orders he gave to Mr Shrubles. He says to pay him his salary, that he never gave any orders about eating or drinking.

Mr White says Mr Willson was to pay him something also, as he was to look to Mr Willson's business as well as the duty of the Post Office. It seems probable the last 4 articles on the Bill Wm. Sargeant contracted on his own account, but I submit to yr Lordships that the six weeks salary amounting to 3 guineas should be paid by the Office.

All which &c

T. Hasker.

So, a lowly servant of the Post Office, having (on official instructions) lent the Government the sum of £4 16s. 6d. for a period of six years, instead of receiving this back with interest, is to have £1 13s. deducted in repayment. That White (Hasker's clerk) 'fixed' the supernumerary there, seems to imply that he was not a native but an importee and would have to pay for his meals. That Wilson should disown anyone so flatly who looked after his business suggests that while he made the huge charge for the special service to the King he was himself making use of it in the ordinary way, for parcels and perhaps passengers, not credited against the bill, and now better forgotten. I feel sure Hasker would have had a few sharp words with him about this and got the matter put right.

Sargeant's uniform would have been returned to store, doubtless to his great regret. But he was not the only one who had been allowed to wear these plumes for the sake of appearances.

G.P.O. Apl 30/94

My Lords

I would not trouble you with the enclosed but that I thought it was very likely the writer would apply to your Ldshps, as I have answered him that he is not the Mail Coach Company's Porter but Mr Stark's, and that I do not see the propriety or necessity of his appearing in a uniform, or that the Office should be at the expense.

His predecessor being Porter there when the Mail Coaches started had one, and it was occasionally continued. But, having left the service, I do not see the necessity of giving it to another.

All which &c

T. Hasker

Mr Stark was presumably the proprietor of the Gloucester Coffee House in Piccadilly. Mail-coaches for the West of England started from here, the bags being brought by mail-cart from the G.P.O., driven by contractors' horses. The coffee-house porter would naturally help in transhipment and, in recognition for this, had been allowed to wear a Post Office uniform. Perhaps a small fee went with the uniform which the thrifty Office was now unwilling to grant. It will be seen in a further letter (p. 79) how the writer of the above was able, on economic grounds, to get Hasker on to his side.

*　　*　　*　　*

The Premier Guard

The next letter is one of four which give the final history of the man who took the leading part in the jubilant send-off of Palmer's plan.

Genl Post Office

May 5, 1794.

My Lords

I beg leave to observe in answer to the Memorial of J. Carter and the letter of his wife that I am very sorry to say that he is unfit for the service, having given himself up to drinking very much of late, which fault, on great promises of amendment being made, and in consideration of a good Wife and many Children, he has several times been forgiven, but to no good purpose.

I recommended him to Mr Vidler, but he has been so long in the service of the Post Office that he can't work—has never been used to it. He was the first Guard that started with the Bristol Mail, before which time he had been the driver of a Mail Cart into Marlboro I believe near twenty years—that I fear he has no way of gaining the least support for his family.

I, sometime since, thought of submitting to your Lordships to

69

allow him the superannuated pay, having been so many years in the Service, but I did not, and now, being dismissed for misconduct, I find it irrelevant.

All of which &c

T. Hasker.

The further story of poor Carter can be read on pp. 74.

*   *   *   *

Diversionists and the Milford Mail

People who thought the Mail ought to deviate from its now established route to suit their own or their friends' convenience were one of Hasker's trials. These 'Memorialists' as he called them generally took the precaution to get some influential person to back their 'resolutions' and then secured the favour of the P.M.G. or at least the Secretary before the matter was referred to the Mail-coach Department. When the request did arrive, T.H. generally ensured its demolition by taking infinite pains in drawing up a balanced statement of *pros* and *cons*—*cons* to win. This is well shown in the next letter.

General Post Office

May 6 1794

My Lords

I have considered of the resolutions of the Merchants of Cork enclosed in a letter to Mr Todd of the 15th ultimo requesting your Lordships to direct the Milford Haven Mail Coach to go via Oxford, Glocester, Monmouth, & Brecknock, and beg leave to observe, that the road is not so much nearer as they state as the Mail Coach must go by Nettlebed and Cheltenham to Glocester which is 112 miles and from Glocester to Milford is 152 miles, so that from London the road proposed is 264 miles, and the other road by Bristol, at present travelled, is 277 miles, the difference only 13 miles—of course there would not be so great a saving of the time as they expect, and the Mail Coach from London to Bristol travels faster by a mile an hour than the Mail Coach does from Gloster or than the Contractors can ever be induced to do it—the state of the road is so different. The road through Brecknock, to balance that, is much better than the one at present travelled through Cardiff and Swansea so that something might be gained there, and I think the delay on the ferry on the average full half an hour. An hour is allowed (sometimes two or three) but then it must be remembered they get on their way 3 miles during this time.

On the whole, my Lords, as near as I can calculate, if it was to go via Glocester as proposed, about two hours would be gained, up and down, it would I think arrive two hours earlier than it does now at Milford, and I think might set out two hours later from there, namely at 10 o'clock instead of 8.

But there are some things I must state for your Lordship's consideration, having talked the matter fully over with Mr Freeling. Bristol, through which the Mail Coach travels to Ireland, is a kind of metropolis of South Wales, the business of the Inhabitants lies very much with that City as does the Commerce of Cork, Waterford, and the South of Ireland in general—and it appears by the resolutions that the Gentlemen of Cork did not fully consider this—for tho the Correspondence might go as regular, yet the cutting of all communication for Travellers and Luggage by coach between Milford and Bristol would be a very great inconvenience between that part of Ireland and I believe I may say half the Passengers have concerns with Bristol, Bath, or the West of England.

If therefore it should be found feasible to send a Mail Coach via Glocester & Brecknock to Milford I conceive it could only be done three times a week, for that the communication between Bristol, Bath, &c must not be cut off.

Yet even for the alteration of three days a week depends on the following circumstances which I submit to your Lordships, whether the Contractor at Glocester is to be depended on for so great a trust, whether Contractors can be obtained from that place to Carmarthen who will undertake the business and will do it well and in time, and whether the old Contractors on the other (Swansea and Cardiff) road will continue the Coach (or if it can be properly fitted to the duty) 4 times a week between Swansea and Carmarthen, for it must continue every day from Swansea to Bristol, and whether your Lordships may approve of the additional expense, the amount of which will be nearly as follows.

Regular Mail Coach from London to Glocester, which City is at present served with a branch Mail Coach from Oxford but which would by no means give the accomodation requested, 112 miles, 50 miles of which is paid already.

Additional Expense

	£	s	d
Sixty two miles at £3:0:10 pr mile pr Ann	188	11	8
Two extra Guards at £32 pr Ann each	64		
Mileage for a Mail Coach from Gloster to Carmarthen 3 days a week 112 miles pr Ann	144	2	
Two Guards at £32 each from Gloster to Carmarthen pr Ann	64		
A Ride from the New Passage to Ragland three times a week, 14 miles, with the Letters to and from Bristol and Ireland the three days the Coach would not travel between Swansea and Carmarthen, as it must go quick, suppose	42		

502:13:8

Reduction

	£	s	d
Twenty six miles of Mail Coach between Carmarthen & Swansea 3 times a week amounts to pr Annum	34	0	7
In which case a Guard will be saved pr Ann	32		
Ride from Llandilo to Carmarthen pr Ann	32		
Ditto between Llandilo & Llandovery pr Ann	30		
Ditto between Llandovery & Brecknock pr Ann	40		
Ditto between Brecknock and Abergavenny pr Ann	40		
Ditto between Abergavenny & Monmouth pr Ann	30		
Ditto between Monmouth & Ross pr Ann	26	12	
Ditto between Ross and Glocester pr Ann	43	16	

308: 8:7

Additional Expence 194: 5:1

502:13:8

The above statement may not be exactly as it may prove on the alteration taking place but I dare say very near it. If on the sight of this your Lordships desire the matter to be further gone into the best way will be to call a meeting of the Contractors of the old and intended new line of road at Carmarthen and request Mr Woodcock to attend. But the alteration appears to me of such magnitude that if on further investigation it should seem advisable, I do not think there would be a possibility of making it at the July Quarter and as it would be improper to begin it at the eve of Winter I do not think the change can take place before next Spring.

All which &c

Probably Hasker had put his finger on the chief grievance when he mentioned the ferry across the Severn estuary. This was called New Passage[1] and the direct course lay exactly above the line of the Severn Tunnel. It was a most awkward crossing at any time except at high tide and in fair weather when neither wind nor rapid current interfered with navigation over the three-mile voyage. At the ebb there would be a long slimy walk for passengers on either side along low wooden causeways, submerged at every tide, and if a sou'wester blew, they would be assailed by its force and the heavy rain with which it is usually charged—this after spending a day and night boxed up in a coach following a rough crossing of St George's Channel where the violence of the Atlantic is not modified. The alternative of getting safe and dry to Gloucester and thence direct to London (never mind if time or distance were shorter or longer) was naturally more attractive.

Hasker took a wider view, and the letter shows his great knowledge of national needs as well as local conditions which, like Allen and Palmer, he could apply to every part of the country as he had travelled everywhere his coaches ran. His notes on New Passage will be found on the time-bill of the Milford Mail (p. 252).

The establishment of a mail-coach to Milford Haven was the most surprising of all Palmer's early enterprises, launched at his own expense. The date given by Joyce is 1786, while that for the establishment of the Post Office packet is 1787, so that the coach must have got there before the ships. However, the first year's profits from the packets were unusually high when 'the proceeds from the passengers alone amounted to more than £1,200'.[2] This shows that there was considerable traffic between the Haven and Waterford already in being. The odd thing is that there was then no place at the Pembrokeshire end. The packets sailed from a creek in the sparsely populated parish of Hubberston.

[1] Closed by Cromwell after the drowning of 50 of his troopers by a royalist stratagem. Reopened 1718 'as new'. Old Passage is the Aust–Beachley ferry higher up.

[2] Joyce's *History of the Post Office.*

The town first called 'Milford', now 'Milford Haven', was only started a year or two later.

The lord of the manor of Hubberston was Sir William Hamilton, British envoy to the Court of Naples, where he lived. This estate and others in South Wales came to him through his first wife. The idea of developing his manor by making a dock in Hubberston creek and building an entirely new town in connection with it was either his own or that of his nephew, the Hon. Charles Francis Greville. At any rate, Sir William made Greville his agent with full powers to go ahead with the enterprise and the first Act of Parliament authorising the construction of the dock was secured in 1790. Greville was well known in London society as a dilettante and patron of the arts and was no doubt one of Palmer's many acquaintances. One may imagine that the two may well have put their heads together over their respective schemes, both so new and so bold, and come to some understanding about mutual aid, otherwise it is difficult to understand why a coach should have been placed on this long, difficult, and highly speculative route before even the Great North Road was served. Incidentally, it was C. F. Greville who first introduced his mistress, Emma Lyon, to George Romney and, later, to his uncle, who made her the second Lady Hamilton—the friend of Nelson.

But the Milford Mail proved the worst bugbear of all to work, as will be seen from Hasker's letters and his final denunciation on the time-bill of 1797. It is next mentioned on page 119.

*　　*　　*　　*

John Carter again

Now comes a new gleam of hope for John Carter (previous mention p. 69).

To Lord Chesterfield
marked '(Seperate)'

G.P.O. May 10th 94

My Lord

I had the honor to receive your Lordship's letter of yesterday respecting Carter. You will conclude from my report that I feel for his family and, being at Marlboro, their sufferings coming to your knowledge, it is no wonder your humanity should feel too.

I should not have been justified, consistent with my duty to have tried him again without such requisition, but now will find him a situation in a few days. The Contractors on the Bath and Bristol Coaches do not approve him and, by being such fast carriages they require very great exertions of a Guard at changing places, which I am afraid he does not use. Therefore I think he should not be put on that road again. If he could move his family to Bath or Bristol he may have a situation on the Bath & Exeter, the Oxford & Bristol, or the Bristol & Birmingham Coaches, and perhaps this might wean him from his own tipling companions.

I am &c

T. Hasker

P.S. If his wife will let me know where he is I will send to him, and if he should reform, the salvation of the family will lay at your Ldshp's door.

(Further news of Carter on p. 107.)

★　　★　　★　　★

But we soon hear that a successor on the Bristol Mail—though of a very different sort—is in trouble.

G.P.O. May 12th/94

My Lords

I have the honor to inform your Lordships that while Stanroyd, the Bristol Guard, was packing his sacks in the Mail Box at Thatcham last Wednesday morning he was called off to attend some other duty and forgot to pack his road sack containing the Chippenham, Caln, Marlboro, Hungerford, and Newbury Bags.

The Guard of the Mail Coach going for Bristol found the Bag in the Warehouse at Thatcham and took it forward to Newbury, the next Post Town, and there left it very properly at the Office, from which place Mr Barnes the Postmaster sent his assistant to Town with it. The expence of the Chaise, Tolls[1] and drivers is about 4 guineas which, with a guinea for the person troubled who came up, if it meets yr Lordship's approbation, I mean to make the Guard pay as a

---

[1] Tolls should not have been charged. A post-chaise hired to carry the mail did not pay toll.

punishment for such negligence. He is a very sober Guard and, but for this, a very careful one. He is very unhappy and willing to pay the Expence and hopes no greater punishment will follow. The expence of the second delivery I have spoke with Mr Freeling about who is of my opinion that as the Guard is of so good a character, if you approve that, he should be excused.

All &c

T. Hasker

(Further on p. 77.)

Thatcham was an important stop and junction-point for the Bristol, and one of the Exeter Mails. The proprietor of the King's Head, where both these coaches halted for regular meals, was Fromont. He horsed both Mails between Thatcham and Brentford—an extensive ground (46 miles) with several changes. The family, who remained in the coaching business down to its latter days and were finally represented by Maria Fromont (p. 285), were all great characters and cared little for the many rebukes from the Post Office or their private customers.

*　　*　　*　　*

Press Gang

G.P.O.

May 13/94

My Lords

I beg leave to enclose your Lordships two papers respecting the Liverpool & Hull Mail Coach being obstructed by a Press Gang. I do not think there is any blame to be laid to the Mail Coach servants and I merely enclose the papers that your Lordships may see the facts, as it is probable that you may have heard something of the affray. I am very glad no mischief was done tho' I think the Gang very reprehensible. If your Lordships approve I will write to Mr Statham the Postmaster of Liverpool to apply to the Mayor that he may give such directions to the Lieutenant of the Gang that such a molestation may not happen again.

All &c.

T. Hasker

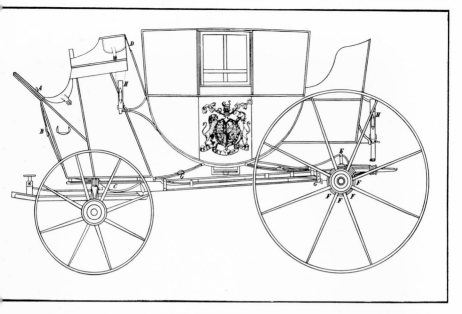

Besant's patent mail-coach. Specification drawing, 1786

A mail-coach of post-Vidler design, 1836

Sir Francis Freeling, Bart., Secretary to the Post Office 1798–1836

John Palmer, aged about seventeen

This is one of the very few allusions in all the letters to war-time conditions in England. The war with France had now been going on for more than a year and was destined to continue. Elsewhere, there are two mentions of how it impeded the mail to the Continent and one where a guard has asked if he can get exemption from military service. The book of printed instructions which has been preserved, covering the duration of the war, which ended in 1815, makes no other reference to it either, except to warn guards in the later stages to treat persons with suspicion who might be escaping French officers who had broken their paroles. Press gangs had become active and unscrupulous, but we hear no more of them. Excisemen, however, not only held up a mail-coach but confiscated it and its team on justified suspicion of smuggling (p. 278).

Guard Stanroyd again (from p. 75)

G.P.O. May 20/94

My Lords
    In consideration of Stanroyd being a good Guard, as your Lordships are so kind to think the whole of the expence attending the bringing up the Bags from Newbury as rather too severe a punishment, I beg leave to submit to your Ldshps that he may pay half the expence and that the other half may be charged in the PMr of Newbury's Incident account.
                    All which &c
                    T. Hasker

So he is let off with loss of five weeks' pay. But he maintained his character as a good guard, and we next hear of him two years hence as one of the picked men chosen to guard the 'Royal Weymouth Mail'.

*   *   *   *

The York and Edinburgh Mail
    The next letter gives an indication of the increase in correspondence. It also points to some of the drawbacks of the patent coach. The York Mail carried letters, newspapers, and magazines, not only to that city (where it made connection with the coach to Edinburgh) but also for several branches and the cross-post between Hull and Liverpool. It travelled along the Old North Road through Ware, Royston, and

Huntingdon, joining the Great North Road at the top of Alconbury Hill. The letter also foreshadows the plan T.H. was maturing to put a second coach on for Carlisle by taking over the line of an existing stage-coach (p. 99).

G.P.O. June 5th 1794

My Lords

Mr Willan and several other Proprietors of the York and London Mail Coach concern have been with me at the G.P.O. and complained of the great weight they carry on the roof of the Mail which they say, as do the Coachmen and Guards, was the cause of the late overturn by which a man was unfortunately killed. They say the weight of the mail with the additional weights of the Coach in consequence is very injurious to their stock of horses tho' they keep a greater number than would do the duty if their load was no heavier than that of other Mail Coaches.

I have already stated to your Lordships by Reports Feby 22nd & 25th, 1794, No 21 & 26 A—that the Mail Box is much longer to the York Mail Coach than to any other, on which account the Coach is obliged to be built much stronger and heavier, it must also be built stronger in consequence of the great weight loaded on the Roof of the Coach—for Carriages must be made strong according to the weight they carry and the Velocity they travel with—the Mail sent by this Coach last Saturday weight 517 lb[1] it has weight 525 lb it is heavier than when the Coach first carried by 140 lb.

The part of the Mail that is tied on to the loop is nearly equal to two Passengers perhaps to more, for when the Coach is on an enclining plain it may shift if not well fastened and accelerate an overturn. The plan of Mail Coaches is to carry only one outside and that on the Box that the body may not be loaded to assist the lateral motion but in this coach though they carry no outside passengers on the roof the Mail is equal to Two. I wish it was to be avoided that the Danger to Passengers by the Coach being so loaded might be done away, that the safety of the Mails might be complete by being all locked in the Box—that the Injury to the Stock the Contractors complain of might be remedied.

If a Contractor would undertake to work a Coach from London

[1] Apparently nett and gross weights, the latter to include the bags.

to Ferrybridge for £200 or £250 instead of 1d per mile each way all parties would be accomodated, the Merchants of Glasgow would have their Memorial granted. It might go by Hatfield by which that road by Alconbury Hill would be supplied with a Mail Coach, the riding work of which amounts to about as much as would pay the Guards so that the additional Expense would only be the sum agreed for as above, £200 or £250, instead of 1d per mile which would amount to £535 it being 176 miles.

I hope your Lordships will see my only motive for addressing this to you is to comply with the repeated solicitations of the Contractors from London to Carlisle (upwards of Thirty in number) and to see the Mail in safety every night.

I beg leave to enclose your Lordships a copy of a letter I sent to Mr Bonner on this subject in July 1792.

All which

T. Hasker

What the 'Memorial' was does not appear. Until very lately, Glasgow had only been served by a riding-post from Edinburgh but the city had improved matters by subsidising a mail-coach from Carlisle (p. 144).

*   *   *   *

Uniform bargain with the Coffee House Porter (from p. 63)

Leicester
June 15/94

My Lords

If it meets yr Lordships approbation on reading the enclosed, to continue the Uniform to the Porter at the Gloster Coffee House, it will I think be very properly bestowed, on condition that he does always assist in helping to load and unload the Bags in the manner he represents he does. His not being a servant of the Post Office, this was not considered a part of his duty, nor had the Office any control over him. But if he engages to do this daily for a Uniform it will be one very advantageously given.

All &c

T. Hasker

*   *   *   *

The Dover Mails

There were two mail-coaches to Dover, one carrying the inland mail for Canterbury and East Kent, the other, the foreign mail for the packets sailing to Calais and Ostend. The former left London at the usual time—8 P.M.—but the other tried to fit in with the tide at Dover and left at no fixed time. The sailors of the packets seem to have made a point of reaching and leaving England on a daylight tide, and the contractors did not want to keep their men and horses waiting indefinitely at Dover, and so left London between the hours of 2 and 4 in the morning. On that account, it seems, travellers to the Continent preferred to go by the regular coach and wait at Dover rather than hang about in London. But now, owing to the war, this Mail was getting few passengers except for local destinations, for Calais and Ostend had both been closed by the revolutionary French Government. A Dover packet still went to Flushing, but most of the Continental mail was being sent via Harwich either to Flushing or Sluys. The question was whether the Dover route ought not to be cancelled, together with the coach which served it, and to send all via Harwich? The usual optimism about the war being over quickly prevailed (it lasted another twenty-one years) and Hasker believed that by personally haranguing the contractors he could at least persuade them to keep the Dover inland mail going. He did, in fact, succeed in keeping both on the road. But after three months—the war showing no signs of coming to an end—the foreign mail contractors called on him again (p. 97).

G.P.O. July 14th/94

My Lords

Two of the Contractors of the Dover Mail Coach have been in Town representing that in consequence of the travelling to and from their Port and the Continent being nearly anihilated the Mail fills very ill and that they think they shall not be able to continue it. Though travelling may be very scarce for the present I cannot conceive that this can be the opinion of the Company in general and have therefore called a meeting at Canterbury tomorrow morning at ten o'clock. I shall go by the Mail Coach that their real opinion and interest may be known, after which I will immediately inform your Lordships, tho I cannot think that for a temporary check to travelling that road they can scarcely think of relinquishing the Mail Coach to Dover.

The above is respecting the Inland Dover Mail Coach. But with respect to the Foreign Dover Mail, if your Lordships approve, I will consult with Mr Braithwaite for, as all the Flanders mails are now received via Helvoet Sluys and Harwich, it may probably be best to send them the same way. They have hitherto been sent by the Dover Foreign Mail to go by the Packet to Flushing but, as now the South bank of the Scheldt is in the possession of the Enemy, I submit this to your Lordships.

I am &c

T. Hasker

P.S. Since writing the above, my Lords, I have seen Mr Starr who says the Flanders Mail should go to Flushing by all means, and of course by the Dover Foreign Mail; therefore the latter part of this report is void for the present.

*   *   *   *

Exceptional tolls

G.P.O. July 22/94

My Lords

I beg leave to explain to yr Lordships the reason that more Tolls were paid on some of the roads in the last Quarter than in the preceeding one.

The Portsmouth Coach in the preceeding Quarter, and part of the last, paid 1/2 per week, but in consequence of orders given that no Coach should be sent out of a Sunday afternoon that came in that morning, this Coach is obliged to pay 8d more for Street Toll in going out, which encreased the sum to 1/10.

The Pool & Exeter Coaches pay 2d more weekly in the last Quarter than the preceeding at Hammersmith gate for watering the roads.

The Bath, Bristol, and Gloucester Coaches pay each 2d more at Smallboro Green & Hammersmith gates for watering the road, which encreases the Tolls for those Coaches from 4/- to 4/4 per week each.

The Shrewsbury Coach from the 11th May pays 2d per week at

Southall gate on account of the Toll being advanced from 8d to 10d.

The Norwich Coach paid in the preceeding Quarter 1/4 at Hackney Gate but, in consequence of the Coach being changed every Sunday since the 20th April they pay 2/8, which encreaced that Toll from 2/6 to 3/8. It would be 3/10 but they pay 2d less at Shoreditch.

The Ipswich Coach, since the above date and for the same Reason pays at Mileend 2/4 instead of 1/2 per week. The other Coaches are in general the same as the preceeding Quarter, except that some variations may have happened in the Tolls paid by the Mail Coaches travelling from Northampton as the Coach which arrives last at Northampton is ordered to bring up the strap bags.

All &c

T. Hasker.

The above seems to contradict the statement of the Postmasters-General 'We are exempted from paying tolls' (p. 146), and also what is said in all books on the subject about the mail going toll-free until 1813, either in a coach or any other conveyance, when this privilege was waived in favour of the Scotch turnpike trusts. But these five gates at the near approaches to London and the 'Street Toll' (charged again if the same coach did not come and go in the same day) were evidently exceptions of which no other evidence except this letter of T.H.'s appears to have come to light. 'Smallboro Green' is Smallberry Green, a mile beyond Brentford Bridge. The name as well as the gate has now vanished off the map.

*　　*　　*　　*

The Royal Weymouth Mail

The story of how the first cause of friction between Palmer and his superiors arose, when Lord Walsingham took on himself to detail a special mail-coach to attend the King at Cheltenham in 1788, has been fully told. The custom was continued during the succeeding annual visits of George III to Weymouth, though with an expenditure much curtailed. This seems to have been largely achieved by allowing the contractors to collect fares from the passengers and make their usual charges on parcels, both of which had passed free on the first occasion. This service, henceforth known as the 'Royal Weymouth Mail', was intended by Hasker to be the perfect model of regularity, and he took the utmost pains to see that it should be so, concentrating all his available staff on that one single route. Yet something always went wrong, to his great grief and vexation. I really believe his zeal was not entirely due to his natural wish to achieve perfection in the working of this specially Royal Mail. He was evidently a strong Hanoverian and had the same feelings of attachment and personal loyalty to George III shared quite fervidly by many, including the intelligent Fanny Burney.

The coach left Lad Lane and the G.P.O. early in the afternoon and, calling at the Horse Guards and the Queen's House at Kew, went on to Windsor and then to Weymouth. It arrived at Gloucester Lodge, where the royal party stayed, in good time for breakfast the next morning. Gloucester Lodge had been built by the Duke of Gloucester on the recommendation (it is said) of none other than Ralph Allen. Allen was well acquainted with the royal family and had lent his huge mansion of Prior Park at Bath to the Duke of York and Princess Amelia while he went to stay at Weymouth, where he was a regular visitor.

The forthcoming run was the sixth and, though Lord Walsingham had just left the Office for his new appointment, Hasker felt that he (the founder of the supreme event) should be kept informed. He wrote accordingly to say that Lord Chesterfield had fixed the following Saturday for the first journey, ending, 'I hope your Lordship will think the connection is a good one though I could not get Mr White of Staines (a contractor) to give an answer for some days, so I continued to do without him—and I do not doubt that it will be better done, as he began the misconduct of the last Royal Mail.' Also, on the same day is a letter to Lord Chesterfield marked 'Private'.

G.P.O. Augt 6th 1794

My Lord

I have the honour to enclose your Lordship a Time Bill of His Majesty's Royal Weymouth Mail Coach, and I have further to inform your Lordship that I agreed with each Contractor to have his horses ready at the proper time in their Places, and have since given them all their full direction in writing; but lest there should be any negligence I send Mr Wilkins on the road, Friday, to see that everything is ready—horses, harness, breechings, &c. Mr

Charlton goes down to Blandford with the first Coach & Mr
Wilkins will attend it to Weymouth & wait yr Lordship's Commands. Mr White will daily go with the Coach from Lad Lane
to the Horse Guards & the Queen's House. I shall be at Windsor
on Saturday to see the first Coach off—& afterwards shall be for
a few days on the Road. I hope & think, my Lord, all will be
smooth.

I am &c
T. Hasker

Wilkins and Charlton were deputy superintendents, White one
of the two clerks. Hasker specially mentions breechings as, although
they should always have formed a regular part of the harness, for
more safety in descending hills—the coaches having no brakes—the
contractors were apt to omit them, as costing a little more and giving
more trouble in the change. The Queen's House is Kew Palace in
Kew Gardens.

The next letter shows that Hasker's pains were at least appreciated
in the highest quarter.

G.P.O. Aug 12/94

To Lord Chesterfield

My Lord

I have the honor to enclose yr Lordship a Time Bill of the Weymouth Royal Mail Coach, as I have now altered the Time between
Blandford and Weymouth. I thought as the horses were changed
at Piddletown[1] that I could cribb a few minutes but, on practice,
finding they had not time enough, I have given them Ten Minutes,
which is as much as was allowed former years except two mts.

I enclose your Lordship the Time Bill that returned this morning.
Everything is regular except a little time lost by Mr Weeks.

His Majesty came down to the Park Gate to see the Mail Coach
the first and second day and told me he was much pleased to see it so
well done & regular and that he was glad Mr White did not work it.

As this night, my Lord, the Servants of their Majesties begin

---

[1] Correctly so-called until this and other similar place-names taken from the
same river were Bowdlerized in the early 20th century to make them fit for
'Tolpuddle Martyrs'.

travelling with it, I have fixed a man at Windsor to help tie on the Luggage with additional cords and straps should they be necessary. I hope everything will be regular and give your Lordship the satisfaction you wish.

I am &c

T. Hasker

Some unforeseen difficulties crop up, and Hasker feels he must send his only other clerk, Nicholas, a man who had more knowlege of the peculiar working of the whole system and perhaps more tact than any other of his assistants, to reinforce Charlton, who may only have known how things were done in the West Country and have been an unequal match for the London contractors.

General Post Office
August 18th/94

My Lord

I had the honour of your Lordship's letter of direction respecting parcels directed to the King, the Queen, or Mr Gorton never being detained which I had anticipated and I hope it was strictly adhered to; but it is possible a parcel might have been left in the outset as the Glut of Luggage was so great that being now over, I hope every parcel for the whole household will be forwarded by the first Coach, it was so yesterday & today.

I gave direction in Lad Lane that they must not book any luggage to go by the Royal Mail for a few days which, the Proprietors complained very much, injured their earnings—however I said it must be done and it was.

Though I had Charlton at Windsor fearing things might not be quite regular, I sent Mr Nicholas and enclose for your Lordship's perusal his letter and as the very great glut of parcels are now gone if we can scape an overturn I do not doubt but the Royal Mail of this year will give great satisfaction.

A mistake I must mention to your Lordship happened on Friday relative to the Messengers which I beg leave to state to your Lordship. A place is taken for one Messenger every day by Mr Napean—a second Messenger being that day to go he, Mr Child sent up for a place for the Messenger and received an answer one was secured for him. At the Bookeeping Office they conceived it was by the

Messenger booked by Mr Napean as he did not send word that he wanted a second seat for a Messenger & let the other three places and the Coach went with three passengers to the Horseguards and Mr Child got in which filled the Coach—presently after Mr Tims, the Messenger booked for by Mr Napean, came—and a horrid dispute was the Consequence and some detention, but the other passengers were good natured and lade 5 in the Coach to accomodate matters.

I am &c

Earl Chesterfield   Tho Hasker

The 'Messengers' were King's Messengers. They don't seem to have had either the dignity or good manners of later members of this distinguished corps and, as will appear (p. 125), they dodged paying their fares which, under the revised conditions, everyone had to do. Wheeler-Holohan in his *History of the King's Messengers* admits as much when writing of the year 1795. He says: 'As a result (of a change in the system of making appointments) a very mixed lot of men were to wear the silver greyhound for a time.' However, things were settling down nicely and T.H. writes:

Marked 'Private'

My Lord

To all appearance the Royal Mail is going on very well. I have the honor to enclose a letter to your Lordship from Mr Nicholas who I planted at Windsor, as I think it will give some information to your Lordship's satisfaction.

I am

Earl of Chesterfield   T. Hasker.

But soon the King and his court are discovered to be breaking Hasker's fundamental rule of punctuality and he sends Lord Chesterfield a polite but firm protest—almost a rebuke. As the time-bill three years hence shows that the coach is still leaving at 4 P.M. it looks as if the hint was properly taken, and the time not put back, which would, incidentally, have hurt the state correspondence by an inconveniently late arrival in London, where the coach was normally due at 10 A.M.

Marked '(Special)'

G.P.O. Aug 21 1794

My Lord

As I perceive the Royal Mail Coach is generally kept at Weymouth beyond the time affixed for its starting I suppose that it is
convenient to His Majesty or your Lordship that it should stay
longer than four o'clock, and therefore submit for your determination if it would not be better to fix it to start every night at either
5 or 6 o'clk as your Lordship may think best.

The only thing I wish strictly adhered to is that it always starts
exactly at the same time settled—there are many reasons for it as
Coachmen, Guards, and horsekeepers knowing when to expect and
be ready for its arrival at the different stages and for passengers to
know when to meet it on the road or they will prefer and go by
other Carriages which will be to the disadvantage of the Contractors'
earnings and if they have but a slight cause they will soon marvel it
to a Mountain. I hope your Lordship will see the propriety of this
proposal—

which &c

Earl Chesterfield   T. Hasker

We gain no idea of how the Duty is being done on the other far-
flung routes, now that the inspectorate and the clerical staff are all
away from them and the Office, leaving De Quincey's 'conscious
presence, over-ruling all obstacles' alone to battle with the daily influx
of time-bills and correspondence. Still he might well think he had now
cured all the troubles arising from the Royal Weymouth Mail. But
then:

Marked '(Separate)'

G.P.O. Aug 23rd 1794

My Lord

What I most dreaded has happened—an overturn by Mr Week's
Coachman, Cook. I beg leave to inform your Lordship that before
the Royal Mail started I had heard a bad account of this man and
wrote to Mr Weeks desireing Spenny, a man I well knew, might
drive, or if he disliked him he should have either Pullen or Scarlet,
in reply to which I received the enclosed answer. As Mr Weeks had
been so long in the Mail Coach line, and as I knew he had bought

some horses, I did not like to look out for another person at Salisbury. I thought it would be acting too dogmatic and therefore let him have his way hoping the Coachman would not prove so bad as had been represented to me. I have some other Mail Coach duty to attend this evening that renders it impossible for me to leave Town till tomorrow. I have took a place by the Exeter Mail Coach, the Royal Weymouth being full and will attend your Lordship's Commands Monday. Mr Wilkins was with the Coach when it overturned at Salisbury.

Which &c

Earl of Chesterfield   T. Hasker

*   *   *   *

Other matters

The letter written to their Lordships on the following day gives a sidelight on Hasker's flexibility and essential humanity. In spite of the disaster and disappointment caused thereby we hear no more of the Royal Weymouth till it is due to wind up. Instead, there is an appeal for the better accommodation of two humble folk, an office cleaner, Mrs Danders, and her husband who live in a poky garret, that they may 'occupy a small room up two pair of stairs which is become vacant by the Dead Cross-road Letter Office[1] being removed from it'.

*   *   *   *

The Portpatrick diligence

After that kindly representation on behalf of the humble couple, whose success is not recorded, Hasker did not write a single line to the P.M.G. for a whole month. The vexed question of the Portpatrick Mail had cropped up again. It will be recalled that Walsingham's refusal to endorse Palmer's agreement to pay the contractors on that route at the rate of 2d. a mile (4d. the double mile) had infuriated Palmer to such an extent that he cancelled the services of four of the most vital Mails—a worse but more honest row than that over the King's coach. The following letter reveals that a compromise had been

---

[1] Dealing with letters in the cross-posts which could not be delivered through misdirection or some other cause. Deputy postmasters were entitled to the unpaid postage due on them.

88

patched up and the Portpatrick service restarted on the basis of $1\frac{1}{2}$d. a mile (3d. a double mile). Part of the bargain seems to have been that a lighter coach, drawn by two horses instead of four, should be used. Among the Palmer Papers there is a note from Woolmer dated 1792 to say 'It was some time ago intended that the P. Patrick Mail would, next Spring, be carried on a light Coach or Diligence with a pair of horses' which, incidentally, explains the meaning of the word *diligence* as then in use on the roads in Great Britain though not on the Continent. Hasker was particularly anxious to maintain this northern link with Ireland. But it happened that on the very day when the first mail-coach ran (August the 2nd, 1784) the Irish Post Office was separated from our own under a Home Rule Act. Following that, the P.M.G. in Dublin behaved in such a strange and obstructive fashion, both towards England and his own fellow-countrymen, as to cause Walsingham to 'lift his hands in amazement that such perversity was possible'.

General Post Office
Sep 24th 1794

My Lords

I beg leave to state to yr Lordships the situation of the Carlisle and Port Patrick Mail Diligence which for many reasons is a very desirable object to the Genl Post Office to keep it on the road.

This road first had a Mail Carriage on it when Packets for the Passage from Port Patrick to Donaghadee were contracted for by the Marquis of Downshire and then I, with much importunity and difficulty persuaded the General Post Office, Dublin, to meet them at Donaghadee by which a compleat Mail Rout is established between London and all parts of Britain via Port Patrick passage to Belfast, Dublin, Limerick, Cork &c &c—in Ireland. From the great opposition given to it by the Innkeepers in Galloway (who will not work it though they lower the price of their post Chaise to 6d pr mile[1] to beat it off the road) the Contractors are reduced to the necessity of giving it up if a temporary aid cannot be allowed them, their pay for carrying the Mail is three halfpence per mile[2]—one

[1] The regular price for a post-chaise and pair was a shilling a mile with a tip to the post-boy at the end of each stage.

[2] 3d. the double mile, while the Glasgow Mail contractors got 4d. In addition, this coach had been subsidised (p. 145).

penny pr mile less than the Mail Carriage is paid from Carlisle to Glasgow. I therefore, finding that it must be given up without such aid, wrote to ask them if such pay, namely Two pence pr mile each way, the same as from Carlisle to Glasgow, was allowed them for the ensueing half year by your Lordships, if they would undertake it and if they thought it would be the compleat establishment of the Carriage to the discomfiture of the Innkeepers who had took up arms against it, merely because a Public Government Carriage should not accomodate the Country [and] the Nobility and Gentry who are very fond of it and desires its continuance, as yr Lordships will see by Letter No. 3 from Mr Gordon, High Sherriff of Kirkudbright Steurartry and, if they succeed by Crushing it, would Triumph exceedingly and it would be setting a very bad example elsewhere.

It would also be the means of Establishing a Carriage from Carlisle to Dumfries by the oppositionists and, which opposition as soon as a road is opened from Sanquhar to Muirkirk would be continued down to Glasgow, to the great injury of the Carlisle and Glasgow Mail Coach if not to the entire anhilation of it, for two Carriages cannot lie on that road; they might exist for a while but discontents in the Mail Coach Contractors would ensue.

The addition I therefore propose for your Lordships to give for the Winter half Year amounts to £46:7:8 pr quarter. That your Lordships may fully see the necessity of the addition I have the honour to enclose two letters, No 1 and 2 from Mr Woolner my assistant at Carlisle received yesterday & today.

All &c

Rt Hon P.M.G.   T. Hasker

(Replies)

Allow for the Winter & by way of experiment the advance Mr Hasker recommends.
> Ch

By all means Contract as Mr Woolmer recommends
> Ch
> Lei

Next letter on this subject (p. 115).

*　　*　　*　　*

Wind-up of the Weymouth Season and the King's Coach

To Lord Chesterfield

marked 'Separate'

G.P. Office Sept 25. 1794

My Lord

I have the honor of your Lordship's letter directing the discontinuance of the Royal Mail Coach after Saturday, the fourth of October, which I shall consider final if your Lordships should not give further orders in consequence of the enclosed letter from Mr Gorton.

If you should not wish to have the Coach continued so long as the fourth you will be so kind as to give your Commands. Had I not received your Lordship's minute of today I should have proposed for your determination for the last Royal Mail Coach to leave Weymouth Sunday next, the 28th Inst., but now it stands till the 4th of October. If I hear no further from your Lordship.

That unfortunate Coachman, Cook, has ruined our reputation for this year. I suppose your Lordship has been informed of the overturn, there does not appear to be any blame attached to any one else, as you will observe by Mr Wilkins's letter. I wish Mr Weeks would have been advised. Mr Willson is inconsolable; his reputation, he says, was so much at stake to outdo his opponent, Mr Willan. If yr Lordship should think it necessary I will attend at Weymouth the last day of the Royal Mail running.

All &c

T. Hasker

(Answer) Sept 27

The Mail may as well continue running to & from Weymouth till 4th Oct. I am very sorry for the Accident which has happened & hope Mr Weeks will in future be more attentive & select proper & approved drivers.

Ch.

Certainly
Lei.
Cook's case reviewed, p. 99.

G.P.Office
Oct. 7. 1794

My Lords

During the time of the Royal Mail Coach running, the Duty of 3 Gds. between London and Salisbury was done by two and the Duty between London and Northampton was done by one Guard less than the Establishment by which the Guards did extra Duty and I thought it better that it should be so done by those acquainted with the Duty than by new ones, especially as it was but for a little time and as the extra Guards if put on would be out of employ now the Weymouth stopped and be destitute of a place till a Vacancy might happen.

I therefore have to submit to your Lordships as a reward to those Guards who have done extra Duty that they have the extra pay being 8 Guineas divided amongst them, it will be no more expense to the Office than it would have been [had] the Weymouth never started.

All &c

T. Hasker

(Answer)

Divide Eight Guineas in the manner proposed by Mr Hasker.
Ch.
Certainly
Lei.

*   *   *   *

Domestic consultation

Gen. Post Office
Octr. 12 1794

My Lords

As I find by your Lordships minute that Mrs Nicholas is to quit her employment of cleaning Mr Freeling's Office, by which she will only have Mr Bannars to do—I therefore beg leave to propose to your Lordships for her to clean my Offices below stairs which have been hitherto done though very indifferently by the extra Guards and which with Mr Bannar's Office will be sufficient employment.

I find that her Bill for Washing soap &c has hitherto amounted to about £12 a year but as my Offices are much smaller than Mr Freeling's that it will not amount to near so much.

All which &c

T. Hasker

Guard's blunderbuss, pistols, time-piece and pouch, bag (?) for powder-horn and shot

An early private bag; the pattern is similar to that of the bye- or strap-bag

A coach snow-bound. The guard, riding the near-side leader, gets the mail forward

(Answer) Oct 16th

No objection strikes the P.M.G. to the employing Mrs Nicholas to clean Mr Hasker's Office—if there are any objections let them be stated.

Ch.

Lei

How different from Palmer methods!

*   *   *   *

Mail-coach robbery

This is the first I have found on record since armed coaches replaced post-boys. But it was not a hold-up. These were not attempted until the opening of the 19th century, when they increased in frequency (p. 280).

Gen. Post Office

Oct 12 1794

My Lords

I have the honor to state to your Lordships the case as far as it has transpired of the property being stolen from the Bristol Mail.

It appears that Tho. Thomas who is committed to prison for the examination of the offence took a journey down to Bristol by the Mail Coach about 10 days prior to the Robbery and returned to London by the same Mail Coach the next day no doubt with an intent to do the deed, but not having an opportunity then he repeated his journey on the 2nd. 3rd. & 4th Inst., and by the Guards not adhering strictly to their Instructions (delivered repeatedly to them as your Lordships will see by the enclosed papers) he succeeded and I have no doubt by waiting for a fit time for his purpose when the Mail Box was carelessly left unlocked or by the guards permitting him to ride on their seat, as it plainly appears that they both were guilty of a breach of those parts of their Instructions.

I am very sorry that any officers in my department should neglect any part of their duty, but I assure your Lordships that it is not for want of frequent admonitions and directions in every way I can think of to make so wide and troublesome a Business as regular as possible in that so necessary a part of their duty namely keeping their

H   93

Mail Box locked—and I have been both by myself and assistants very watchful to meet them on the road when not expected to detect and punish this fault and so recently as the 14th June last S. Pendleton the Liverpool Guard at S[toney] Stratford was dismissed for this fault, and on the 23 of July Wm Emanuel the Oxford Guard and on the 18th Sept C. Allen in the very same Town. All those dismissed were stuck up in the Office that they might see it every night and from such noteriety avoid such neglect and tho every possible endeavour has been made by the entreaty of friends and representations of distress and great family [hardship?] yet I have not restored them for I look on the crime too great.

I beg leave to enclose your Lordship several papers by which you will see every possible attention and direction on my part has been given.

Both the Guards upon their examination fairly owned that they locked their Mail Boxes at such places as they were afraid of meeting a Superintendant or any person who would give information that they might be punished. Thos. Hawkins the Guard from Marlboro to London on being asked why he locked his Mail Box at Caln-break though he neglected it all the way from Thatcham said he perceived the Worcester Mail Coach was coming up to them and he did not know but a Superintendant might be in it.

In domestic concerns it is notorious that servants do not frequently do their duty even though their director can inspect their duty constantly, it is therefore less surprising that when Guards are left to themselves not dreading detection that they do not do their duty.

One of these men, L. Williams, has been in the Service 5 years and was promoted to the best place in it from Marlboro to Bristol for that it was thought he might be depended upon. Thos Hawkins is also a respectable man in appearance and has an excellent Carracter from various respectable people. I can only assure your Lordships that I have been for some months past more severe with Guards for this fault than heretofore as your Lordships will see from extracts from the Black Book several having been turned away and I beg leave to say that I will pay every possible attention in every way I can devize and meet them constantly where unexpected and endeavour to prevent such misconduct in future:

No 1. Guards Instructions that they sign and give £20 Bond to perform with two sureties.

2. Their Oath of Office.

3. A letter sent to every Guard in the Kingdom April the 4th 1794 to the very purpose of locking their Mail Box.

4. A letter finding fault of their negligence and desiring more attention or they would be discharged.

5. Extracts in print from the Black Book which I am sorry to say the example with these Guards has not had the desired effect.   (Several are reproduced in Chapter XI.)

I am constantly sending them other letters of directions as well as giving it verbally but as these are all that concerns directly the present case [such as?] they are I send to your Lordships.

All which &c

T. Hasker.

(Answer)

Oct 15th

The PMG have not the least doubt that as far as Mr Hasker's attention & that of his deputies goes every possible care is taken to guard against any losses by the Mail Coaches [and] in the instance of the late robbery of the Bristol Mail no blame is imputable to them. The Guard of that night doing duty with that Coach must be suspended if not dismissed. The Gds appear frequently to be riding on the Box with the Coachman. Would an order saying that all Coachmen who suffered the Guard to ride on the Box with them should be dismissed prevent this happening? I know that the Coachmen are not appointed by the P.O. but surely no Mail Coach Contractor would desire to be excepted or excused from obeying such an order.

Ch

Lei

The Bristol Gd must be desired [sic] in some way or other so as to be forthcoming as evidence at the trial of Thomas Thomas.

Ch

Certainly

Lei

The suggested order shows how little the P.M.G. understood the difficulties of working the amorphous system. To embarrass the already delicate relations between guard and coachman by making them spy on each other would have been disastrous. The two guards were duly dismissed, but Hasker could not afford to lose such good men (he must have been much impressed by the unvarnished candour of their confession). He kept his eye on them and eventually had them back.

*   *   *   *

The racing urge

G.P.O. Oct 20th 1794

My Lords

The enclosed is from Mr Cooper, Postmaster of Preston in Lancashire who is also a Mail Coach Contractor. Your Lordships will see by his letter that the Mail Coach and a Gentleman's Carriage were running together on the road and that both were Overturned—if the Gentleman should bring an action against Mr Cooper how far it may be your Lordship's opinion to reimburse him his expense I submit for your determination but Mr Cooper certainly hopes rather too much when he seems to expect your Lordships to order an action to be commenced. There is no doubt but Mail Coaches though they travel for public accomodation are a good deal obstructed, and if the Coachman to the Gentleman had been good-natured he would have given way—his Master should have reproved him for not doing of it for it is for the convenience of every Gentleman that the Mails should be carried expeditious.

I have written to Mr Cooper and desired he will send up the depositions of the Guard and outside Passenger and have desired him to get the opinion of the Inside Passengers, as Guards and Coachmen do not always tell the truth nor do Juries sometimes believe them.

If your Lordships should be inclined to support the Mail Contractors in this (as it strikes me) the only way will be to let them defend their own cause and for you if you think it is a just one to reimburse some part of the expence.

All &c

T. Hasker

To race and overtake are chronic temptations by no means banished from the roads. But in the case of the mail-coach, the coachman had full right to overtake a private vehicle which, on its part, was bound by law to give way. As competition on the roads increased racing between stage-coaches became a common menace, and in spite of strict orders to the contrary, the Mails occasionally indulged.

*   *   *   *

Cary's final account

G.P.O. Oct 1794

My Lords

About two years since the great roads of the Kingdom were begun to be measured by your Lordships directions—the saving by this ascertaining the real distance amount to about £60 pr Annum. The admeasurement already paid is £150 and I beg leave to enclose for your Lordship's signature a bill for the remainder if it meet your approbation.

I also enclose a sketch of the manner[1] 3700 miles of it is copied in a large Demi Folio which is kept in my Apartment for the use of the G.P.O.—the person who has copied it and reverted [? converted] many of the admeasurements to make all the calculations from London wanted to be paid by the Mile which would have amounted to about £30 but I have settled with him if your Lordships approve at 20 Guineas—it is very neatly done and is very deserving of that sum.

All &c

T. Hasker

The work, besides reducing the 'reputed' mile to its statutory length, thereby cutting the contractor a little more, must have brought in additional revenue from the increase in postage, now based on mileage and not, as formerly, on stages. Previous mentions of Cary's commission and his Road Book are on pp. 2, 67.

*   *   *   *

Dover Foreign Mail again (from p. 80)

G.P.O. Oct 25th /94

My Lords

Several of the Dover Foreign Mail Coach Contractors have been

[1] T. H. appears to mean ' a *precis* of the matter'.

in London and have represented that in consequence of the Continental travelling being thrown into another Channel they are obliged to reduce the number of their Carriages which will make it impossible for them to continue carrying the Foreign Mail provided their Lordships cannot consent to its leaving London at 5 o'ck in the Morning. At present it leaves London at no fixed hour but generally from ½ past 2 till 4 A.M.—They say they will agree to carry it down by the Time they now do on those days the Tide serves for it to leave Dover early. Now frequently though they set out a Coach at an uncertain hour in the Middle of the Night without Passengers to carry the Mail to Dover, it 4 times in 5 has to wait there some hours before the Packet departs. I therefore submit to your Lordships determination as I see no impediment to it if, during the time the principal despatches for the Continent go via Harwich if it will not be proper to accord with their request especially as when the Tide serves early they will strain a point and be down as soon as now which we shall be able to direct from this Office by having a Tide Table.

All which

T. Hasker

P.S. I must further inform your Lordships that the present expense of conveying the Mail by Coach does not amount to half what it would do if this Company was to cease carrying of it and it was to go by express—as it did some years since.

This last cry seems to have been answered to the satisfaction of the contractors as the coach continued to run until the following year when Holland was overrun by the French, and Dover packets could no longer make use of Dutch ports. All mail for the Continent went thenceforward from Harwich to Hamburg (the 'Hamboro Mail' of future references). The discontinuance of the Dover link was another nail in the coffin of poor J. Carter, the doyen of the mail-guards. Having been barred by other contractors he had been put on that worst paying of all grounds. His next adventure is recorded on p. 107.

*   *   *   *

A plea for Thomas Cook (from pp. 87, 91)

G.P.O. Novr. 1st 1794

My Lords

His Majesty's Bounty of 30 Guineas, which he generously gives to be divided equally amongst the Coachmen and Guards of the Royal Weymouth Mail Coach, for their care of that carriage and the luggage, is all distributed at 2½ Guineas each, except to Thomas Cook, Mr Weeks's Coachman, who had the misfortune to overturn the Coach twice. It has hitherto been a custom that if any overturn or misconduct happens, the person guilty of the error does not receive his share of His Majesty's Bounty but it is divided among the remainder. This was the case two years ago when John Guppy, for misconduct, had no share given to him and, it being withheld certainly has had an effect in inducing the servants to do their duty properly. Therefore I submit to your Lordships whether Thomas Cook should have his share—he twice overturned the Coach but, in the accident, he had the misfortune to break his thigh. Tho an indifferent coachman, he is otherwise a very good kind of man and his punishment has been very great.

All which
T. Hasker

(Answer, Nov 3)

Let Thos. Cook partake of His Majesty's Bounty, but let him be told that he receives it in commiseration of the misfortune he has had to break his Thigh, for that his conduct would not otherwise have entitled him to it.

Ch.
Lei.

A second Carlisle Mail

To the Earl of Leicester. Marked 'Separate'

G.P.O. Dec 31/94

My Lord

I have the honor of your Lordship's commands enclosing a letter of Lord Sandwich's respecting Mr Homes of Alconbury Hill whom I know very well, and whose house and self are very respectable. But

I must beg leave to state to yr Lordship that when the present Coach, called the Princess Royal or Carlisle Coach, is made a Mail Coach it will not be a new connection, for at present Mr Sibley of Stilton works past Mr Holmes's door to Huntingdon and when it runs up the other road must certainly work to Bugden, for it would be too short a stage to stop at Mr Holmes's at the Wheatsheaf.

Perhaps if Mr Holmes would work a stage from home, namely above Bugden, he may be accomodated. I only say perhaps, my Lord, for your Ldshps know, as must Ld S. that these people all run in connections and it may not be possible to join them—for he, at present, houses Coaches in opposite concerns. But at the meeting, which will be about the end of July, I will be very particular in remembering yr Ldshps desires, and everything that can shall be done for Mr Holmes.

I am &c

T. Hasker

Hasker is using Lord Sandwich's request to reinforce his plan to relieve the congestion complained of (p. 78) by running a second coach to Carlisle with connection to Glasgow. This would travel by the Great North Road (at present only served by rides) and share burdens with the York and Edinburgh Mail which went down the Old North Road. The time-bills for those Mails in Chapter X show how the suggestions in this letter were being carried out. In the *Torrington Diaries* (Ed. John Beresford) a bill of the Wheatsheaf at Alconbury Hill is reproduced bearing Mr Holmes's name. It was a simple but welcoming little inn to which John Byng paid many visits. [Carlisle Mail established (p. 113.)]

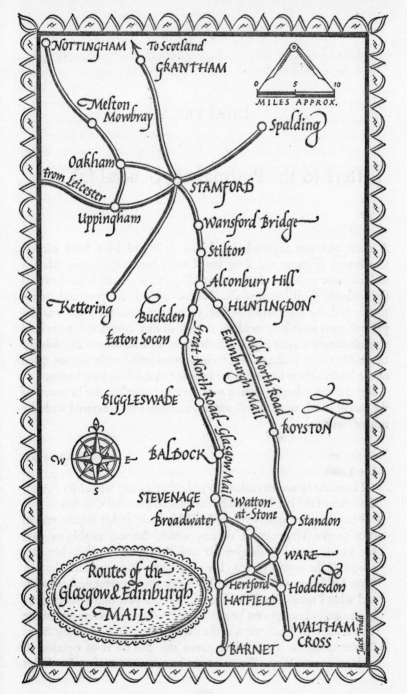

NOTTINGHAM   To Scotland
GRANTHAM

Melton
Mowbray

0   5   10
MILES APPROX.

Spalding

Oakham

from Leicester

STAMFORD

Uppingham

Wansford Bridge

Stilton

Alconbury Hill

Kettering

Buckden   HUNTINGDON

Eaton Socon

BIGGLESWADE   ROYSTON

BALDOCK

STEVENAGE   Watton-
Broadwater   at-Stone   Standon

WARE

Routes of the
Glasgow & Edinburgh
MAILS

Hertford   Hoddesdon
HATFIELD

WALTHAM
CROSS

BARNET

Great North Road—Glasgow Mail
Edinburgh Mail
Old North Road

Jack Trodd

CHAPTER V

Letters to the Postmasters-General (2) 1795

A COLD and wet September had been followed by a hard winter. Conditions of snow and frost lasted until late in February, when a sudden thaw caused widespread flooding and a general breakdown of the surface of the ill-made roads. The harvest had been poor and owing to this and the dislocation of foreign markets caused by the war the price of corn was rising steadily. In spite of that, contractors were held to their bargains with results which showed themselves in the debility of their horses, which perforce were kept underfed, reducing the speed of the Mails. These hardships are reflected in the following letters.

But the series begins with a plea for the 'relict' of the inventor of the patent coach who, as will appear, could not be honoured with the title of 'widow'.

G.P.O. Jan 14/95.

My Lords

I have the honor to enclose to yr Ldshps a letter from Mrs Besant, the relict of the late Mr Besant, Patentee of the Mail Coaches.

I beg leave to state to your Lordships that as Mr Besant was in debt to the Trade at his decease which she was unable to pay, Mr Vidler agreed to forgive her such debt [and] to allow her 12/- a week if she would give up her share of the Patent, which she did. Your Lordships will see by her letter that she is a great deal reduced, and what I mean to solicit in her favour is a post office, should one be vacant and no interest be made for a successor, nor any one of the Town offer, as I believe was the case at Hounslow not long since. I have spoke to Mr Freeling about this and he is of opinion iff such an opportunity offers it might be convenient, if yr Lordships approve, to appoint her. She is a very industrious methodical woman & I really think in a small office would make a good Post-master.

All &c
T. Hasker

Considering what John Vidler stood to gain by the above-named bargain, seeing that he was in possession of the exclusive right to manufacture every mail-coach put on the road, with the exception of a very few stage-coaches modified to meet the needs of the Post Office, the allowance was slender and inadequate. But the inventor's 'relict' was evidently conscious of a weakness in her claim clearly exposed in the deceased's will. Herein he leaves '£500 owing by me on bond to my reputed wife, Johanna Brown, widow, who now lives with me . . . it being the money that I actually borrowed and had received from her'. In addition, he made her his heir in his equal share of the partner-ship, including the patent rights of the mail-coach. We do not know what his debts amounted to, but feel that if she had been made of the termagant stuff like the widow who plagued the unjust judge in the Bible, instead of the homely body described by Hasker, she could have done better for herself. As she is never mentioned again I fear the Post Office was even more ungracious than the coach-builder.

*　　*　　*　　*

Awards for valour

G.P.O. Jan 29 1795

My Lords

I beg leave to solicit a small reward for some guards who have particularly exerted themselves to forward the Mail in time, in con-sequence of impediments occasioned by the precarious weather as per list enclosed—

John Rees, Guard from Swansea to Bristol, in consequence of the Waters being so rapid, was obliged to proceed by horse and, near Bridgend was up to his shoulders and, in that condition, in the night, did not wait to change his clothes but proceeded on his duty— I propose a guinea.

Thomas Sweetman, Guard of the Chester Mail, was obliged to alight from his Mail Box at Rockcliff to fix the Barrs and put on some traces, up to his hips in water, in the middle of last night, after which it Froze severely. He came in that condition to London—I propose 10/6.

John Jeffs rode all the way from Cirencester to Oxford and Oxford to Cirencester thro' the snow and water—the Coach not being able to proceed either way. He was not wetted but thro' great exertion was in time with his Mail—I propose 5/-.

James Taylor, whose letter I have the honour to enclose—I propose 5/-.

Many other guards have suffered very much from the intense cold last. As they are now resting, and some attended by surgeons, I shall have the honor to submit their cases to your Lordships hereafter.

All of which &c

T. Hasker

Hard weather continues in the North.

G.P.O. Jany 31st 1795

My Lords

I have the honor to state to yr Ldshps that in consequence of the very heavy snow in the North between Press and Dunbar, at Pease and Dunglass Glens in particular, the Guards have with great difficulty for 4 Days past been unable to get the Mail to Newcastle on horseback in time to proceed by Coach the subsequent day for, in spite of all their efforts, near twenty hours time was lost each journey between Edinbro & Newcastle.

I would have sent Mr Woolmer across from Carlisle but judged that his exertions would soon be wanting in the West of Scotland, which expectation is realised—by a Letter I received from him this morning which I beg leave to enclose to yr Ldships. I therefore have sent Mr Wilkins on the east side of Scotland to see that regularity is established as soon as possible after the snow is removed and the roads open.

The snow, I beg leave to observe to yr Ldshps has been pretty general but not so deep as in the North. The thaw, too, was of great help in clearing the roads in the South—but I do not hear there has been any thaw North of the Humber. The *Coaches* therefore are tolerably regular except the above, the North Letters of which have lost only one day, with the difference only that the Snow on Newmarket Heath & below Cambridge impedes the Norwich and

Wisbech Mail Coaches about two hours a journey. On these roads I have sent Mr White.

T. Hasker

A further letter arriving from Woolmer describing local conditions and his own strenuous endeavours, T.H. takes the opportunity of appealing for an improvement in the salaries of his two senior deputies who are not only wretchedly underpaid but unequally, the one who worked harder and took more responsibility getting less than the other for no apparent reason.

Gen Post Office
Feby 5th 1795

My Lords

I have the honor to enclose your Lordships a letter from Mr Woolmer, Deputy Superintendant of the Mail Coaches, by which you will see that he is particularly active at this inclement season, as indeed he ever has been on all occasions—and I beg leave further to state to your Lordships that he was the oldest Depy. Supt. & with Mr Wilkins received £54 : 12 :—per Annum salary till the establishment about two years since, at which time Mr Wilkins's salary was raised to £80 a year & Mr Woolmer's settled at only £50.

Perhaps it might have been conceived by yr Ldshps that as he was stationary in the North his duty did not require an advance of salary, but I humbly submit to yr Lordships that he has a very troublesome situation, for the Contractors in the North demand very laborious attention to keep them regular and the roads being worse and the carriages paying but indifferently, if it was not for his being with them and using constant exertion, the Mails would frequently arrive too late at Dumfries, Carlisle, Ferrybridge, & Manchester. I have communicated this to Mr Freeling who, knowing the Duty and the exertion of Mr Woolmer, perfectly agree with the propriety of this solicitation which I have now the honor to lay before yr Lordships.

All &c
T. Hasker.

The application was not granted—probably it was negatived at a personal interview by a mere shake of the head. Two days later another letter from the same source is forwarded again emphasising Woolmer's zeal and difficulties with a louder pedalling on the importance of the North Mail. But as his deputies are not to get any more there is a touch of perhaps intended irony in his refusal to act without authority in the matter of spending a few shillings on getting the snow cleared at that vital spot near what is now known to both road- and railway-men as Beattock Summit.

Gen Post Office Feby 7th/95

My Lords

I beg leave to state [to] your Lordships that as far as common impediments occur I always endeavour to remove them for the regularity of the Mails without troubling yr Ldshps, but when they are very great and likely to become very expensive I think it my duty to apply for your approbation.

So great a Commercial and Manufacturing City & vicinity as Glasgow should have the correspondence conducted regular if possible, on which I directed impediments as circumstances should direct to be removed. I requested Mr Woolmer would use every exertion possible to get the North Mail up for this day's (Saturday's) delivery, that it might not loose two days. By his letter of the 3rd from Moffat, which I beg leave to enclose, you will see he has been completely frustrated in his attempt by a very heavy second fall of snow, and that he pauses at the expense that may be occasioned in cutting it thro. I therefore entreat your Lordships further direction. By this rout the whole of the Correspondence from England is conveyed to the third part of Scotland & *visa versi* [*sic*].

T. Hasker

(Answer, Feby 7th)

So many days must elapse from the date of Mr Woolmer's letter to the receipt of an answer that possibly the impediments may by that time be removed. However, the P.M.G. wish Mr Hasker to direct Mr Woolmer to use every exertion at as moderate an expense as possible.

Ch
Lei

*   *   *   *

More news of the premier mail-guard (previous references, pp. 69, 74).

John Carter, last heard of on May the 10th, had been put on the 'worst ground'—the Dover Foreign Mail—where passengers and their tips became fewer and fewer till the service was extinguished. He then had to dree his weird as an extra-guard. But the hard weather suddenly promoted him to guarding the Dover Inland Mail—still a well patronized coach, but it once more placed temptation in his way.

> Gen Post Office
> Feby 2. 95

My Lords

I have the honor to enclose a letter from Mr Johnson, Postmaster of Gravesend to Mr Freeling for your Lordship's inspection respecting the loss of the Gravesend Bag.

A guinea has been given to the finder very properly which, together with the expense of the express, should fall on the Guard if he had been an established one but from the late severe weather so many of the regular Guards have been ill that sometimes, though there was an additional number of extra Guards, there was great difficulty to find men we could confide in to send out. This was nearly the case on the Dover road, for the Guard being unable to go out, and all the extra men was engaged on duty, I was obliged to send J. Carter, whom Lord Chesterfield may remember he interceeded for at Marlboro and who, on account of his great family, he directed to be a foreign Mail Gd, which he was till the Dover Foreign Mail Coach dropped. For though this man was the very first Mail Guard, he has took so to drinking that he was not fit to be trusted with any other duty. But from the above cause that no other person on the emergency even so fit could be obtained, and as he knew the road so well, it was hoped he would do the duty till the other recovered.

The above is the case and I beg leave to state to your Lordships that he is so poor and has so large a family that he is not able to pay the expense of his default.

> All of which &c
> T. Hasker.

(Answer, Feb 3)

I perfectly remember the circumstance of my recommending Carter to be again tried. It was at the particular desire of the principal people at Marlboro where I was quartered at that time. I do not know whether we ought to forgive him the fine of the guinea. I think it should be stopped by installments out of his pay.

	Ch
Certainly	Lei

The final letter on the subject is on p. 116.

*   *   *   *

The thaw
A rapid thaw and heavy rain has caused flooding everywhere.

G.P.O. Feb 16/95

My Lords
I have the honor to state to your Lordships that the Mails are recovering [from] the late deluge. They all arrived in time for the first delivery this day except the Exeter, on which road the snow which fell between Thursday night and Friday morning lays very deep, which was the cause of its arriving so late as past 12 o'clock.

But I fear for some time they will not arrive so early as they used to do, for the roads are dreadfully bad and there is not one I believe where, in consequence of broken bridges or some other impediment they are not obliged to go a circuitous rout the flood has been so very general.

In Scotland too I find by a Letter from Mr Wilkins this morning that they have had a third fall of snow and that tho every exertion is making by the Surveyor, Superintendents, &c., that it is impossible to get the Mail to Newcastle without the loss of a day.

I should suppose the snow is deeper in the West of Scotland than in the East side for there is no branch in from Glasgow to Ferrybridge and of course no information from Mr Woolmer.

T. Hasker

Sticky conditions also prevailed in South Wales. The Presidents alluded to in the next letter were the senior clerks of the Inland Office.

General Post Office
Feby 28th 1795

My Lords

I have the honor to state to yr Ldshps in answer to the Presidents'
remark, which is herewith enclosed, that the Presidents have mistook
the matter.

The facts were these. The Bristol, 4 Irish, and the whole of
West India Mail came up to Thatcham by the Bristol Coach.
There, the Guards very properly put as much into the Bath Mail as
they possibly could carry, namely, the Inland, the 4 Irish, and the
Agent's Bags; but being unable from height and bulk to take the
other part it was obliged to come by the other Coach and,
the horses of one coach happening to be stronger than the other, the
Bath Mail Coach arrived earlier—at 8.45—the other not till 9.55.
And immediately on the arrival of the first Coach, namely the
Bath, a note was written from my Office by Mr Nicholas to the
President to inform him that the *Crediton Bag* was arrived (it being
so inserted in the Bill) and that an East India mail was coming by the
Bristol, for so it was written on the Bill.

Better conduct and discipline could not be observed than by the
Guards dividing the weight—indeed the whole conduct of the
Guard of this Mail from the time it arrived at Swansea was good—
for the Coach being full of passengers' luggage and mail—so that
he could not take the Jamaica mail—rather than leave it behind—
he took a Chaise and, finding from the state of the road when he
reached Cardiff that they were likely to be too late at the Severn side
for the ferry to cross in time to reach the Bristol Mail Coach at
Bristol, he left his passengers and proceeded by Chaise with all his
mail and was in time; and it all reached London as soon as the
Coaches could travel.

All &

T. Hasker

(Initialled by P.M.G.)

It is a pity that T.H. has omitted to mention the name of any of these
well-recommended guards, particularly him of the Milford Mail, for
neither guard, coachman, nor contractor on that route ever earned
another good word from him. But the story is rather confused, perhaps penned without his usual deliberation in a fit of annoyance with

the unfounded complaint of the said Presidents, who may have still borne the ancient grudge against mail-coaches. By the 'Bath Coach', the Exeter Mail travelling the northern route is clearly intended. It should have carried the mail from the West Indies out of the Falmouth packet. That it didn't may have been due to the dislocation caused by new snow in the Exeter area reported in the previous letter when additional mail may have been sent by the riding post between Exeter and Bristol. The procedure of dealing with the mails on the Exeter-Bath and Bristol coaches at Thatcham is given in Hasker's note on Time-bill 5. The 'East India mail' is a mystery unless it confirms the suggestion that the letter was written in haste and wrath and Hasker made one of his occasional mistakes, meaning 'West Indian'. It was an old complaint of the Post Office that all mail from India and the East Indies was brought in boxes by ships of the East India Company to East India House and paid only the inland rate of postage.

*　　*　　*　　*

Another cold snap in the north and East Anglia

G.P.O. March 3/95
½ past 8 A.M.

My Lords

I beg leave to enclose you a letter which I received this morning from Mr Wilkins, by which your Ldshps will see another fall of snow is a new impediment to the Mail Coach travelling yet regularly to Edinbro. There was a great deal of snow on Saturday in various parts which had impeded the Mails both going from and coming to London, particularly the Ipswich, it having been very heavy below Colchester, and the Mail being obliged to go 5 miles round by Nayland is the cause of its arriving so late & I fear will cause a second delivery—tho they have had 6 horses to the Coach all the way from Ipswich to Rumford for some days.

T. Hasker

P.S. Ipswich just arrived—8.58 A.M.

The diversion through Nayland (as appears in the next letter) was obviously caused by a breach in the bridge over the Stour at Stratford-St. Mary made by the floods about February the 10th which, for some hidden reason, Hasker does not yet mention. This Mail was due to arrive in London at 7. A.M. (*see* Time-bill 18) and a delay of two hours, less two minutes, under existing conditions, was pretty good going. A second delivery was an additional expense (? employing the super-numerary Letter Carriers) as will have been gathered in the case of Guard Stanroyd (p. 75). With six horses, a post-boy would have to be paid to ride the leading pair as only four horses could be controlled by the reins from the box.

G.P.O. March 6th/95

My Lords

I am happy to state to your Lordships that the rot is to a great degree getting out of the roads and that they are in most parts recovering their hardness. There are in many places very deep holes which obliges the coachman to drive rather slower than they used to do over such spots, and where they do not see them they are often attended with accident. The York Coachman and Guard were both chucked from their seats going down to Huntingdon last journey and, coming up, the Guard is lost this morning, supposed from the same cause, as the passengers say he was blowing his horn just before they missed him.

This is only to show yr Lordships that there are yet some deep holes, but you will see that the arrivals are pretty good except the Ipswich, the cause of the detention of which is going five miles round, and the road being narrow and very thinly made, by no means calculated for the high road to Norwich, Ipswich, Yarmouth &c.

I forbore to say anything of this as I understand the Surveyors were sent to examine Stratford Bridge from both Essex & Suffolk. They afterwards met the Commissioners but could not agree to come to any resolution. I therefore submit to yr Lordships if Mr Parkin[1] should not write to them and, if not directly attended to, indict the Counties, for this impediment not only retards the delivery in London near an hour every day but is very expensive, for additional horses are put to the Coach to fetch up the lost time in going round.

All of which &c
T. Hasker

[1] Solicitor to the Post Office.

(Reply)

Let Mr Parkin write & say if the road is not repaired immediately the G.P.O. must indict.

Ch

Lei

Parties at the meeting would be the Parish and Turnpike Surveyors (whose powers overlapped) and the Commissioners of the Peace—the Justices of the two counties. The upkeep of roads throughout the country was the responsibility of each parish which appointed its own Surveyor of Highways. He was given power under the Highways Act of 1555 to demand six days a year free labour and the use of carts and horses from parishioners. In the case of a turnpike road, managed by a Turnpike Trust, control was in the hands of the Commission of the Peace, though the parishes were still responsible for supplying statute labour to augment work paid for by the Trust. The Commission of the Peace was the nearest approach to the County Council of the present day.

The remedy for getting an impassable or decayed road seen to was to indict or 'present' the responsible authority (parish or Commission) at the next Quarter Sessions. Here a fine for neglect could be imposed (paid by an extra rate levied on the unfortunate parishes concerned) and an order made for repairs forthwith. Where a bridge, dividing two counties and two Turnpike Trusts, collapsed the parties on either bank hesitated to rebuild what they might thereby be committed to maintain. In any case, the Post Office was not a favourite customer of any Trust as its vehicles were driven more furiously than the stage-coaches but, unlike them, paid no toll. But the Post Office was far more active than anybody else in the matter of indictments, for Hasker was constantly stirring up his indolent masters to act drastically that his coaches might keep time. It has been often pointed out that the magnificent system of roads which we came to possess by the middle of the 19th century was entirely due to persistent pressure on all local authorities on the part of the Post Office. This is true enough, but it should not be forgotten that the Post Office was not the least interested in the speed of the royal mail until John Palmer forced it to adopt his mail-coaches. That great national development with all depending on it should therefore be put to his credit.

To return to Stratford Bridge, after a further fortnight of *laissez faire* Hasker wrote more urgently—

G.P.O. March 20/95

My Lords

I have the honor to enclose to your Lordships two letters I received this morning in one from Mr Parkin the Solicitor. Your Lordships will see the Contents and, as the bridge in question has been washed down since the 10th Feby, full six weeks, and nothing is yet done or given orders for, I submit to yr Ldshps that an indictment ought to be immediately made.

T. Hasker.

He followed this up the next day by another saying that the contractors were complaining that it was impossible to go on attempting to get the Norwich and Ipswich Mail up to London in time for the ordinary delivery until the bridge was repaired, and goes on to suggest a more effective line of attack than letters from Mr Parkin. It was to insert notices in the local papers warning people that the coach will now have to start the up journey an hour earlier to 'induce the Public in those Counties to complain of the inconveniency they suffer by the tardiness of the Commissioners whose disputes prevent the necessary accomodation'.

Whether or not this cunning plan was ever carried out and the parties thereby shamed into action does not appear in the Letters. But repairs must then and there have been expedited as we hear no more of this 'impediment'. The bridge is shown in Ogilby's map of 1675 and was probably of medieval construction. The present iron bridge replaced it in 1876.

Meanwhile, other matters were being attended to.

The second *Carlisle Mail* (from p. 99)

Arrangements to replace the stage-coach *Princess Royal* by a mail-coach which would travel the more easterly route and carry the mail for Glasgow were now practically concluded. But a diversion to serve Hertford had been proposed of which Hasker did not approve. The objection which he gives was probably not the fundamental one. To call at Hertford, the coach must take a different route out of London to that followed by its former proprietors, who were going to be the contractors under the new arrangement, and Hasker's carefully matured plan would be entirely upset. The *Edinburgh* travelled by Ware and Huntingdon (Old North Road), waiting at three places, the passengers breakfasting at Huntingdon. It was not due at Stilton until 6.10 A.M. The *Glasgow* would go by Barnet and Biggleswade (Great North Road). This was four miles further but there would be no wait, and it was timed to arrive at Stilton at 5.17. Passengers must hold their appetites till they reached Stamford at 7.2.

G.P.O. March 13/95

My Lords

I have the honor to state to your Lordships that I have had the road measured from the 17 miles stone in Hoddesden to Broadwater via Hertford and have gone over it myself, and that I find it is more than a mile & ¾ further than the road thro Hatfield, which road is also almost 4 miles further than by Huntingdon & as this Mail Coach must be at Stilton before the Mail Coach that goes via Huntingdon so as to give the Postmaster time to send the Bye letters brought down the Biggleswade road for that Coach to carry them on—it will be impossible to go further round than the 4 miles thro Hatfield road.

The Proprietors of the present Carlisle Coach will all meet on Monday next to sign an agreement for carrying this mail from 5 April next by a Patent Coach in the way your Lordships have approved & I have the pleasure to say that this Coach will ease the York Mail of 2 fifths of its great burthen.

I have consulted with Mr Freeling who says he will send a Surveyor to the road to meet Mr Wilkins, my assistant, before the Coach starts to arrange the correspondence, & I shall be a day or two on the road at the same time, that everything may be regular.

T. Hasker

But the result of the meeting is not reported till the end of the month as T.H. has been having trouble with Mr Sibley of the Bell at Stilton through shifting his old ground for horsing the Edinburgh Mail. This was due to a desire to meet Lord Sandwich's wishes (p. 99) that Holmes of the Wheatsheaf at Alconbury Hill should be given a turn. That T.H. succeeded in making a workable adjustment will be seen in Time-bill 15.

G.P.O. March 31st 1795

My Lords

I had the honor to state to yr Ldshps after the meeting at Ferry-bridge N.B. that everything was settled and the Contract signed—but since that Mr Sibley has been twice in Town dissatisfied with the ground allotted, the only ground that he could have and by which he is much better off and has more than he had in the Coach before it was a Mail, as the enclosed from Mr Willan will explain and all his horses employed in it one 3 forths of the time at home or 36 hours out of 48.

I would not have troubled your Lordships with this any more than I do with many other busines of this nature only that he has been with Lord Sandwich & Ld Hawke and it is probable your Lordship might hear of it and conceive it misconduct or mis-management of mine. I always told him that he should be better off and have more ground than before and I have kept my word—but some people are not to be satisfied—nor was he till last Friday morning when I was obliged to tell him if he gave any more trouble he should not have it at all & that if he played any tricks and did not work his ground well & do his duty properly hereafter he would not keep it. This brought him to his senses and he requested no more might be thought of his Conduct, that he saw he had been wrong, was much obliged to me, & would do it well. I had some thoughts of sending a copy of this & the enclosed to Ld Sandwich & Ld Hawke but as they are his friends I desist as it may hurt him in their opinion.

T. Hasker

* * * *

The Portpatrick diligence again (previous references pp. 28, 88).

G.P.O. March 14/95

My Lords

Yr Lordships will recollect the great trouble the Carlisle & Portpatrick diligence has given for some years past and notwith-standing the additional pay of 1d. per mile that you gave them this winter they wrote to me in January to give it up on various grounds that they lost much by it which they now state to your Lordships by memorial. I told them by return that as they had agreed to do it till Aprl 5th that I wished they would fulfill such agreement—knowing that it would be difficult to get the riding work established at that inclement season—and I likewise informed them then that I would endeavour to get yr Lordships to continue the additional price a little longer if they found an inclination to continue it. Yr Ldshps will see they say even the extra pay will not enable them to renew their Contract from the great opposition of Innkeepers &c &c &c, for even the Farmers of the Post horse tax in many instances I am well informed renounced their Post horse duty to induce people to ride in Chaise to the injury of the earnings of the Mail.

Therefore on the whole I submit to yr Lordships that the Mail diligence from Carlisle to Portpatrick shall cease after the 5 April next and that the riding work shall be re-established.

Respecting the further prayer for yr Lordships to reimburse them some of the loss they have sustained, I beg leave to submit that if your Lordships should be so inclined I will get from them some other Accounts and Documents. They have only sent me up one Month's earnings and that for the Month of January—of course in that Country the dullest time in the year.

T. Hasker

*　　*　　*　　*

The last of Guard Carter (previous reference p. 107)

G.P.O. March 19/95

My Lords

I have the honor to state to yr Lordships that J. Carter was, from his infancy, employed to drive a mail cart on the Bristol road, and that when the Bristol Mail Coach started he was the first Guard that travelled with it and continued as such from Marlboro to Bristol till about 2 years ago he was removed to the upper ground for being often seen in liquor. He afterwards was discharged at Marlboro for drunkenness. By much intercession he was again restored & put on the Foreign Dover Coach and continued till it stopped. Being so addicted to drunkenness I could not trust the Mails under his care but submit to your Lordships' consideration his being a servant of the Office near 40 years and the extreme distress of his wife & eight children if he could not be allowed the pension given to superannuated Guards.

T. Hasker

(Answer, Mar 20)

Certainly
Ch
Lei

I think this plea for the old scapegrace who had given him so much trouble shows Hasker's innate humanity. The retirement pension (7s. 6d. per week) and sick benefit fund for guards was started by Palmer who deducted 3s. a week from their then authorised wage of 13s. This was one of the first causes of friction with Walsingham, as he had introduced the scheme without authority. It continued in being, however, with the only modification that the regular wage was fixed at 10s. 6d., the surplus being apparently put aside for the pension though not named as a deduction. But sick-benefit and a contribution of two guineas towards funeral expenses were paid by the Post Office.

*　　*　　*　　*

Costs of de-icing

G.P.O. 21/95

My Lords

I have the honor to enclose for your Lordships perusal a letter from Mr Dunhill of Doncaster. He is both Postmaster and Mail Coach Contractor. I know he was very prompt in getting the Ice removed at the time of the floods. He says he was at 20/- expence, but as this was not directed to be incurred by the Office I do not pay it without your Lordships approbation, but I submit to your Lordships that such payment would be very proper.

I also enclose a letter from John Raper, the Mail Guard, which corroborates Mr Dunhill's as to the dreadful situation of the roads. I understand that three bridges are down between Doncaster and Ferrybridge and that Trent Bridge is one of them.

All &c

T. Hasker

(Reply)

If it is usual pay similar demands.

Ch
Lei

*　　*　　*　　*

A noble nomination
Ld Leicester

G.P.O. March 27/95

Marked (Separate)
My Lord

I have the honor of Ld Exeter's Letter recommending Anthony Sturdy to be a Guard on the Carlisle Mail Coach with your Lordship's and Lord Chesterfield's directions at the back of it and beg leave to inform your Lordships that some of those who assisted during the hard weather [had first chance]. All that are necessary have been fixed some time and their cloaths made, it being only a week to the starting. But as you are so very desirous of his being appointed I will, the first vacancy that happens any where, either take a Guard from that road to make room for him or give him the place, that is, if he, on examination answers the established description under 30 years of age.

I will be down at Stamford in a few days and will then see A. Sturdy and, if fit, send him to the Manufactory[1] till he obtains the necessary knowledge of repairs. This will take him 10 days or a fortnight and will then take him on as an extra Guard till the vacancy happens.

My Lord I must further beg leave to observe that this is not the easy duty expected by those who only look at it; any man may do it if he will, but if he swerves from his instructions he is suspended or dismissed and I am sorry to say necessity obliges it for the service could not be done with partiality to any recommendation[2]—and if discipline was not so rigid the proper conduct of the Correspondence and the Coaches would not be performed. I will trouble your Lordship with a sheat of Guards general instructions for your perusal and will write a further line as soon as I have seen the man.

T. Hasker

[1] Vidler's coach-building works at Millbank.　[2] Ditto to Greville, p. 182.

Hasker thus makes it tactfully plain that he reserves to himself the sole right of having the last word in the choice of his men, even when the nominee is backed by two earls and a marquess.

*   *   *   *

Ginger for contractors

Genl Post Off
Apl 5th 1795

My Lords

A few days since, I stated verbally to your Lordships that it was necessary a few of the Contractors should have notice to quit the 5 July next—that if, on meetings being called or further communication, they should not be brought to a sense of their duty, others may be appointed in their stead. They are as follows—

Mr Hare of Taunton, Bath and Exeter Contractor, for losing time and not being under any management of the Office, will not pay a Bill for greasing and cleaning his Coaches which, for their reputation and safety, I was obliged to order and pay, and for not accepting the last wear and tear Bill. This destroys all system, it being a necessary security for Mr Vidler. I had much trouble with him more than 12 Months ago to get him to accept these Bills and do many other necessary things. He was the last that paid for the moiety of the Contract.

Mr Noseworthy of Collumpton, the next stage in the same Bath and Exeter connection, for losing much time and abusing the Office. Mr Thompson of Exeter, for not appearing satisfied with the Coach; will not do his work in time; wants 2hrs 10mts for 12 miles, and an allowance from your Lordships for taking the Coach into his house, it being in the night.

Mr Fromont, the Bath and Exeter & Bristol Contractor, has also notice. He does not keep time and has frequently been heard abusing the Coachman for driving fast though behind time. And to Mr Pickford who works the stage from Macclesfield to Manchester. He has lost much time and having other great occupations does not attend to the Coach duty.

The connection from Bristol to Milford—the whole being so shamefully performed, Horses, Coaches &c—and tho they have been applied to for upwards of two years in the most pressing manner to furnish a place of safety for the Mail, some of the Coaches has not got that conveniency yet, but the Mails is carried in the boot with common luggage, this too is more shameful as the principal Contractor is a Postmaster.

I did not give notice as I proposed to Mr Weeks, for he has done his duty better of late, nor to Mr Bruce of Leicester or Mr Lathom of Ware, but have wrote to them that it was so intended, yet in hopes of amendment your Lordships had passed over their misconduct for this year.

All which &c

T. H.

Although the same threat was repeatedly issued—sometimes in more drastic language—every one of the above accused is found to be still in 'the Mail-coach Concern' in the time-bills for 1797. The most noteworthy among the names is that of Mr Pickford. His 'other great occupations' were those of general carrier between Manchester and London on which account, in our own time, his name has become a household word. In the case of Mr Hare of Taunton, Hasker was under a misunderstanding, as will appear (p. 124).

The *quarter days* named in the letters, when contracts were terminable, were not the same as at present. They were the 5th of the months January, April, July, and October.

*   *   *   *

The Royal Weymouth (previous references p. 82)

Genl Post Office

Sept [for Apr] 9 1795

My Lords

I have endeavoured to reform some errors that remained to (the) Royal Mail at Egham. Mr Cooper had fixed the Coach to stop at a small Public House, the White Lyon, where there was very bad accommodations in every respect. I therefore yesterday agreed with Mr Graves to find stabling gratis for Cooper and to accommodate the Passengers which he can do very well as he keeps a very large commodious Inn, the Red Lyon, is very civil as at present he has not much business.

It is necessary the Coach should stop at a good house at Egham for one Coach generally arrives 8 or 10 mts generally before the other and to reload[1] the things generally occupies a quarter of an hour.

I applied to Cooper who agreed to go to the Red Lyon tomorrow. This I am very glad to have obtained as the Servants of the Household generally come from Windsor in a hurry and want tea or something, the Passengers too will want something and, returning, if any person should want a bed or a chaise they can have it at this House.

It appears to me that the business this year will be very compleat, Coaches weigh 1 cwt less than before, and not carrying any outside, 1 cwt, 2 qrts, 0 lbs; more so that there is less to carry by 2 cwt, 2 qrts, 0 lbs and not so long a journey by 9 miles and nearly as much time that with all nursing if any irregularities creep in I shall be more disappointed than I ever was. I will trouble your Lordships again tomorrow after seeing Demezy, Weeks, &c.

All which &c

T. Hasker

This Mail was not due to start running until August the 10th, but Hasker, most anxious to avoid any hitch this time, makes preparations early. Instead of sending the coach round by Windsor, he is arranging a shuttle service to connect with it on the main West Road. (Next reference p. 125.)

*   *   *   *

As witness

Gen Post Office Apr 21/95

My Lord

I suppose Mr Freeling has informed yr Ldshp of the order from the Committee of the house of Commons to inspect into frauds and abuses of Public Offices, in consequence of which order I attended and was examined for upwards of 3 hours yesterday on the abuse (for so they call it) of sending and receiving parcels free. I first delivered in the papers 1, 2, 3, containing yr Ldshp's Orders to Contractors to charge for all parcels addressed to the P.M.G. or any

---

[1] From the Coach or conveyance from Windsor Castle. Letter written by a clerk and not in H's handwriting which accounts for so many 'generally's.'

other person belonging to the Office which has been strictly adhered to. On this I believe I was interogated for 2 hours to know what parcels now came free, by whom directed if they were sent free, and to whom &c, &c.

My answers were that all parcels charged were paid for, that if Proprietors freed a parcel it certainly was received so that the persons now receiving parcels free if the Proprietor pleased were Mr Freeling, Mr Todd, myself, and some of the Surveyors. They asked if you did not receive them so. Sometimes you might, I said, and sometimes you did not; that was not an answer, I was to say yes or no. But did I not even send Game to the P.M.G. free?—I certainly had—and on the whole they made me fix the sum I thought all free parcels received and sent amount to in a year—I could not guess but was sure much under £50. I was then asked which seemed the sum of all if such parcels were paid for if the Contractors would not perform their Contracts for less mileage. I said no— your reason?—because even supposing it to be £50 there were 200 Contractors and if divided it would not amount to 5/- each. The Honourable Committee then wanted to knoe if the Mail Boxes had not been made larger in consequence of so many things sent that ought not to be sent both in and out of the Bags—my answer was no, but in consequence of the increased Correspondence & Newspapers. The above took up half an hour.

They then wanted to know if Contractors did not memorial for more pay 3 years ago in consequence of their Coaches being so loaded free and if the Contractors did not complain; I remembered Mr Fromont did—he is to be ordered [to attend and give evidence]. How were these Contractors claims to be got rid of?— By my informing your Lordships that if they would not do it I did not fear but I could get others. I believe they have ordered Mr Fromont, they have also ordered Mr Needle who sees the mails packed of a night and Barker who was dismissed about a fortnight since for bringing up his mail on the roof of the Coach and converting the Mail Box to his own use. I suppose, my Lord, he is to be examined to see if not turned from the Service for a crime that those higher in Office practice, tho' my answer was clear, that if there was at any time a parcel the orders were that tho' for Majesty himself the Mail must take the place of it in the Mail Box.

I was next examined about sending down Catalogues which,

being informed would happen, I wrote down the facts—which I herewith enclose yr Ldp—. The last question asked me on this head was if I could not have vented [?] Bills and Cards to as much advantage by having them Posted [i.e. displayed] at Post Offices in the County Towns or at Booksellers shops or Libraries. My answer was no—The reason? Because Post Offices in many Towns are private houses and all Offices should be accessible to Post Office Officers only; besides, I had no business with Post Offices. I also delivered into the Honourable Committee a list of Mail Guards Instructions & orders and spoke with great respect but freedom of the Herculean labour it was to keep such a System regular. And my Lord I must say that it appears to me that this Committee instead of going into the abuses of franking only are examining into the minutiae of Offices—and if they go as extraneous from the point in every Office as they have respecting the Superintendant's department of this it will be perhaps at these times a very dangerous investigation.

I am &c

Ld Chesterfield   T. Hasker

(P.S) I have seen Mr Willson and Fromont today—I think both will be examined. They seem quite in good spirits and talk of more mileage in consequence.

I was also examined respecting the new Mail Coach, the purport, if it was not obliged to start in consequence of the encrease of Parcels, pamphlets &c. I answered no, that it had been solicited these 3 years in consequence of the encreased Correspondence & Newspapers which were when the Coach first started 450 lb—now 550 lb wt—such encrease and 2 or 3 overturns very dangerous, induced yr Lordships to grant it, and so far as parcels *talked* of being a grievance it is performed for about 3/5 of the price given on any other road.

The object of the enquiry was to get evidence as to the extent to which the privilege of franking (sending letters and newspapers free) was being abused, preparatory to framing the Act of 1795 designed to remedy this which, however, it quite failed to do. The examiners evidently cast a wide net.

Mr Needle, referred to, was probably the same sharp fellow as that porter of the Gloucester Coffee House who had been prepared to serve the King for the sake of a uniform (without profit). Only a week after the above, Hasker presents his name again to the P.M.G. as 'a very active person who understands the duty' to supervise the loading of the mail not only at the Gloucester Coffee House but also at Lad Lane and the Bull and Mouth 'as Guards are still negligent in putting all the bags into the mail-box and locking it. His report and attention I could depend on', so he now recommends that he should be paid 1s. 6d. a night, which is confirmed.

At the same time an application is put in to institute another amenity designed to cost the Post Office even less. The guards were ordered not only to clean their three firearms after every double journey but also to reload them to ensure the powder being dry in case of need. It was now requested that one William Broadrib should be installed in a room hired at 3s. a week to relieve these hard-worked men of a task which would rob them of that much sleep. But those who availed themselves were to have 6d. per set stopped out of their wages, on which fees Mr Broadrib must subsist. This request was also granted with unusual dispatch.

*　　*　　*　　*

Mr Hare of Taunton again (previous ref. p. 119)

G.P.O. April 30/95

My Lords

I have the honour to enclose your Lordships an extract from my report respecting Mr Hare of Taunton & his Partners which will show that I only wanted them to do the business in the same method as the other Contractors in the Kingdom do. The notice sent produced Mr Hare's extraordinary answer *No. 1* which I did not trouble your Lordships with as I intended to call a meeting, but the attendance on the Committee of the House of Commons prevented it. I this day received his letter *No. 2* signed by the other Partners also. I humbly submit to your Lordships that the notice I gave ought to be put in force for their refractory conduct. But if your Lordships approve I will call a meeting of them in London and give them a fair offer of paying the Bill, of accepting Mr Vidler's bills, which if they do and promise to perform the Duty well and good-humouredly I will then inform them they may continue another year, if not that they must quit.

They really all deserve to go out of the Mail Concern, but if they do, Mr Willson of Lad Lane will loose one of his Coaches, namely the Bath & Exeter; this is the reason I act with so much lenity to them.

All &c

T. Hasker

As already said, Hasker was under a complete misapprehension about this claim. In the next letter the mystery is revealed.

P.O. May 6/95

My Lord

Mr Willson of Lad Lane has requested I would inform your Lordships that he has been solicited several times by his Partners in the Country that he is yet unable to settle the Mail Coach accounts for the Royal Weymouth of last year owing to his not being able to get a settlement at the Secretary of State's Office. He has received at the Duke of Portland's Office £76:2:6 and says there is still due £144:7:6 as by the enclosed sketch he has delivered. He desires me to inform yr Lordships that it is an invariable custom for all passengers to pay their fares before they travel their Journey and that he and his partners hope yr Lordships will not object to the Messengers in future paying at Windsor either on their way down or returning.

All &c

P.S. I also beg to enclose an account from Mr Heaven, Proprietor of the Portsmouth & London Mail Coach for the fare of two Messengers while his Majesty was at Portsmouth last June.

(Other references pp. 85, 131.)

Apparently the expenses of the Royal Weymouth Mail were paid through other than the usual channels. It was explained earlier that under the revised arrangement for this special service the contractors were due to get their usual earnings from parcels and passengers, but the King's Messengers had been using their position to get free rides. The 3rd Duke of Portland referred to was at that time Home Secretary. This is one of several sidelights (the case of Mr Shrubles on p. 64 was another) on the prevailing difficulty of getting accounts settled promptly. It will be seen later how Hasker, himself, was once badly out of pocket from the same cause.

Two other accounts are dealt with. One is from Peach the Leeds contractor who has incurred legal expenses in getting his stretch of road indicted at Quarter Sessions. It is his third application for the money. T.H. demurs at settling a number of other items and says (referring to the whole amount), 'I do not think that or any other pay will satisfy Mr Peach, and it is very probable it will induce him and Mr Gray [see Time-bill 13] to solicit pay for other articles. I have marked with a tick of red ink such articles in his bill as are for indictments, the amount is £68:11:8—which should yr Lordships be inclined to pay I will direct him to send a separate bill for such articles only.' He is to be sent a copy of 'the report'—presumably by Mr Parkin, the Post Office solicitor—but only in part 'as I conceive (in its entirety) it would be improper for his perusal, for that it would probably make him more troublesome'.

The other is a bill from the Postmaster at Exeter for nurse and lodging of J. Mathews, late Mail Guard who 'employed no Apothecary' and which 'as there is no Doctor's [bill] I submit to yr Lordships for approbation to pay it—The sum of £2:2:0 for Funeral is according to the standing order of the Office'. This is approved to be settled by the Postmaster, Mr Jackson, and charged to his incident account.

Hasker next went down to Bristol to meet the erring contractors of the Milford Mail 'in consequence of their having notice to quit for their negligent inattention to the Mail Duty', but 'as they have promised the Coach Mail Boxes &c shall be put in compleat order in one month, I have (with your Lordships' approbation) on those conditions promised the continuence another year'.

*　　*　　*　　*

The Liverpool Mail

Two 'memorialists' have applied to have this important Mail diverted. Hasker gives plausible reasons why neither should succeed.

Gen Post Office
June 29 1795

My Lords

I have the honor to state to your Lordships that in consequence of your Lordships commands I have surveyed the road from Birmingham to Stone via Walsall, the memorial of the latter town having solicited the Liverpool Mail Coach to go that rout, and find that road near three miles further and much worse than the present road, besides which, was the Liverpool Mail Coach to go by Birmingham, by arriving earlier, both down and up, than the Shrewsbury Mail Coach does it would annihilate it. I have entered the particulars of this survey in a book of Roads I keep for that purpose and therefore shall only state further to your Lordships that the majority of the Liverpool Company would be unhappy at the change and that the Shrewsbury Mail Coach is of great consequence to the Office as it leaves Bags at every Town from Hyde Park to Salop and though the Liverpool Mail Coach might leave the Bag at Birmingham going down yet the Shrewsbury Mail Coach must take it up on its way to London.

All which &c

T. Hasker.

(Answer, June 30)

Copy to the Principal person who signed that Memorial.

Ch.

Lei.

Walsall gained a service by branch diligence in the autumn of 1796 —an unusual turn-out with coachman-guard (p. 191). The second appeal is from Henry, 3rd Baron Vernon, whose principal seat was at Sudbury House near Uttoxeter. It was obviously an unworkable proposition and would have entailed discharging many tried contractors and a doubtful search for new ones.

Gen Post Office

June 29 1795

My Lords

I beg leave to state that having your commands in consequence of the memorial to your Lordships for a Mail Coach to go to Liverpool via Atherstone, Ashby de la Zouch, Burton, Uttoxeter, the Pottery, Sandbach, Middlewich, Northwich, Warrington &c, I made a survey and find it to be 15 or 16 miles further than the present rout and [a] very indifferent road in many parts, sandy, deep, rutty, hilly, narrow &c—

If the present Liverpool Mail Coach was to travel this road it

127

would not [arrive] at either end for five or six hours later than at present and if a new one was to be established it would cost seven or eight hundred pounds per annum to go through a Country that is already well served with their Correspondence. Every Town has a daily post except Uttoxeter, and I think the Pottery would not be so well accomodated as at present, for the Postmaster of New-castle serves them twice each day and waits for their answers as long as the returning post will admit. The London letters do not arrive till after 6 o Clock evening, and he immediately dispatches two riders and they wait for the return till midnight.

I do not know any person that could be found to work such a Coach—nor do the memorialists for a continuance; and this would, could it be possibly established, destroy the present Liverpool Mail.

I have entered the remarks of this survey which are more des-criptive in the book of roads kept for that purpose should your Lordship want to use them, therefore shall not in this report be more minute.

All which &c

T. Hasker

(Answer)

Copy to Ld Vernon.

Ch.

with the P.M.G's Compts

Lei.

In spite of their hard bargains, the established contractors seem to have been contented as none served notice to quit. But new offers for the mail contract from stage-coach proprietors to open fresh routes were rare. In early June, however, one came from the proprietor of the Gosport coach. This was to serve as an auxiliary mail-coach (one carrying the mail and a guard only part of the way). The proposal was to serve a district in Hampshire between the mail routes to Ports-mouth and Poole, picking up bags and guard at Alton, where the Poole Mail made the connection. T.H. would no doubt have liked to adopt the plan but believed the contractor could not make it pay and would soon wish to resign and he was strongly against any short-lived plan as he felt sure it was bound to affect the reputation of the service.

Accordingly he wrote of Mr Nicholls' vehicle, 'It is a six inside passenger coach and they carry as many outsides as they can get and I think it would not be in their Interest to make it a Mail Coach and conform with the regulations of Mail Coaches [maximum load allowed, four insides and two outsides], for 30 miles, as it must travel 50 afterwards (between Alton and London) without adding to their load, or but trifling, as the towns are but small it passes through. The money is the same as paid on every other road, the Expense being, Guard inclusive, £125 per Ann.' On the other hand 'it would save the greatest of the ride from Alton which is £84 to Bishop's Waltham, but as the Coach would be down very early in the morning in the very populous neighbourhood of Weston, Warnsford, Droxfield &c, I fear it would not accomodate so well as the present Post. It might carry the Fareham-London bag, for which £40 per Ann is paid I think, but could not save any of the cross ride between Portsmouth and Winchester'.

No comment from on high, but the proposal not adopted.

*　　*　　*　　*

More bills for last winter

G.P. Office July 22/95

My Lords

I have the honor to state to your Lordships that I have collected all the bills for Post horses for conveying the mails in Scotland [over] the Mail Coach routs during the last severe Season. They appear very considerable, much more so than any that have been laid before yr Ldships; but the impediments being much greater than they ever were before will appear to yr Ldshps the cause. Mr Ronaldson who was on the Berwick road even says that the exertions were so great, as yr Ldshp will see by his letter herewith enclosed, that he thinks something more should be given to them. I suppose at that time he had not seen their charge which is 4d ½d per mile, per horse, *each* way, and I therefore submit if yr Lordships pay such bills it will be [as a] reward for the horses actually employed in the Service of the Correspondence and tho they get nothing by their Cash earnings during that season I do not see that the Office can make them any compensation—it would be opening a wide door to a very expensive example.

During this 6 weeks, the two Guards employed between Berwick and Edinbro could not ride the full distance, 60 miles a day, therefore two others were procured who have for such duty received 10/6 per week each but as neither they nor the regular Guards received any vails (tips) or other emoluments for this severe duty, I submit to yr Ldshps approbation 10/6 per week each in addition. Mr Wilkins was down there the whole time and is of opinion that no pecuniary reward will compensate for the dangers encountered but join with me in requesting the above.

The expense of conveying the mails is according to the enclosed abstract £   . It is to a greater amount than the like duty of all England comes to, which I account for that though the winter was severe here it was nothing like [the] season there. There is a small bill that does not come directly within this cause, but as it is for Post horses to draw the Mail on the Port Patrick road I submit to yr Lordships with others.

T. Hasker

The provender situation

As the year advanced the scarcity of fodder for the horses, due to the poor harvest of 1794, became more and more acute and prices rose steeply. The next two letters show the dilemma in which the Superintendent of the mail-coaches was placed when his attention was again, and more forcibly, drawn to this situation. Levi, the contractor, who horsed both the Leeds and the old Carlisle Mail between Dunstable and Northampton, came up to London to take up the matter personally and beg for a temporary increase in pay to tide over, stressing the dearness of corn and hay and saying that it was almost impossible to get it at any price. Hasker reports the interview.

He says that a temporary allowance is given for the soldiers and it must be for this, or that they cannot proceed in the Business. I do not see how any allowance, even if temporary, can be given to them without amounting to an Enormous sum which I fear, if once given, would be Annual, for I do not think it would ever be reduced. I have therefore told him that I cannot make any solicitude for them; that they are obliged to buy corn and hay for their other Coaches and must for these; if they do not like to continue them they may give notice to quit. [At the same time T.H. fears that their horses may get weak and, when the roads get heavy] so faint that the Duty will not be performed in Time. And even if the Harvest should produce plenty, new Corn is bad to work on immediately and will give Diseases.

Nevertheless, Mr Levi is still found horsing his two Mails at the basic rate in 1797. A much more formidable applicant was Mr Wilson of Lad Lane whose teams carried six principal Mails over the first stages out of London and who was chairman of several associations of contractors. He had an additional lever in the old complaint about the fares of the King's Messengers, still unsettled after nearly nine months of repeated applications.

Genl Post Office, July 22/9

My Lords

I have the honour to inform your Lordships that about a week ago, in a conversation with Mr Willson, it was thought proper that those who worked the Royal Weymouth Mail last year should be wrote to and informed that it would start for the Season the beginning of August next and, as I had some idea that the Dearness of Provender would be an objection from some of them, I settled with Mr Willson, that they should have no complaint against the Office, that he should share the fares of the Messengers of last year as if they had really paid them, which finished last year's accounts. This was done, and Mr Willson's Book-keeper is endeavouring to get the rest of the money from the Secretary of State. Should he not succeed in getting the whole I must report further on the subject.

Mr Willson mentioned to me the dearness of Corn, Hay, &c and said it would be impossible for the Coach to be worked on the Terms of last year, and that they must memorial for a larger mileage and he wrote in his letter that he intended so to do. But not one of them have sent any answer. I therefore have sent to Mr Willson to accompany me down tomorrow morning, and if I find objections it must be held out to them that if they do not perform the Royal Mail that they cannot keep the Exeter. And it may not be wrong to say that it will be given directly to another connection. Horse keep is dear no doubt, but they know that the Royal Mail must be horsed and therefore hang about to make their merit and pay the greater.

T. Hasker

Hasker writes of the settlement of the outstanding debt as a *fait accompli*, but it is most unlikely that it could have been paid from official funds without reference to the P.M.G. (of which there is no trace in the letter-book) who had to be consulted in such matters as the hire of the charwoman, the small rent for Mr Broadrib the weapon-cleaner's room, and (as later appears) that he should be allowed a scuttle of coals to make him a fire in the winter. It is more likely that Hasker advanced the money from his own private account to appease Wilson as he evidently did later on for a much larger amount.

Opening of the Weymouth season

Lord Chesterfield, marked 'Separate'

G.P.O. July 30th/95

My Lord

I have seen Mr Gorton this morning and His Majesty has fixed his Journey for the 17th of August. If you approve, the Mail Coach to be regular by that time may start about the 10th or 11th.

Before I had the honor to see your Lordship at Bailis, I had some conversation with Mr Willson [and] Mr Gorton to gain another hour for the travelling of the Royal Mail Coach between London and Weymouth, and he thought if we were in before 9 o'clock always, so that His Majesty might have his despatches when he sat down to breakfast, it would be quite in time. Willson's reason for asking for this hour was that it would be difficult to purchase Corn to keep the horses in the highest condition, as well that the additional hour would add greatly to the safety of the Coach. I enclose your Lordship a proof of the new bill for your approbation. I have allowed additional time from Weymouth to London to which I do not see any objection and, should you see any to the addition [of an] hour, as the Proof now stands, on its way to Weymouth, I will have them printed as last year.

T.H.

Lord Chesterfield, marked 'Private'

G.P.O. July 31st/95

My Lord

I have been over the road from Windsor by Ascot Heath to Bagshot, but I do not recollect if it passes near enough to Gloster

Lodge[1] to take up the Basket of Vegitables &c. If it does, it will certainly be the best way. I will wait on your Lordship next Wednesday morning to go over the road if necessary and take any further orders.

I sent the spare Coach down to Blandford yesterday (one of the new ones) it was weighed in the morning by a pair of Stillyards [steelyards] that I had proved, and it is only 16 hundred—rather lighter than the common Mail Patent Coaches. I was very much pleased to see it weigh so light, for I dare say the Contractors will complain of its heaviness. I did not weigh the other two for, as they are all made on exactly the same scale, the weight must be nearly the same.

T. Hasker

P.S. Willson is very busy with his Hay, but I will inform him of your Lordship's Command, though if I find that it is inconvenient to him I will not press him to accompany me to Baylis. I have made preparations to start Monday the 10th August.

The steelyard was an old-established and very reliable weighing-machine on the principle of unequal-arm balance. It could weigh up to several tons, but objects had to be suspended. A good example remains at Woodbridge, Suffolk. It was superseded by the weighbridge. Most of the early coaches weighed from 15 cwt. to a ton.

Lord Chesterfield, marked 'Private'

G.P.O. Aug 3/95

My Lord

I had the honor of your Lordship's letter and am attending to every part of the Weymouth Royal Mail business, that it may be started Monday the 10th Inst; and next Wednesday morning, between 9 & 10 o'clock, Mr Willson and self will attend yr Ldshp at Bailis to lay anything that occurs before you and take your further Commands.

Notwithstanding what I wrote your Ldp of my having weighed one of the new Royal Mail Coaches I received the enclosed very extraordinary Letter from Mr Demezy this morning, in consequence

[1] Not to be confounded with Gloucester Lodge at Weymouth where the King stayed.

of which I have directed all things to be ready for another weighing tomorrow morning—not that I have the least opinion that the first was erroneous. I have desired Mr Wilson [to attend] in your Lordship's name, and I have engaged Somners & Son, Scale & Stillyard makers to attend and prove the weighing just.

Mr Demezy having been told that his earnings should be made 1/9 each way or 3/6 per (double) mile and asking for an additional pair of horses over his good stages is shameful and extortionate & I hope yr Ldp will think such discontented, troublesome conduct on this occasion ought to be punished at a proper time. [To threaten him] with the loss of the Exeter Mail is a very good one.

The appearance of the Coach is remarkable light. But how inconsistent and selfish Demezy's conduct must be if he supposes it heavy, to ask for the passengers to stay and sup there.

If Mr Willson's Coachman has reported such falsehood of the Coach, without such falsehood being drawn from him by Mr Demezy, he ought to be turned from the Service—for such report down the road will make the already too discontented contractors more so.

T. Hasker.

Demezy's rate for this special coach at 1s. 9d. per single mile is 3d. less than the usual charge for a post-chaise and four horses. In addition, he gets earnings for passengers and parcels though these were probably not much in mid-season.

Genl Post Office
Aug 7th 1795

My Lord

Supposing Mr Brown would inform your Lordship of His Majesty's approving of going by Egham I shall proceed to observe that on my arrival in Town I took Mr Vidler to see the long Coach at Mr Boulton's and finding that the hire of it with the alteration, painting &c would be attended with so much Expense—and that there was a probability of extortion, and that it was possible some of the Passengers in going from Windsor tho' they would be detached from the Luggage yet being in the same appartment might complain. Then things made me turn my thoughts to another Coach, and after weighing it well in My Mind, I thought that a

Patent Coach with a very large Mail Box would be better to go between Windsor and Egham, I returned to the Manufactory and fixed on a York Patent Coach that is New Painted and well fitted up altering the inscription to *Weymouth & Windsor Royal Mail*. By this the Passengers from Windsor if 4 as will be the case sometimes with His Majesty's Household from the 12th to 17th Mr Gorton has booked it full will have the inside entirely to themselves. The Mail Box will hold the greatest part of the luggage, as I had the lid took off and the Guard's seat, as it will give more room, and he may stand 5 miles or go with the Coachman, and a leather cover put on that will let out to the Load. I have also put staples on the Roof of this Coach besides which there will be the whole of the Boot for rough Luggage; on reflection, too, there was another motive for the Patent Coach, namely if the New Royal Mail should at any time be broke before it reaches Egham this might be its substitute all the way to Weymouth.

I hope your Lordship will approve of this and so for a few Journeys my ordering Mr Cooper of Windsor, at the additional expense of 3/ per day to put on 4 horses that there might be a respectable appearance at Starting.

Lord Chesterfield.   (Not signed or initialled.)

The long coach was the progenitor of the omnibus, the one in question probably had a single door at the end instead of one on either side. It has already been seen (p. 78) that the York Mail was now given a larger mail-box.

The service was duly started (first for servants and luggage). But once more there was a slight hitch from an unexpected quarter, due to the usually reliable Vidler being an hour late in delivering the coach.

Lord Chesterfield (private)   G.P.O. August 12th 1795

My Lord

By the inclosed Time Bill your Lordship will see the Royal Weymouth Mail Coach was pretty well conducted for the first journey, both down and up, and I do not doubt but it will soon be quite regular.

The reason it did not start till past four, Nicholas has informed your Lordship, but to prevent a repetition of such error in Mr

Vidler, I have ordered an Extra Guard for a few days, to do nothing but see the Coach fetched and returned in proper Time, as your Lordship will see by the copy of his direction. I will wait upon your Lordship on Friday after Noon to receive your commands prior to my going on the Weymouth Road, and to Weymouth, which will be the next day.

T. H.

The next letter is of particular interest as it contains the only reference extant about the regulation of the time-pieces. It would seem that at that date they were set to gain to correspond with local time when the coach went east (making for punctuality on the more important up journeys to London) and only later that they were also set to lose when going west. Postmasters, where watches were handed in, were entrusted to wind them and adjust the regulator, which was made much larger than on an ordinary watch. The letter also shows what a profound dislike the guards had already taken to this early method of 'clocking in'.

'Unofficer-like' is on a par with, though not allied to, the expression current in the fighting services 'an officer and a gentleman'. Officials of superintendent status in the Post Office called each other 'brother officers' (see p. 201). Subordinates were also called officers, as in the present police force.

Genl Post Office
Sept 1 1795

My Lord

I saw your Lordship's observation on the Royal Weymouth Bill respecting the time piece, in consequence of Mr Charlton's remark which was very unofficer like on his part. Every possible attention is daily paid to the Time pieces to keep them in repair, in despite of which to cover negligence and form excuses they are very ill used on the road by Guards that their own irregularity may not be discovered. Guards frequently throw the time piece in the Pouch from one to the other when they change. When they are discovered they are punished for it, but that is not one time in a hundred.

The Time piece in question is a very good one. [It] had been two journeys down the Exeter road for the purpose of trying it, therefore had been ill used by some person before Mr Charlton made his remark, for the chain was broke, and this is the first timepiece that has stopped on this road this year, tho' while I was on the road I had very many complaints—for every proprietor is fond of complaining and thinks he has a right if they are not with his Town Clock. We have them regulated to gain about 15 minutes in 24 hours, that when they are travelling Eastward they may be with real time, therefore they gain about 10 minutes in their way to Weymouth which, added to the Clocks so far west, being a few minutes slower than in London, is the cause of the variation in the time Bill at Weymouth.

Considering how time pieces are thrown about I do not calculate that they can travel above 4 or 5 journeys regular. But even if they were not to travel one half of the journeys correct they would be of infinite use, as on those very journeys we could show the Contractors their errors past their excusing and shuffling from very necessity if they ever are accused.

I have told Mr Charlton in future not to write on the Bill to give the Contractors an opportunity of excusing bad performance but to write to Mr Delafons who is always very ready to correct and repair errors.

(Apparently for Ld Chesterfield but not stipulated or signed.)

Hasker refrains for a fortnight from disturbing the holiday of the P.M.G.s but then feels bound to let them know that the Postmaster of Dorchester is falsifying a time-bill. It appears that three coaches set out from Weymouth each morning, the R. W. Mail, the ordinary Mail, a branch coach which went only as far as Dorchester and transferred bags and passengers into the up Exeter, and a stage-coach. Delamotte, the contractor of the branch mail, applied to have his coach timed to leave Weymouth earlier. As this would simply be an unnecessary annoyance to the passengers from their longer wait till the Exeter came up Hasker looked into the matter at once in person. He found the Dorchester Postmaster was marking the bill twenty minutes earlier than the actual time Delamotte's mail arrived, 'I was Eyewitness of His Coach being the last of the three,' and he correctly surmised interested motives on the part of the deputy. 'This improper way of dating the Time Bills has often been represented, and I cannot see why the Post Master of Dorchester should persevere in it, except that he has a Coach from Weymouth [the said stage-coach] that runs before the Mail, that by keeping the General Post Office from the knowledge of the real Time of arrival they could not regulate the Duty accordingly, and his Passengers by that, to the injury of the Weymouth Mail, had the preference of Places in the other Mail Coaches (the Exeters) both up and down.' This local scandal was actually investigated by Lord Chesterfield who minuted a confirmation, on which T.H. promptly re-timed the branch Mail. Freeling doubtless took appropriate measures with the sinner.

Their Lordships were left alone for a further week, when they were written to on two heads; on September the 21st, to say that agreement had been reached to continue carrying the mail by coach from York to Scarborough, though at a higher rate of pay than hitherto. Time-bill 31 shows this service in operation, the coach running to Malton every day, going thence to Scarborough on four days and to Whitby on three. The other is a claim by Vidler who 'is so very importunate' in the matter. It related to one of those unfulfilled promises of Palmer to pay him a guinea each for cases for the guards' firearms. T.H. says he 'was in hopes that when you agreed to take the payment of oiling and greasing and drawing the Coaches to the Office, to the great ease of him and the Mail Contractors, that it would have covered every trifling expense of this sort and have kept me from further importunity, but as it does not, I refer it to your Lordships with his letter'. The argument is not easy to follow as the contractors were certainly paying a large part of Vidler's bills for lubrication and draft.

Hasker chose the last moment of the great seaside holiday to forward a humble prayer for better pay for his two hard-worked clerks.

G.P.O. Sept 30th 1795

My Lords

I have the honor to enclose to your Lordships a letter which I received at Weymouth from Mr Nicholas in behalf of himself and Mr White the other Clerk in my department respecting that they conceive themselves much underpaid for the constant and active duty they are employed in.

At the time the general arrangement was made throout the Office I, on finding that it was Ld Walsingham's intention to fix my Clerks so low as £60 & £70 per Ann., took the liberty of representing to him that their duty was *very* very great and

required great zeal and execution as occurrences might happen—
that every other day, Sunday included, they were obliged to attend
the Office from 6 o'clk in the morning till the mails were dispatched
at night and the other days full office hours, during which time they
have full employment. But I was not so successful as to persuade his
Ldshp to what I thought reasonable and just.

I therefore most Humbly entreat yr Ldshps to consider the case
and grant such addition as to yr Ldshps may seem proper.

T.H.

But this strongly worded and most deserving appeal met with no
better success than Hasker's earlier one on behalf of his deputy superintendents. There is not even a comment on it recorded.

Weymouth finale. Arrangements for Egham shuttle service

To Lord Chesterfield
Marked 'Private'

G.P.O. Oct 1/95

My Lord

I have the honor of your Lordship's commands from Andover
and have wrote to Mr Cooper to inform him the different times his
horses will be wanted at Egham on Sunday and Monday morning
Thus

Sunday Morning

First Turn

The Exeter Mail Coach passes through Egham at 3 o'ck in the
morning. The Coach must then be ready to take His Majesty's
servants to Windsor—return immediately to Egham.

Second

The Royal Mail Coach will be at Egham at 6 o'ck in the morning.
It must then be ready as usual to do its own duty to Windsor and
return directly to Egham.

Third

The Mercury [stage-coach] passes thro' Egham about 9, 10, or 11
o'clk in the morning. It must then be ready to take His Majesty's
servants to Windsor.

At night do their usual duty from Windsor to Egham as heretofore and Monday morning the Duty as above repeated.

I have sent Mr Charlton a copy of Mr Cooper's instruction and lest any contingencies should arise I will be at Egham Saturday and Sunday night for as this business has gone on so properly this year I should be much Vexed was it not to finish with eclat.

As the first turn will be in the morning before it is light I have sent a pair of Lamps and so[me] Oil to Egham.

I shall attend yr Lordships on Saturday or Sunday at Baylies to see if you have any further Commands, except you direct the contrary or fix any other time.

T.H.

After this there is an unexplained cessation of correspondence for more than a month. It may be assumed that Hasker was on tour, inspecting remote posts of his empire, before the winter set in with all its dangers and difficulties—for there is nowhere any suggestion that he ever took a holiday or was laid up. Perhaps the next letter was inspired by him after observations made in the course of travel. Mr Hodgson has not been identified.

*   *   *   *

The Bramham Moor cross-roads

G.P.O. Nov 11 1795

My Lords

I have the honor to represent to your Lordships relative to Mr Hodgson's proposal of the 28th ultimo for the York and Liverpool Mail to go via Witherby,[1] that if it was probable the Mail Coach Proprietors and the Passengers would agree to it, that it would no doubt be the proper rout for the Mail, but they will not, it being so far round. For the additional travelling the former ought to earn three hundred pounds pr Annum more than at present, instead of which the [Coach] would earn less, as the Passengers would find another mode of Conveyance rather than travel so much about.

Mr Hodgson may recollect that the whole of this was fully talked

---

[1] *Wetherby.* Many 'e's' were formerly pronounced as 'i's'—Greenwich is a survival.

The Leeds Mails passing midway. The Coachmen salute with whips in the approved fashion

The York Mail. The horsekeepers put to a fresh team at the Marquis of Granby Inn

over when the Coach was established and I met him at Leeds, prior
to which I had travelled three different roads to Witherby from
Leeds in hopes of finding one sufficiently good and new to send the
Mail that way to York—there was then a rumour of their making a
direct Road from Witherby to Leeds between the Kidder[1] Lane
Road and the Harwood[2] Road, and if such road was made I should
still be in hopes that the Mail might go through Witherby, but can't
think of its going 6 miles round, for what would the passengers say
to be only 14 miles from York at Bramham Moor and then travel
5 miles more to Witherby, and then be a mile more from their
journey's end, York?

I wish a House was built near where the Roads cross each other on
Bramham Moor where the Mail Coach from the North might have
the Bags for the West, and the cross Coach going west from York,[3]
about an hour or two after, would take them. In like manner the
cross Coach going to the East would have the Bags, and an hour or
two after, the Coach going to the North[4] would take them—this
would save the dangerous ride that Mr Hodgson speaks of, which
costs £32 per Annum, and I do really think it is worth while to see
if Sr Thomas Goodrich,[5] Sr Walter Vavasor,[6] or some other
neighbouring Gentleman would not Build a Cottage and put a
Shepherd or labourer into it, to whom a comfortable Salary could
be afforded by the Office to make it a receiving house.

Respecting that part of the Letter which proposes that the Liverpool Mail Coach[3] should leave York at 10 o'clock or a little after to
take all letters for the line of Road between Alconbury Hill and
Barnet[4]—I do consider it would be very big with Evil and not
answer the calculation. It often happens that the Coach[7] is not
arrived at York from Edinbro by 10 o'clock—of course then the
Coach would not be able to start till half past ten and as some part of
the road is but so so and rather narrow to Wetherby (15 miles),
they could not drive there in less than 2 hrs 15 mts—that would be a
quarter before one, and the Mail from the North[4] is generally there

---

[1] *Kiddal, Kiddall* or *Kiddhall*.
[2] *Harewood.*
[3] The Hull and Liverpool Mail, Time-bill 33.
[4] Glasgow Mail, Time-bill 14.
[5] *Goodricke* of Ribston Hall.
[6] *Vavasour* of Haselwood Hall.
[7] Edinburgh Mail, Time-bill 15.

by ¼ past 11, so that the wait there would be an hour or more. Which waiting is not the worst of it for, in defiance of orders, Coachmen, Guards, and Proprietors would find out below that they could not leave Wetherby till late and would procrastinate their arrival there, which would delay the departure of the Borough-bridge Ride for York, which I am afraid with all possible exertion is often not there in time to forward the letters for the east of that City, and if this was to be put in Practice passengers would be very discontented, and with propriety, for after travelling 6 hours in the Night they would not have got on their journey more than 24 miles, not being able to leave Leeds till 4 o'clock in general. At this time we find it difficult to get the Mail Coach from London down by that time, Roads so bad and Provinder so dear.

I agree, Coaches should be independent of each other if possible and I looked every way to obtain that before the Ferrybridge was established,[1] but I see no way of making it so. I have shown above that you cannot get the Mail from York in time for this Coach without keeping it waiting at Wetherby, nor can you get the Mail to Alconbury Hill to catch the Glasgow going down—for the Post from Cambridge arrives at Huntingdon about the time of the Edinboro Coach—often behind it. The Edinbro Coach is dispatched as fast as possible and seldom catches it even at Stamford, where it Breakfasts. Of course if there was such a ride the Cambridge and Norfolk letters could not go by it and it would be a very considerable drawback on the saving proposed. And altho the up Glasgow waits for the Edinbro at Stamford it is at dinner time, an hour and half or two hours in Summer and about 3 quarters or an hour in Winter, and it is so near London the Office has not the least inconveniency from it. Going down, they seldom are at Ferrybridge longer than the supper time before it arrives—they often arrive there together, and I am happy to say I have not had one complaint on this head from either passengers or Contractors.

T. H.

The direct road from Wetherby to Leeds, predicted above, was eventually made and is now A58. The cottage at the cross-roads was a first-rate idea for the improvement of the service. Palmer would have

[1] Glasgow Mail, Time-bill 14.

had it built and manned by a retired or an extra guard without asking leave. But a labourer or shepherd would have suffered badly from broken nights. Nothing further is heard of the suggestion.

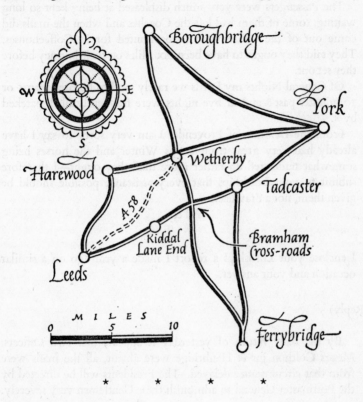

The G.P.O. accused of laxity

G.P.O. Novr 24/95

My Lords

I beg leave to state to your Lordships that the mails have been for some time past [occasionally] very late from the G.P.O. Last night some of the dispatches were as late as 48 past 8.

I should not have troubled your Lordships with this if it was not so very big with evil. It gives the Contractors, Coachmen, and horsekeepers cause for excuse to augment the delay and for throwing the Coaches into great irregularity, too much so naturally in the

Winter Season, especially this, horse keep being so very dear. And if at any time they can fix a blame on the Office there is no bounds to their negligence.

The Passengers were very much displeased at being kept so long waiting, some of them had left the Coaches and when the mails did come out of the Office were to be hunted for in Coffeehouses. They said they ought to have been Six Miles on their journey before they set out.

Of General Nights my Lords we rarely used to be later than 5 or 10 minutes past 8 and of bye nights were frequently all dispatched by 8.

From the Dearness of Provender I am very sorry to say I have already had very great trouble this Winter and the horses being somewhat under fed do rather more than they ought—I therefore submit to your Lordships that every assistance possible should be given them, not a drawback.

All &c

T.H.

I enclose your Lordships a report I made a year ago on a similar occasion and your answer.

(Reply)

By the daily return of yesterday it appears that two Officers, Messrs Colthon jnr & Hanbridge were absent, all the mails were from that circumstance delayed. The Presidents will be directed by the Postmaster General to admonish these Gentlemen very severely.

Ch

Lei

*　　*　　*　　*

Glasgow told to mend its ways

G.P.O. Novr. 26th 1795

My Lords

I have the honor to inform your Lordships that in consequence of the very bad state of the roads I addressed a Letter to the Lord Provost of Glasgow, the enclosed of which is a copy and also an extract of Mr Woolmer's as far as marked with commas, which I could not have expected would have drawn from them [*i.e.* the Lord Provost and his people] the enclosed answer which I send to your Lordships as they desire it; not that I think it needs any answer, for if they do not chose to mend the road they had no need to wander into extraneous matter to avoid it.

Respecting that part of the Letter which expresses that they have contributed about £300 towards purchasing the four Mail Coaches which run betwixt Carlisle and that City—such sum certainly was given to the Proprietors of the Mail Coaches by them, who were fearful without additional aid of undertaking a Mail Coach through so dreary a Country for so many miles where a coach had never been before, and the Office were further obliged to give them double pay for carrying the Mail, namely twopence per mile instead of a penny, which pay is continued to this day, though the only road in the Kingdom which has it, this additional penny per mile, is more than £300 per year.

They state in the next paragraph that they agreed to pay 10d upon a Single letter from London or Liverpool &c and that the Inhabitants of Edinbro, the same distance, pay only 7d—and from this they draw that there is probably an extra revenue of £1000 per Ann and hope that something may be allowed therefrom to keep the road in Repair. I must here beg leave to state to your Lordships that I never knew an instance of the G.P.O. being at the charge of mending roads, & further, that the Inhabitants of Glasgow pay only the same for their Letters now that they did before the Mail Coach run, when they had [them] via Edinbro or through some barrier Town as the Act expresses.

The next paragraph wherein they think the Mail Coach ought to pay tolls which would induce the Trustees to keep good roads would be to get roads mended at an expense [of] £10,000 a year & upwards which, as there is an Act of Parliament to avoid, I presume that neither your Lordships nor Mr Pitt will be inclined to saddle the revenue with.

I should not have sent your Lordships their letter but that they desired it, and as I do send it I thought it necessary to write this in explanation for your Lordships, for I do not think their letter requires any answer.

T.H.

(Reply)

We can have nothing to do with repairing roads—we are exempted from paying Tolls.

Ch
Lei

The Scotch, however, scored their point in the end. The story of
how it came to pass is quite typical of the way things do happen.
The British Society for Extending the Fisheries and Improving the
Sea-Coasts of the Kingdom had for a long time been pressing the
Government to develop the Highland ports and the land communications to them. Their arguments at last prevailed and, in 1801, Telford
was commissioned to make a survey of that wild and neglected
country. His report was accepted and, two years later, he set to work
on the enormous task of improving the harbours of the northern
seaboard and more than 900 miles of road leading to them, complete
with the many bridges involved. This prodigal spending of public
money on up-to-date facilities north of the Highland line set the
Lowland lairds agitating for improvements in their turnpike roads,
where they had financial interests showing poor or nil returns. They
represented that they could not possibly afford to make these roads up
unless the Mails paid toll. In 1813, in spite of strong resistance from the
Post Office, the Government gave way. In that year an Act was passed
repealing the exemption of tolls in all Scotland for 'mail-carriages with
more than two wheels'.

The result of that Act was to increase running costs of the Mails by
£6,865 a year. The Post Office felt bound to take some measure to
modify this sudden and unexpected burden and imposed a surcharge of a halfpenny for every letter crossing the Border. But the
Northern Kingdom, feeling itself secure in its new powers, retaliated
by raising the price at all its toll-gates, costing the Post Office a further
sum amounting to nearly £6,000, and there was no alternative but to
cut mail-coach services in Scotland. Several new ones had been
established, doubtless through Hasker's energy and contempt of
difficulties—just at the time when Telford was opening up not only the
Highlands but much of the Lowlands, too, with fine mail-coach roads.
Hasker was still in office when these things occurred but no record
seems to have survived as to what he thought about them. After

twenty-nine years of unremitting endeavour to make perfect the Palmer plan throughout the United Kingdom it is not difficult to imagine his feelings. But this was not all. Almost at the same time, the new Chancellor of the Exchequer, Nicholas Vansittart, in an ill-considered economy sweep, caused nine recently developed mail-coach services in England and Wales to be discontinued. On this last move, Joyce comments, 'By Pitt, the mail-coach had been regarded as the pioneer of civilization; in the eyes of Pitt's successors it was a mischievous encumbrance.'

CHAPTER VI

Letters to the Postmasters-General (3)
January to June 1796

In the year just ended, while life in England went on as usual, there had been great changes on the Continent. The flame of the Jacobin Terror in France had burned itself out. The protestations of equality and fraternity were already outmoded. Paris was not only orderly but gay, the newly rich spending money lavishly on luxuries, the poor kept from troubling by the National Guard. Only the citizen army mobilized by the Revolution preserved the impetus which had launched it, now translated into a passionate fervour of nationalism. Holland was overrun and compelled to join the French in the war on England, and Spain, also under compulsion, was about to do the same. Across the Italian frontier, in Piedmont, another French army was fighting and about the time when Thomas Hasker returned to his office after another unexplained absence of two months, young General Bonaparte was preparing to set off to take command of it.

The only effect of these momentous happenings on the British Post Office was that the packet station at Dover had to be closed and the main Continental mail diverted to Yarmouth. A Post Office packet crossed from there to Cuxhaven at the mouth of the Elbe, whence the mail was carried by road to Hamburg for distribution. On that account this foreign mail is always alluded to by Hasker as 'the Hamboro Mail'. Portugal was still our friend, and a Falmouth packet sailed once a week to Lisbon. The letters were made up in London on Tuesday night and dispatched by the Exeter auxiliary coach at 4 o'clock on Wednesday morning (Time-bill 4a).

There is no clue as to the reason for this second and larger blank in the letter-book. On New Year's Day Hasker had sent off the quarterly batch of mileage warrants for the contractors to endorse before they could be paid. After that, there are no letters until the beginning of March when the series is resumed, almost the first being the following:

(previous reference p. 124)   G.P.O. March 8th/96
  My Lord

    The weather being so very cold, Mr Broadrib, the 1st Instant, informed me he could not clean the Guards' Fire Arms if he had not a Fire for immediate use. I directed him to take a Scuttle of Coals from my Office and have now the honor to solicit your Lordship to allow him a fire when necessary in such very cold weather.

Freeling's armed horse-posts

    Three 'memorialists' apply for alterations in the service. One from Manchester asks that a mail-coach should run from there to Chester via Knutsford. T.H. explains that this route which is served by a ride has suffered much from robberies. But the horse-posts are shortly to be armed, and that should put matters to rights—'In the request for Mail Coaches the memorialists seldom have an eye to any correspondence but that of their own Town or, at most, that to which they are immediately concerned.'

    The proposal to arm the horse-posts had just been put forward by Freeling and he was pressing for it to be done immediately. But his plan entailed radical alterations in the time-honoured mode of conveying the mail, still in operation in many cross-posts and branches all over the country. The old type of post-boy, 'many not yet fourteen years of age', was to be replaced by those not less than eighteen, or older than forty-five, and of approved character. They were to be issued with a brace of pistols, a cutlass, and a strong cap for the defence of the head. The reform was an obvious one which ought to have been put into effect years before the advent of the mail-coaches, and it was evidently taken for granted by officials in the Post Office that it would now, at last, be done. But opposition came from a quite unexpected quarter—the Prime Minister. He fully appreciated the point of the argument; but the additional cost was estimated at not less than £6,000 per annum, and the expenses of the war had reduced the national exchequer to such an extent that he felt bound to turn the proposal down. The news of failure must have taken some little time to get back to the Office as Hasker confidently mentions it in future letters as something just about to be done—as indeed it was eventually.

A number of requests are received from 'the Inhabitants of Carlisle and Dumfries and Galloway'. The troublesome Carlisle-Portpatrick diligence had been taken off the road in the spring of the previous year (p. 115) and the petitioners are begging 'that it might be continued from Carlisle to Dumfries as had been the case when it ceased to Port Patrick before [by Lord Walsingham's orders, see p. 28] which Mr Edwards [the Surveyor at Carlisle] & self, conceiving of advantage to correspondence, I represented it to your Lordships; and also that if those Proprietors would performe it for the Turnpikes [*i.e.* the privilege of driving toll-free] and the sum it would cost the Office to send the mails by run to Annan and ride to Dumfries, that it would be very proper for many other reasons which you, approving, so directed up to October 10th last. It was heretofore at /3d per mile, and after that time £15 per quarter—the sum the mail would have cost was it done by horses &c'. But the coach-masters do not seem to have fallen for this bargain.

And there is a memorial from 'the Inhabitants of Bury St Ed's', requesting that one of the two Norwich coaches should call there. Hasker points out that the only plan would be to run an extra coach which ended at Bury. But that would overlap the Ipswich Mail as far as Chelmsford (30 miles). Chelmsford to Sudbury was already covered by a ride, though the fifteen miles from there to Bury 'a post does not travel', the town being served at present by a ride from Newmarket. He estimates the cost:

Expense of mileage, 73 miles, per Ann.	£225	
3 Guards & cloathes do.	96	
Washing & Greasing Coach	36 : 10	
	357 : 10	
Present expense of Rides about	£135	
Addition	£222 : 10	

He doesn't recommend the scheme. But only two days later (March 10th) he has a personal call from Sir Charles Bunbury, who was a noted man of the turf, a founder-member of the Jockey Club and winner of the first Derby. He was naturally interested in affairs at

Newmarket, and his principal seat was at Barton Hall, Bury St Edmunds. Hasker reports 'Sir Charles Bumbay is very anxious to have a Mail Coach to Bury, any road'. He was probably more impressed by the breezy demands of this forceful baronet than those of other memorialists. By a happy coincidence there came on the same day a letter from the contractors of the Wisbeach mail-coach asking for an immediate meeting at Cambridge. The Wisbeach coach had not been paying its way and they wanted in future to run it only as far as Cambridge and complete the journey by mail-diligence (a light two-horse coach). 'It struck me,' says Hasker, 'that it might make the Cambridge Mail a good Coach to extend it to Bury (an addition of 27 miles, costing £82:1:6) and save the Ride from Newmarket to Bury, 14 miles, £58:13:4. But as the mails are soon to be guarded,[1] there will be but a trifling encreace in expense.'

The meeting was held within a week and Hasker could report that his plan had been adopted in entirety 'to carry the mail by Coach from London to Cambridge, and by diligence from Cambridge to Wisbeach and . . . to run a branch Coach from Cambridge to Bury to join their connection . . . I have been over the Road and it is remarkably good'. The new arrangement was to come into force the day after the next quarter-day, April the 6th (*see* Time-Bill 16). In case there should be any misunderstanding in the sporting world as to whom the credit for granting this boon was due, their Lordships write under the letter—'Copy to Sir Charles Bunbury with PMG's compliaments. Ch. Lei.'

Other and quite different matters in East Anglia were now engaging Hasker's close attention. Due to the war, the foreign mail was all coming to Yarmouth but arriving at irregular times. One never knew now when the packet from Cuxhaven would arrive, though as soon as it did, it was essential to get it forward as quickly as possible, but at the same time, as cheaply. On one occasion the 'Hamboro mail' had come into Harwich after the Continental service from that port had been given up and the mail-coach had ceased to run there. The contractors who used to work it were asked to make a special journey, during which they only managed to collect one passenger, so they sent in a bill for 9d. per mile which T.H. forwarded, recommending payment, 'If it was an extra journey and they did it to forward the Mail, tho the price is double, it would be right to pay them without a murmur.'

[1] *i.e.* by Freeling's armed horse-posts.

The guard had already been given half a guinea. Later, Hasker laid down detailed instructions about how the 'Hamboro mail' was to be dealt with if it missed the regular coach (p. 162).

There were other difficulties in working the Yarmouth and Norwich services, partly due to a falling-off in passengers and parcels since pre-war days, making these mails less profitable to the contractors. A sub-contractor on the ground worked by Forster between Yoxford and Yarmouth, called Roberts, ran a stage-coach of his own, the *Telegraph*, between Yarmouth and London. He had applied for the agreed rate to be trebled, threatening that if it wasn't he would refuse to horse the Mail any longer. At the same time he was taking underhand means to divert patrons of the Mail to his own coach. His nefarious practices are denounced by Hasker in the following letters. From time to time his name crops up throughout the year after he has left the mail-coach company. The most curious reference is that on page 201. It shows to what lengths T.H. could go to score even one point against this sworn enemy who appears to have been the proprietor of the White Horse, Fetter Lane.

> Gen Post Office
> March 25 1796

My Lords

I have the honour to enclose to your Lordships two letters from Yarmouth, one from the Agent, the other from the Postmaster, by which you will see how very unfair Mr Roberts is acting.

I have recommended to Messrs Willson, Boulton, and Crouse[1] to go or send to Yarmouth and give such explanation of their conduct as may prevent such false representation from being effective, as it would be very improper for the Office to take it up in the manner Mr Seaman[2] proposes, though it shows his zeal for the service.

But I submit to your Lordships Mr Warmington's[3] remark and if means should not be taken to prevent the petty officers of the Custom House delivering cards and otherwise being agents for an established opposition to his Majesty's Mails, and for a man who has behaved so very improperly as Mr Roberts, and against an establishment that it will be the interest of the Government to support at this

[1] The Norwich contractor.
[2] Postmaster of Yarmouth.
[3] The Post Office Packet-agent.

crisis and prevent discontented spirits from such conduct in future—for, should he succeed, it would be a lesson to the Mail Contractors to follow his example or obtain such extravagant pay as they would demand.

All which is humbly submitted

T. Hasker

(Reply)

Officially we cannot interfere with any recommendation the C.H. officers chose to give. If Mr Todd could get a *private* hint sent them it might answer the desired effect.

Ch.

Lei.

Less than twenty years before, Customs officials on the Harwich station were found to have been in league with the captains of the packets in smuggling in a large way. Hasker probably had this in mind when accusing the Yarmouth men of disloyalty. (Next reference, p. 157.)

*　　*　　*　　*

Road repairs

Early in April T.H. forwards a letter from Sir Christopher Willoughby, Chairman of the Grand Jury at Oxford, 'by which you will see that they dread an Indictment from the General Post Office'. A promise is given that if this measure is not proceeded with the road will be made up. Lord Leicester thinks that they should be given another chance. Hasker is clearly sceptical but writes tactfully 'I hope the promise will be kept and the conduct of Coltman, the Surveyor of the road, will be agreeable to your Lordship's opinion'.

A report (with map) on the road south of Nottingham has been made by a Mr Gray. Hasker forwards it to Lord Leicester asking if he can take any steps to mend and complete the road which would 'certainly expedite the [Leeds] Mail'. There is a reply signed by both Lords. 'The Northampton road must, I fear, remain out of repair. The Corporation have as yet made no proposal which the Gentlemen of the Country think it proper to accept.' . . . Oh for the Palmer days! . . . One wonders if the particular stretch referred to

was that described by a competent eyewitness only six years before?
'The part I saw of it between Trent Bridge and the top of Bunny Hill,
may without prejudice, be deemed one of the worst kept roads in the
kingdom. The steeps torn into inequalities, strewed with large loose
stones, and set with fast ones, in the true breakneck crush-carriage style,
and the levels loaded with mud to the footlocks.'[1]

*   *   *   *

Once again! (previous application, p. 138).

Gen Post Office
Apl 28/96

My Lords
    I beg leave to remind your Lordships of the enclosed memorial
from Messrs Nicholas and White, the clerks in my department,
petitioning for an augmentation of Salaries, which petition is waiting
the consideration of the Lords of the Treasury, and from the multi-
plicity of business it may not be attended to for a considerable time.
I therefore humbly submit to your Lordships to reconsider the case.
They have only Salaries of £60 and £70 per Annum though their
duty is so great, and if to your Lordships it shall appear meet to
allow them a Temporary assistance till something permanent is
done, as their Situation from the smallness of Income is really very
destressing and their long and constant services are deserving of it.

All which &c
T. Hasker

(Reply)

    Pending the memorial at the Treasury it would in my opinion be
highly improper to allow any money to the persons who are the
objects of Mr Hasker's Letter.

Ch.
Lei.

Yet it does seem that Thomas Hasker was ready, at a pinch, to
advance money from his own private purse to get the mail forward.
In spite of the above chilling and thankless rejoinder, the very next day
Hasker composes the most energetic and masterly of all his epistles.

[1] *Rural Economy of the Midland Counties*, W. Marshall, 1790.

29 April 1796

My Lords

I have the honour to submit to your Lordships a Letter enclosed from Mr Crouse, the Norwich Contractor. In order to bring it fully to your Lordship's recollection it may be proper to restate the heads of this troublesome business, from the time of Mr Roberts letter to your Lordship which declared that unless he was paid 6d per mile, instead of 2d, that he would take the horses from the Coach the next Thursday sennight, which request if complied with would have made a difference in the payment to them of £1800 per Ann. and as all the other Contractors would have expected the same it would have made a difference of £26000 per Annum to the Office.

This claim was made very pressingly about four years ago & I coincided with your Lordship's opinion of fully resisting it, and as Mr Roberts had been wavering and very Troublesome for some time this new claim had been frequently fully talked over by your Lordships and me, by which you had made up your minds to act prompt and give orders on this; better, to furnish another Contractor rather than the additional pay. Messrs Boulton and Wilson undertook the mails—London Contractors have great advantages from the bookage and porterage of parcels that Country ones have not, that they were readily obtained—but I had great Difficulty in getting two or three others on the Road at Newmarket and Colchester.

But to return to Messrs Crouse and Watson, who both live in Norwich and work the different Mail Coaches, from Yarmouth to Ipswich, from Norwich to Ipswich & from Norwich to Newmarket, who, on Mr Roberts falling off as these Coaches did not more than just save the Contractors, their receipts barely covering their expenses, there was some difficulty in retaining them (Messrs Crouse & Watson) and blending them with the new Contractors (Messrs Wilson & Boulton) and they would not sign the Contract. They now propose each to have a sallary and to be indemnified from loss. The former cannot be complied with, for if there was no other impediment to it I should state it as my opinion that if they were to have salleries every other Contractor in the Kingdom would claim it, as they would also if their mileage was raised. Yet these proprietors must be retained if possible, for were they to leave the Concern, it being a loosing one, by the opposition that Mr Roberts now makes to it others could not be obtained and even Messrs

Wilson[1] and Boulton would not work the Coaches thro to Norwich without additional pay which, as I observed before, must not be given as it would involve the whole. Nor can such an indemnity as they hint at be given, for if they were to [be] hired to do the duty at so much per mile they would have no interest in the Coaches; and this would be the ruin of their other partners, for it would be their Interest to have the Coach light or empty instead of full, as by that they would have less for their horses to draw.

But, my Lords, as they cannot be paid a salary, nor have their mileage raised, nor be hired to do the duty, and they must be retained or the Mail Coaches drop—to the exultation of Roberts and the Down fall or disgrace of the Mail Coach system.

I have to propose that as since the present conection have had these mails they have earned not quite two shillings a mile, which sum will not pay their expenses, that I should be empowered to agree with them to give them a sum not exceeding one shilling and four-pence per mile for half their earnings for one year, which sum may be an expence of two hundred or two hundred and fifty pounds per Quarter to the Office and by which I will undertake to beat off the opposition of Roberts and Shaw, Mail Contractors, that, as Government will support their plan, that it will be in vain for them to act as Mr Roberts has done, who, I learn, has been corresponding with all the Mail Coach Contracting Malcontents in the Kingdom, not doubting to overturn the system or raise the price—which would have been done had your Lordships complied with Mr Roberts's demand he claimed first. They were all ready to follow had he pro-ceeded. Therefore, my Lords, I do propose to your Lordships that I may be permitted to make such agreement for one year on these Roads.

All which is humbly submitted

T. Hasker

There is nothing to say what the P.M.G. thought of this very bold proposal. Perhaps they preferred their answer to be verbal and off the record. Whatever it was, Hasker immediately put the plan into action:

---

[1] Of the Swan, Lad Lane. Others contractors of the same name were at Andover and Carlisle.

The stage-coach, Cheltenham 'Magnet', is forced to give way to the Mail

A midnight change, the coachman unhooking the leaders, the guard producing the horsekeeper

and (as I read the context) by advancing funds from his own bank account. Further letters on the subject are in the second book, p. 161.

23 May 1796

My Lord(s)

I have the honour to enclose to your Lordships a letter from Mr King, the Mail Coach agent at Yarmouth and as in the latter part he says the Captains of the Post Office Packets do not attend to the directions sent by your Lordships command, a copy of which is herewith sent, I humbly submit to your Lordships that you direct to your Secretary to sign such letter to of [sic] the Captains.

I fear Mr Roberts by great attention and civilities to them endeavour to bring them to his interest, and I am told he offers them a seat any time for themselves.

Respecting [Captain] Colln Hampack, as mentioned at the former part of Mr King's letter, I cannot see that the Office can interfere. I have therefore recommended to Messrs Willson and Boulton to offer him as advantageous terms by their Coach, or more so, than he has by Mr Roberts's.

All which is humbly submitted
Th Hasker

(Reply)

It is certainly the wish of the PMGl to encourage the Mail Coaches as much as possible but I have my doubts as to the propriety of directing the Secretary to write in the PMG's name such an official letter as Mr Hasker proposes—any intimation to the Captn to the same effect, the PMGl can have no objection.

Ch.
Lei.

This expression of gracious indulgence towards the mail-coaches is no doubt intended to put that department in its proper place.

The Post Office packets on this station were engaged on contract terms but the vessels themselves were owned by their captains.

*　　*　　*　　*

Mr Demezy again

G. P. Off
23 May—96

My Lord

I have the honor of your Lordships letter and am glad Mr Demezy has made you his friend, for he is such an unthinking mortal that tho his untoward behaviour last year did very much perplex and increase the expence of establishing his Majesty's Mails to Weymouth yet it would be too great a punishment to take his Exeter Mail from him.

I will write him a very severe letter and inform [him] that I have your Lordships Command to say that he is only on his good behaviour till the 5th of April next. I shall give him a good jobation and I hope he will feel himself sensible of your Lordship's indulgence.

I believe I can do without him for his Majesty's Royal Mail which, tho he was so scurrilous last year I am sure will hurt his pride. Aris, the Guard, is now at Salisbury. He shall explain tomorrow. I am much surprised at his neglect as he is so steady and sober a guard, and I am very much ashamed to hear that such neglect should have impeded his Grace.

I am making some arrangement for the Royal Mail and shall settle the whole in a few days which I will inform your Lordships of.

(Unsigned).

We have to make a guess as to what the whole of this story is, but it would seem as if Mr Demezy had been trying to curry favour with Lord Chesterfield and improving the occasion by telling unfounded tales on Guard Aris of the Exeter mail.

*   *   *   *

A memorial from South Wales

Genl Post Off.
June 25 1796

My Lords

I have the honour to enclose to your Lordships a letter from Mr Greville with my answer respecting the reasons I had before given to him why an additional Coach should not be established in South Wales. The Innkeepers, looking only at their own road I suppose, say to him and to Ld Rt Seymour that it would answer very well.

It is impossible; it would either itself be destroyed, or destroy the Mail via Swansea. If your Lordships approve of my letter it will be immediately sent after it returns to me.

T.H.

(Reply)

Mr Hasker's letter to Mr Greville is very right.

Ch.

This is the Hon. Charles Francis Greville who was busy building the new town of Milford as agent for his uncle, Sir William Hamilton, whose first wife owned large properties in South Wales (p. 74). The letter in question is copied in full in the second book (p. 164).

Hasker has now only one more page left in the present volume devoted to letters to the P.M.G. and he writes on it the last surviving of the august series on June the 28th. It is a proposal to take the Bristol-Birmingham Mail through Thornbury (spelt Thumbury), a market town on the left bank of the Severn, a little way off the main road. The application is from a Mr Rolph. T.H. says that years ago the road was reported not complete. But Wilkins, now at New Passage, will go and report on it. At present the mail is taken there by a runner at £10 per annum. The decision must be left to the contractors for 'all the Innkeepers and Coachmasters from Bristol to Birmingham are in a Company, thirty-four in number, and if they should say they will not, a new Connection cannot be formed'. For this slight diversion from the present route, to pass through the town, Mr Weeks would be allowed an additional five minutes. We don't hear how the thirty-four voted, but their successors, the Railway Company, thought it worth while to build a branch line to Thornbury from Yate.

CHAPTER VII

Letters to Mail-Coach Personnel
and Others (1)
June to August 1796

HASKER finished the earlier volume of this series almost at the same time as he did that of his letters to the Postmasters-General. There was only an overlap of three days. He opened this present one on June the 25th and closed the other on the 28th. It has already been said that only these two—a single specimen of either series—has survived. Most of the letters addressed to P.O. Staff are short, sometimes as many as four on a single page, so that the number is much greater than in the P.M.G. volume. In the following selection I have again retained for the most part the day-to-day sequence, as showing the relationship between time and growth in the organisation. I have made some small collections under single heads to save the reader hopping continually from reference to reference when the time factor was of no particular moment.

In this book one is looking at the working of the 'mail-coach Concern' from exactly the opposite angle to the other. But, taking an element common to both—the destructive criticism of contractors —it may seem surprising that only a very limited number of those horsing the Mails in all parts of the realm come under the lash, and do so not once or twice but repeatedly. As Hasker was by no means a man for making favourites and the reverse, there must have been some method in his punitive programme. After all, we can only watch him at work for three out of thirty-three years. During that time he was terribly short of staff and had no doubt made up his mind to wage a long campaign of progressive purges. We have seen him concentrating on the western roads. Now he is trying to regulate the eastern routes, letting out an occasional back-lash at the old target. If more volumes had been preserved we should no doubt find the Shrewsbury, Liverpool, Holyhead, and other Mails, which seem to be getting away with everything so easily, having their turn of Haskerian rigour. It would be a mistake to imagine that because we hear nothing about them they were all as good as gold.

The series opens with a letter to Wilson of the Swan with Two Necks who jointly, with Boulton of the Golden Cross, was chairman of the company working in the Norwich (via Ipswich) Mail. From it, it is clear that the plan which Hasker put before the P.M.G. on April the 29th, to the confusion of the despicable Mr Roberts, has been in operation for some time. Those contractors who were neither to be *salaried*, nor *hired*, nor have their mileage raised, were yet, by another convenient formula, to be roundly subsidised. Hasker had evidently gone so far to meet them as to advance pay to one of their number, but they had not even played fair by the first rule of the game, and T.H. is in danger of having the draft he had already drawn refused by the bank. The two coaches must mean the up and down mails. The time-bill gives the distance from Witham to Colchester as 13½ miles, so the agreed subsidy was even being paid on the generous side.

To Mr Wilson of Lad Lane   Southend June 25 1796

Sir

I have paid to Mr Waterhouse one shilling per mile or 28/- per day for half of his earnings on the two Coaches between Colchester and Witham—you & Co. was to have paid into my hands the half of his earnings to help enable me to do it. I suppose the Accounts are made out by this time to the 18th of June, if so, leave me an account, and they have long been settled up to the 25th of March, 3 months ago, though I have not had the pay.

You may remember you was to pay half his earning to me, the other half you was to keep to pay you the debt for your horses &c. Please to give Nicholas a draft for the earnings to 25th March to take to my banker or I cannot pay Waterhouse for I am overdrawn.

                              T. H.

(Next reference on page 182.)

*   *   *   *

The 'Hamboro Mail'

The irregularity of the Yarmouth-Cuxhaven packet service due to
the war and the difficulty of getting the mail up to London quickly,
when landed, was alluded to on p. 151. Hasker's special instructions
on how to deal with it now follow. He tries to make doubly sure by
writing both to the Packet Agent and a coach proprietor at Colchester,
giving the latter a sly, confidential wink about a latent weakness in the
other. Mr Hedge appears to be of Messrs Hedge and Boyce, addressed
elsewhere as Mail Contractors, The Duke's Head, Yarmouth. They
don't appear in the time-bills as horsing the Mail but may have been
proprietors of the auxiliary coach which only carried the mail and a
Post Office guard between Yarmouth and Ipswich, being a stage-
coach for the rest of the journey. The London bags were carried on
from Ipswich by the Norwich Mail which left half an hour later than
the other and arrived in London an hour and a half earlier.

A. Mannington Esq   Genl P Off
H.M. Agent of Packetts, Yarmouth   July 4—96

Dear Sir

I send the enclosed, which is nearly a copy of the instructions
before given, but though they must be the general line for your
government, yet you must in particular cases act *ad libitim* [*sic*]
keeping in your mind that a mail by express, namely by cart or
chaise, will arrive in London in about 21 or 20 hours after you
despatch [it] as, for example, had you sent the mail that arrived the
29th at 5 o'Clock in the afternoon, we should have received it by 1
or 2 on the 30th in the afternoon, and the letters would have been
delivered that day to the Merchants; but by keeping it till the next
morning, 4 o'Clock, it did not arrive till the morning of the 1 July
—of course was not delivered till 9 o'Clock that morning. If any
mail arrives within an hour after the Mail Coach is gone, perhaps a
post chaise and four might catch it at Ipswich. It is worth the trial
especially as by this exertion, should it fail of that point, it is so far on
its way.

If any mail arrives from that time—/½ past 3 P.M. till ½ past 3 or
4 A.M. it should be dispatched with every Possible exertion, for it

will arrive at the General Post Office in 20 or 21 hours after, any of which time will be before 12 Midnight, that is, it will be noon to midnight, according to the time it arrives at and leaves Yarmouth, and such arrivals in London will be of the utmost Moment. If from the 30th past, 3 or 4 A.M. till 8 in the morning, named in the general instruction—tho it will not arrive in the General Post Office to be equally serviceable as in the last case, as it will arrive there from Midnight till 6 or 7 in the morning, yet the mail ought not to be delayed; for if it arrives but an hour at the General Post Office before the Mail Coach, that hour may be of the greatest service to the States.

You will observe the reason why you keep the mail to send by the Mail Coach is that tho you detain it 4 or 5 hours, it arrives as soon at the General Post Office as if sent by Express, for the Coach travels in 16 or 17 hours and the Express in not less than 20 or 21— Sometimes more.

I hope this letter in aid of your instructions will be sufficiently explicit. However, if there is any particular case, you must act *ad libitum* as I said before—and in that Case of the mail arriving at 5, the 29th, your observing as the Guard was not returned with the Cart, and as you had no Guard, you kept the Mail; now in that case you might have got a man you could confide in and sent him off in a Post Chaise.

(In the hand of a clerk and from dictation, evidently in haste, and not signed or initialled.)

Mr Hedge	Genl Post Off
Mail Contractor	July—4—96
Colchester	

Dear Sir

I received yours but not having your letter before me I shall not be able to answer every point. However as far as i can I will, and if any mail arrives at any time, when you have a Coach or Dilly setting off in an hour or two, keep it and send it up by it with a Guard. If you have not one setting out in an hour or two, send him off in a Cart or by Chaise. Do not let them wait at Colchester except if they arrive at 9 at night. Keep them for the Norwich Mail Coach. Wee have from some detentions at Yarmouth been obliged to stir up the Agent, and he may send some mails up at times you may not expect. Don't mind that, as however you send them the expense will be paid.

(In the hand of the same clerk—not one of the regulars—he uses a little 'i' in one place.)

To Mr Warmington   General Post Office
Yarmouth   July 7th 1796

Dear Sir

I received yours of yesterday but do not see how I can make any alteration of the Coach for, though ever so proper a one was pointed out the Coachmasters are such strange beings that they will neither lead nor drive. We make them keep time as well as we can. The Office at Ipswich, too, has so many forward letters to sort that the Coach is there an hour.

T.H.

✻   ✻   ✻   ✻

A second Milford Mail?

On June the 25th the two letter-books were both being used so on the one hand we have the letter to the P.M.G. about Greville's memorial (p. 159), and on the other a copy of Hasker's answer which he had enclosed. The proposal was to put a mail-coach on the more northerly route to West Wales which would go from Gloucester through Ross-on-Wye, Abergavenny, Brecon, Llandovery, and Llandilo to Carmarthen. This would provide an alternative way to Milford, where Greville's new town and dock were being built. It would certainly be much more attractive to passengers than the present Milford Mail as it would avoid the awkward and exposed crossing of the Severn at New Passage. The request was identical with that made by the Merchants of Cork two years earlier and dealt with in full detail by Hasker in his letter of May the 6th, 1794 (p. 70). The four letters on the subject are here put together.

The Hon. C. F. Greville   Genl P.Off.
                                                           June 25—96
Dear Sir

I have the honour of your favour of the 20 Inst and am much concerned that Mr Longfellow still equivocates, as I do not think it would be proper to establish a Mail Coach between Gloucester & Carmarthen except he would turn his coach to a Mail. The reason I have before given, it would establish more coaches on the road than could live. The interest of Messrs Boulton, Heath &c makes them say otherwise, as to them it would be a new Coach—a great acquisition to their houses and, once making it a Mail Coach, the Office would have all the trouble and the disgrace of it if it failed as it would, or destroy the other Mail that runs via Swansea—nay it does not appear to me clear that if an additional coach was put on on the upper road but that they would so distress each other that before the next winter was out there would be [no] Mail on either road.

My real opinion is, as I once had the honour to mention to you, that the only way for the advantage of Milford, the Packets &c is to prevail on Mr Longfellow to make his Coach a Mail—if not, there is no way of having a Mail via Brecon but by persuading the Contractors on the lower road to reduce their coach three days a week and add that to the upper road. If the Innkeepers think the contrary, and will back that opinion, and not let it be only words, let them Start a Coach themselves and run it three days a week from Gloster to Carmarthen for six months, and at the end of that time they shall have the mail to carry. I have talked this over with the Postmasters General and their Lordships see it quite in the Light that I have the honour to state it to you.

I really should be happy to accomodate this and every road to your wish—I am sure the community owe much to such spirited exertions, but looking to the whole, and knowing the private views of Contractors I hope you will think the Office can do no more.

                              T.H.

Hon. C. F. Greville   Genl P. Office
                                                       July—4—96
Dear Sir

I have the honour of yours of the 29 ulto and having talked the matter in question fully over with Mr Freeling we are decidedly of opinion, as is their Lordships the Postmaster General, that the mail cannot go more than three times a week via Llandovery to Carmarthen.

Therefore if Messrs Heath Nott & Co will run [a] light Coach three days a week for six months, at the end of that time the mail will be given them to carry on the usual conditions, as I before described in a letter to Mr Longfellow a copy of which I had the honour to enclose to you.

I am very sorry that you should have so much trouble on this subject, but these are the only conditions that the Post Office can agree to, and I am afraid you will have more trouble yet with the Inn-keepers or Coachmaster—though it is probable if they have courage to start a Coach against Mr Longfellow that he will join them. I think he is a timid man and will not run in opposition.

T.H.

P.S. Sir, you will please to observe by my saying Heath Nott & Co have no objection but the contrary to Mr Longfellow being one, and of converting his Coach to the Mail Coach—or if he will not, if they establish a light coach *three* days a week for six months without him, the mail will at the end of that time be given to them.

Heath and Nott, members of the South Wales Association (of coach-masters), were also members of the company which worked the Milford Mail. Nott's name appears in Time-bill 25 as horsing the Mail between Swansea and Carmarthen. The company was never in good odour with Hasker, as will appear from the sharp letters he wrote to and about its members.

C. F. Greville   8 July 1796

Dear Sir

I have the honor of your letter of the 5th Inst and am much concerned to learn by it that my last did not amount to your wishes and I am sorry further to explain that it is not the intent of the P.M.Gl. to increase the number of Post Days for the Towns and their collateral branches between Brecon and Carmarthen, whether the mail goes by Coach or continues by horse.

Brecon is served now six days a week and, should a Coach start, would so continue, namely, three times by horse and three times by

Coach. Carmarthen is also served every day—and would remain so served. In short, all the Towns, however they may be served, will be served as often as now, though the Inhabitants, should the Innkeepers establish a Coach, would not have their Correspondance worse conducted than at present—but as much better, as the safety of the Coach with a Guard is preferable to the horse post. Should you think any further explanation necessary I beg you will not apologise for the trouble as I shall be happy in the communication.

T. H.

Hon. C. F. Greville   July 12, 1796

Dear Sir

I have the honor of yours of the 9th and am concerned that I am not enabled by any authority from the Postmaster General to say anything respecting the encreasing the post days between Brecon and Carmarthen. Should the respectable Gentlemen you mention, with yourself, apply to their Lordships when the Coach has run six months and is ready for the mail they will, I am confident, comply with your request if consistant with the rule of [the] Office and be most happy to have it in their power to do so.

By the time the Coachmasters can be ready to start the Coach will be a good time of year, for their six months probation will expire in Spring when, if they have performed it well the P.M.G. [hopes] to grant them the mail.

T. H.

Two months later came the following, addressed to Nott, the Carmarthen contractor.

Mr Nott   G.P.O. Sept 10. 96

Dear Sir

I received yours but have not yet seen Mr Greville. I am very glad that all parties have agreed to the proposal I made. I should think that the sooner the Coach is altered properly to a light Coach the better and by such means it will get regular by the time we put the Mail into it which will be at Lady day, for it has been so driven off that it has been impossible to arrange the posts and make the alteration sooner and contrary to the rule of [the] Office, never to establish any Mail Coach after the 5th of July.

T.H.

The new Milford Mail must have been duly put on the road at the time predicted, though it does not figure in the time-bills of 1797. In spite of Hasker's opposition to the plan when it had first been proposed by the Merchants of Cork it proved to be the better way and superseded the other. It has, in fact, left a mark which can still be seen. On the Gloucester-Carmarthen road (A 40), three miles this side of Llandovery, where the little river Gwedderig has scored a deep defile, there stands an obelisk called the Mail-coach Stone. It marks the place where, on a December night in 1835, the Milford Mail, driven by a drunken coachman, dashed into the ravine, with horrible consequences.

Mr Longfellow has not been identified. He seems to have been a stage-coach proprietor in the loose confederacy called The South Wales Association, but working in opposition to Messrs Heath, Nott, and Co. A stray but uncertain gleam is shed on the doings of this alliance by two letters, written midway between the last two quoted, and may have had some bearing on the Milford proposal. Mr Marmont enters the letter-book with a dramatic gesture whose chief aim was probably to impress the great man from London. It does seem to have had some effect, but that soon wore off and, before the end of the year, we find Mr Marmont getting some very hard knocks.

To Mr Marmont, Pyle   G.P.O. Aug 20/96

Sir

I very well remember the meeting when you subscribed £100 in the name of the Mail Coach Company. I was very much pleased at your doing so and thought it was perfectly right, but did not recommend as I thought the Contractors desired it, or undertake to settle it with the Contractors as I conceived you had. They must be a very shabby set of partners if they refuse to pay their shares of it. I have wrote to Mr Bradley & Mr Nott that I think they should allow the above sum to be paid by the Company. If they refuse, give me a line.

T.H.

Messrs Nott, Carmarthen &
Bradley, Cardiff

G.P.O. Aug 20/96

Sir

I have received a line from Mr Marmont respecting the £100 he subscribed in the name of the Mail Coach Company to the South Wales Association. I was present at the meeting and much satisfied at him doing it. I could not conceive that any of his partners would have had any objection to it. It will be hard for it to fall on himself alone, when it was done evidently for the good of the whole connection, among whom it will be but a mere trifle. You will of course settle it with him.

T.H.

*   *   *   *

New ground

It will have been noted that only one out of the many public applications for new coach routes has met with any success and it may have been thought that Hasker was an inveterate opponent of any move towards an expansion of his service. He was indeed bent on consolidating the unstable empire bequeathed to him by Palmer. But after the best part of four years of terrific work under circumstances of enforced stinginess, all routes were pretty well established and he was already planning an advance that showed him to be far from a timid isolationist. This was to the far-off city of Aberdeen. It seems to have been his own idea and, as there is no suggestion of anything of the kind being mooted in the previous book, perhaps it was thought wiser that the P.M.G. should not be consulted until all arrangements were quite complete and contracts laid on the table ready for signature. Edwards is the Post Office surveyor in the North, Drysdale one of the Edinburgh innkeepers. At present he horses the Edinburgh Mail on the ground from Haddington. He is known to be forceful in promoting a mail-coach link with Glasgow (still only a 'ride') and would like to be in on the run to Aberdeen. Hasker knows that his inn and stables would make the ideal junction for the change of coach, horses, gear, and passengers. But Drysdale has other keen competitors.

Mr Edwards, Surveyor   Southend
Carlisle   June 25th 1796

Dr Sir

When you find all obstacles removed, the time of departure from
Edinbro for Aberdeen fixed &c, as it is impossible for me to venture
so far, will you give me a line that I may either direct Mr Woolmer
to accompany you with a Contract or will you take him with you
—The Grand difficulty will be the getting it worked to Drysdale's.
If you find Innkeepers to undertake it, 2d per mile each way will
keep it on its legs and I do not think less than that would, and even
that price will be as moderate as your riding price in those parts.
But I dare say you will think this a little premature for it is not yet
fully determined on that there shall be a Coach.

T.H.

No further news of this for another three weeks (p. 183) during
which, however, the plot has considerably thickened.

*   *   *   *

Name of Pickwick

There can be no doubt at all where Charles Dickens got the name
of his popular hero, for Sam Weller says as much. To quote from
Chapter XXXV of *The Pickwick Papers*:

> As Sam spoke, he pointed to that part of the coach door on which
> the proprietor's name usually appears; and there sure enough, in
> gilt letters a goodly size, was the name of PICKWICK!
> 'Dear me', exclaimed Mr Pickwick, quite staggered by the coinci-
> dence; 'what a very extraordinary thing!'
> 'Yes, but that ain't all,' said Sam, again directing his master's
> attention to the coach door; 'they puts "Moses" afore it, vich I call
> adding insult to injury . . . ain't nobody to be whopped for takin
> this here liberty, Sir?'

Mr Pickwick of Bath and his stage-coach which ran from that city
to the Golden Cross, Charing Cross, were realities. This was the
coach mentioned in the following letter. Pickwick also worked for
the Post Office, providing teams which carried the Bristol-Oxford

Mail between Bristol and Bath. For this he earned Hasker's most unstinted encomium (note on Time-bill 26) though he had failed to conform to rule in the matter of the patent coach. Probably Weller's Pickwick was not this man but his heir. The incident reported below is not made clear in further letters, but it may well be called 'Pickwickian'. It caused Hasker to make use of one of the only two marks of exclamation found in all his letters. He is writing from Southend (where he had been for the last ten days) to one of his clerks.

Mr Nicholas, G.P.O.   Southend
                                                      July 5 1796
Dr N.

Inform Mr Dibbin that I have seen his letter and that I have the greatest confidence in his opinion and report, and that I never take the part of or protect a Guard any further than when they act properly in the line of their duty, that Fennel shall be put on another place till I can further investigate the matter—that I by no means wish Mr Fromont or any proprietor to dismiss a coachman except for the good of the Service, that as the gentleman passenger has told Mr F. [that] Hulbert was not to blame I by no means wish him punished. There is only one thing I would wish them to fathom— why Hulbert took up a passenger and put [him] into his coach from Mr Pickwick's Coach, and he drunk too!—and if the gentleman lives in Town let him send his address that we may enquire fully into the business.
                                                      T. H.

Dibbin was (apparently) Postmaster of Thatcham, Fromont, the proprietor of the King's Head, Thatcham and mail-contractor. It seems to have taken a full month to clear up the affair, after which Guard Fennel was exonerated and restored to his old place on the 'good ground'.

*   *   *   *

Points on uniform

Coachmen were not at that time given a uniform either by the contractors or the Post Office. An exception was the case of those driving the Weymouth Mail and the coachman-guard (pp. 173, 194). Later on, after Mr. Vidler had instituted his Mail-coach Show on the King's birthday, uniformed coachmen on the crack Mails became more general, the dress supplied by the contractors.

W. Wood (Blandford), Ware, Weeks, Demezy   G.P.O. July 7th
1796

Sir

Will you please to send the name and measure of the Coachman you intend to drive the King's Weymouth Coach as the time is so short if the measure is not immediately sent up his Uniform cannot be made in time.

T.H.

* * * *

Special mark of favour

S. Nicholls   G.P.O.
(late Mail Guard)   July 16th 1796
Manchester

Sir

Tho it is customary for Guards quitting the Service to leave their Uniforms for their successors, Mr Hasker, in consequence of your good conduct while in the employ of the Office, makes you a present of them—and your leaving it with propriety gives you a fair claim to a future employment if you desire it.

T.H.

A new dignity for Post Office Surveyors

To Postmaster   G.P.O.
Dover   9 July/96

Sir

The Surveyors being all allowed a Guard each, Mr Bartlett has fixed upon Dover for the payment of his. I have therefore enclosed his sheet of receipts and you will please to fill it up and return it with the 6 guineas & $\frac{1}{2}$ to Mr Hasker. You will be credited for it with the receipts you have already sent up.

H.N.

These were Hasker's men and, like all the other guards, were paid by local postmasters at centres from which they worked.

Small incident

J. Ashby, Mail Guard, Congleton   G.P.O. 9th July 1796

Sir

Mr Hasker received yours and you did very well in getting the Mail forward after the Coach was overturned. There will be a lamp sent down tomorrow night. Send Mr Hasker word if the Coach is sent to Warrington and Repaired.

S.W. (the clerk, White)

     ★   ★   ★   ★

A hard case

The following incident was evidently a 'lark' perpetrated by some well-to-do young fellows—the kind of ill-considered frolic particularly common in the 18th century, usually ending in trouble for the innocent.

To Postmaster   July 9/96
Liverpool

Sir

I received yours respecting Waldron the Guard and [would] be much obliged to you to investigate the matter, as a man should be heard before he is dismissed but I have no doubt but he ought to be discharged as he ought not to have presented a Pistol to the Gentlemen unless they had stopped the Coach with intent to rob the Mail.

T.H.

To Mr Banning, Post Office,   Genl Post Office
Liverpool   July 19 1796

Sir

In consequence of a letter received this morning from J. Waldron, Liverpool and Manchester Guard, denying the Charges made against him in the Letters you was so good as to send up, Mr Hasker would be glad if you would inform him of. It appeared on the information that was given by Passengers and Coachmen that Waldron did so illtreat the Gentlemen (as they represented in their letters) as it is very improper to trust such a man with fire Arms—

if he acted in the way it is represented. We have Truman in London, who I find was Coachman with the other Coach that was in company with the Mail and was eye witness to the whole. He has repeated the Circumstances exactly as the Gentlemen did, only describes the treatment given by the Coachman to the second Gent: to be much worse than he represented it. Trueman says he was examined by Mr Statham and has given him the same information as now he gives us. Waldron says in his letter 3 Gent: on horseback on the road stopped the Horses of the Mail by laying hold of the reins without speaking a word, and nearly overturned the Coach. The Coachman flogged him and his horse that held them, but to no purpose 'when I got down and begged them to be off, and they were going to strike me when I threatened to shoot one of them if thei did not desist, upon which they let us go after losing some time'.

It appears by Truman's information and the Gentlemens' Letter that every word of this is false. Mr Hasker requests you will give him a line on the subject.

(Probably by Nicholas).

Mr Murrel   Genl Post Office
Manchester   July 21 1796

Dr Sir

I have Mr Hasker's directions this morning to discharge J. Waldron, the Liverpool and Manchester Guard, and you will please to make him give up his Cloaths as his Bondman will be sued for the value of them—and he has also directed W. Quick to be put into his place. All this you will be so good to see done immediately and send the uniforms and Hat up directed to Mr Hasker.

(Unsigned)

Murrel (spelt in several different ways) was one of the recently appointed deputy superintendents looking after a large area based on Manchester. He seems to have been young and inexperienced as he gets more raps from his superior than the others. Statham was Postmaster at Liverpool, Banning, his assistant, to whom the letters which follow are addressed. Guard Waldron's case was one of hard luck, whatever the truth of the story. The Post Office received frequent

complaints about their guards' misuse of their fire-arms. They naturally found it irresistible to take an occasional pot-shot at a sitting
pheasant or other edible target when the coach was empty and no
gamekeeper in sight. But what the management was in constant
dread of was being confronted with a case of manslaughter due to
panic on the part of a nervous guard. Cautionary circulars, aimed at
preventing homicide and other accidents with these dangerous
weapons, were issued from time to time. An example is given on
page 280.

＊　　　＊　　　＊　　　＊

Manufacture of time-pieces

Hasker wants new time-pieces made for the Liverpool-Hull Mail
(referred to below as the York Mail). Mr Banning, the Assistant
Deputy P.M. of Liverpool, has persuaded him to give the work to a
local watchmaker and has probably promised a more reliable article
and one more able to withstand rough usage and meddling fingers
than the standard model of London make. But his man is slow in
delivering the goods and Hasker gets impatient, then finally makes an
appeal on the higher plane of national honour. This correspondence
extends over a period of four months, but the letters are put together
here before returning to chronological sequence. It has already been
shown that the guards bore this tell-tale instrument no good will.

Mr Banning, Post Office,   G.P.O. July 7/96
Liverpool

Sir

    Having altered my plan respecting the Time Pieces I am in the
utmost distress for the Time Pieces you was to make. Pray be so
good as to get them done with all possible speed and put them to
work as I first directed—giving me information.

T. H.

Postmaster   G.P.O. July 7/96
York

Sir

    We have a person in London that Contracts to keep the Time
Pieces in repair and he is not paid so much for a whole year for the

175

York Time Pieces as Mr Rule has charged for two months—I must therefore request you, when the time piece wants repair to send it up by the York Coach that arrives here of a Sunday and to have no more repaired at York, as all the bills are paid by the person that contracts for repairing them here, which he cannot afford to do.

T.H.

Mr Banning   G.P.Off
Post Office, Liverpool   Oct 24 1796

Sir

I received yours. When I gave orders for the timepieces I proposed them for the York and Liverpool road only, that they might be intirely under your care and, if approved of, to be extended to another road contiguous to you. I must therefore request you to get them on that road as soon as possible and send the old ones. Your observation that great pains was taken to open it in London without effect is wrong, for we opened it immediately, both before and after the alteration. If one Guard should become acquainted with the method of opening it he would teach all the others. But this cannot happen as those in the secret will not divulge it. It is my opinion that the weight of the case would totally destroy the works should it experience a fall, which would not be so likely to happen with a light wooden case.

T.H.

Mr Banning   G.P.Off
Post Office, Liverpool   Nov 12. 1796

Sir

By the Liverpool and Hull Bill up this morning, it appears that they had no Time-piece. I don't know where the fault lies.

I was in hopes that you would, long before this, have had the new time-pieces on the road. Pray let them be done directly as we shall have the business all in confusion. As soon as the new time pieces are at work send up the old ones to this Office or, if one or two of them is ready, put them on.

T.H.

To Mr Banning, Post Office, G.P.O. Nov 18/96
Liverpool

Dear Sir

Your timepieces not being nearly ready you will see confine us very much on the road—for, in consequence of my supposing they were ready, I ordered the person at York not to repair them. Three Time pieces will do from Liverpool to Hull and back. When will you have three ready for the duty?

Our Duty is not like common business you know, we must be exact, the eyes of all the Kingdom is on us and the Correspondence of the Country is at stake.

T.H.

The time-piece in action

Mail Guard Johnson G.P.O.
Nov 5 1796

Sir

On your journey up to Manchester on the 2nd Inst: it appears by the bill that the Timepiece was delivered safe to you at Lancaster, and when you delivered it at Manchester it was very much broke. It looks very suspicious on your part. Therefore directly write me the particulars what you know of it, and write *truth*, for I am determined to find it out and punish the offender very severely.

T.H.

Mail Guard J. Kelly G.P.O.
Nov 11 1796

Sir

On your journey up to Lancaster the Timepiece was very much broke and, it seems, came into Lancaster buckled to the strap-irons[1] behind the Coach instead of being buckled round you. In that situation no wonder it was broke—it lays between you and Johnson and I will find out the default. Write me every particular you know of it—and write truth.

T.H.

* * * *

[1] The strap-irons were to hang the *strap-bags* on. These were bags containing bye-letters between places not far distant from each other and were hung by straps on the irons instead of being stowed in the mail-box.

The Weymouth season once more

This time the organisation of the King's special coach is presented from the other angle—as from the horse's mouth. The 18th of July must have been a terrific day in the Office. All the movement orders for the start of the Royal Weymouth Mail were issued then and a number of other important letters written on widely different subjects. But in spite of all the detail in the instructions to contractors one thing remains obscure. How were the extra horses provided for this seasonal part-time mail? With the two coaches going in opposite directions there could hardly be less than a hundred additional horses needed for the work.

One of the more dire threats used by Hasker was 'to take away his Exeter Mail' which, by comparing contexts, means that he will find a new set of contractors for both these mails (via Marlborough and via Salisbury). The contractors of both must have shared a common interest in the profits of the Royal Weymouth, though it followed only one of the Exeter routes (via Salisbury), otherwise Mr Hare of Taunton, who was miles off that road, could have had no claim on fares for the King's Messengers. If all were interested parties might not the men on the northern road have helped to make up the additional teams needed? The Exeter Mails were among the best filled and best paying all round the year and the innkeeper-contractors on both these roads must have kept a number of supernumerary horses on hand for resting the regulars and replacing casualties.

Deputies

To Mr Wilkins, Northampton   G.P.O. July 18. 1796

Dear Sir

As I before directed, you will leave Northampton on Saturday the 23rd Inst, and London on the 24th, by the Exeter Mail, seeing the Horses are ready at every stage—Harness &c.—after you reach Andover 'till you get to Piddletown, according to the directions you will see I have written to each contractor by the Letters copied in the Letter Book.

You will come from P.Town by the first Royal W.mouth Coach to be at W.mouth, leaving Mr Lawless at Piddletown to be refreshed, to return with the Coach at night.

T.H.

Mr Charlton,

Meet me on Tuesday next at Bagshot to take the directions for Superintending His Majesty's R. Mail Coach. Should I not be there, stay till I come, as I shall certainly be there the next morning.

Mr Lawless[1]

Dear Sir

You will please to leave London by the first R. M. Coach Monday the 25th Inst. I doubt not but you will find all ready and everything smooth on the road. Should you not, assist as well as you can, and give me information by informing Mr Wilkins at Piddletown, at which place you will stay till he comes to me at Weymouth, making yourself ready to return at night by the up Coach.

Mr White (clerk)

Dear Sir

You will as usual go with the Guard and Bag from the G.P.O. before 3 o'Clock every day on and after the 25th Inst, and with the Coach from Lad Lane call at the Secretary of State's & the Queen's House—doing the duty as usual.

Contractors (Summarized instructions) July 18th

Wilson, Lad Lane.
Horses to be ready in 'your yard' 3 P.M. on morning of 25th. 'You will send a servant to call with it at the Horse Guards and the Queen's House, Kew Bridge, every day as usual, on its way to Bagshot. As the first Coach from Weymouth will not arrive in Town till the morning of the 27th. You will please to direct such horses as you may want to draw the R.W. Mail out on the 26th to be led back.' The up due at Bagshot, 3 A.M. on 27th.

Demezy.
Horses to be ready at Bagshot, 7 P.M., 25th. 'As there will be two Coaches down before one up, you will please to order your horses to be led back if you have not others to drawn down the R.M. Coach on the 26th from Bagshot to Basingstoke.' Up due 1 A.M., 27th.

[1] Recently appointed (like Murell). His area East Anglia.

Weeks.
Four horses to be ready at Andover at 11 P.M. on 25th. First journey up at about 10 o'clock at Salisbury, Tuesday, 26th.

Shergold.
Horses to be ready at Salisbury 1.30 A.M., Tuesday, 26th. Up at about 8.30 the same evening.

Wood.
Horses to be ready at Woodyates 3 A.M., Tuesday, 26th to go to Blandford. Up at Blandford 7 P.M. the same night.

Mrs Bryer.
Horses to be ready at Blandford 'at ½ past 4 on Tuesday morning, the 26th, and every morning after at the same time to draw His Majesty's Royal Mail Coach to Piddletown', returning at 5.30 the same evening.

Warr, Bridport.
Horses to be at Piddletown 6 A.M., the 26th 'to draw H.M. Royal Mail Coach to Gloucester Lodge, Weymouth, and you will direct your Coachman to see to R. Mail being loaded every day before 4 in the afternoon, and that he departs at that hour precisely from Weymouth'. He adds that he will be at Bridport 'on Tuesday next'.

Coachbuilder

Mr Vidler

Genl Post Office
July 18th 1796

Dear Sir
On the 21st Inst you will please to send by your horses the Patent Mail Coach labelled Windsor & Weymouth (as altered) and the Royal Weymouth Mail Coach that is to be left at Blandford as a spare Coach. Direct your servant to leave the former, namely the Patent Mail Coach, at Egham at Mr Graves, the sign of the Red Lyon. I think your man must then proceed with the Royal Weymouth Mail Coach & leave it at the Crown Inn, Blandford, in the care of Mrs Handy or Mr Wood.

On the 25th Ins' you will take care there is a Royal Weymouth Mail Coach at Mr Willson's, Lad Lane, before 2 o'Clock in the afternoon; & every day after till further notice have a royal patent Mail there at the same time.

T. H.

Another spare coach to meet an emergency had apparently been deposited already at Bagshot. Hasker, who was due at Windsor on the morrow, appears to have gone on down to Bagshot the same day and inspected this vehicle himself. He found it deficient of two important fittings.

Mr Vidler   Bagshot
                                                            July 19/96
D. Sir

The spare Coach here is No. 15. There is no cushions in it which I think is not wrong [*i.e.* not one which fits]. There is a spare pole wanting here, for there is not one in the Coach. You will order one sent down by the Royal Mail Coach which you send to Blandford, and order your man to leave it here as the Coach goes down.

T. H.

Nor is that the end of Vidler's omissions.

Mr Vidler   Genl Post Off
                                                            July 26/96
D. Sir

There was no long bar sent down with the Weymouth Coach yesterday. There should be one with each Coach—the same as last year—to go through with the Coaches.

One may gather from the note on breakdowns (p. 210) that a long bar was a kind of iron crow-bar used for a roadside repair of a broken spring (a frequent occurrence). It is not on the official list of spares to be carried on every coach but (if the guess is right) it was an obvious precaution which it must have become customary to take, as the guard in the note referred to is blamed for not having one with him.

Among other letters which Hasker wrote before leaving the Office the three following may be quoted.

181

Mr Crouse (Contractor,   Genl Post Office
Norwich)   July 18 1796

Dear Sir

I received yours and quite approve of your manner of setting the account—but you must draw on me for the balance of the earnings separate from any other matter whatever as the Draft must go to the Postmaster General, Treasury Auditors, &c &c before I gett the cash allowed. Respecting the other sum I will now ask for it, (your trusty Agent) for though I expected they would bring me the needful I have seen nothing from Lad Lane.

I leave Town for Weymouth tomorrow, if I can I will see Mr Wilson.

(Unsigned)

This is a continuation of the subject mentioned on pp. 156, 161 and adds confirmation to my suggestion that Hasker was advancing money out of his own resources to keep the wheels turning. Although the two Norwich Mails were in the same association, this company appears to have had three joint chairmen, Wilson and Boulton of London and Crouse of Norwich. The mileage warrants were always sent separately to Wilson and Crouse for settlement with their sub-contractors. With Crouse Hasker shows himself to have been on terms of real friendship, a side of his nature he does not allow any other employé to share. But this man was in failing health and died before the end of the year.

Greville has written again, but this time not about a second Milford Mail or even a P.M.G. matter. In his reply Hasker asserts more plainly than ever the prerogative which he so jealously guarded.

C. F. Greville   G.P.O. July 18/96

Dear Sir

I have the honor of yours and if you will at any time when at leisure drop a line to the young man you recommend that when convenient he may call at the Office in Lombard Street that we may examine [him] if not above 30 years of age and if otherwise fit for a Mail Guard, that his name may be enrolled to take his routine, tho' perhaps his turn may not come for six, eight, or even twelve months.

I shall ever be happy to oblige you tho' Guards' places cannot be looked on in the name of Patronage. The pay is weekly and the duty strict, very strict, and if found erring, though the recommendation be ever so powerful, for the sake of persons and property I am obliged instantly to dismiss them—I trust your young man will not deserve it.

T.H.

But, on this busy day, the matter which probably engaged his personal interest and sense of adventure more than the rest he dealt with last, but with his usual care to express essentials fully and lucidly. Things seem to have gone forward with the Aberdeen project since the one and only mention on June the 25th (p. 170) in the official letter-book. Perhaps some communications never reached the record.

Aberdeen proposal

To Woolmer   Genl P. Office
Carlisle   July 18th 1796

Dear Sir

Directly on your receiving this you will go to Edinburgh at which place you will see the Postmaster General's Secretary and Surveyors and take any information they may give you respecting the establishing of a Mail Coach or Dilligence the length of Aberdeen via Dundee, Montrose, Bervie[1] &c, after which go over the road and write me a report in the manner of the one I enclose you herewith, the very particular state of it mile by mile. You know it must be a maxim of the Office to bring all the Mails to one Inn at a Central Town that they may assist each other. This being the case, Drysdale's must be the Inn at Edinburgh—and by way of nursing the undertaking I will intreat the Postmaster General to give the first year 2d per mile each way—if the hills are still so bad between Bervie and Stonehaven there is another road via Lawrence Kirk—it may be right if you find it bad to report the Lawrence Kirk road. Excuse haste.

T.H.

[1] Now called Inverbervie.

Nothing more is found on this matter until the last day of October, when Drysdale is written to and told that Hasker will go to Edinburgh in the spring and settle matters with regard to the Aberdeen service and the long delayed mail-coach link between Edinburgh and Glasgow. Now, on his way to Weymouth, he gets off one letter from Windsor Castle.

*　　*　　*　　*

Coachmen and tipping

Severally to   Windsor
Wilson, Lad Lane   July 19, 1796
Boulton, Charing X

Dear Sir
　　You must be sensible how very disagreeable it is to me to desire a Contractor to do any thing contrary to his wishes, yet sometimes for the general good of a concern I am obliged. I have twice before troubled you on this head & would not repeat my request had I not the solicitations of Messrs Forster and Waterhouse added to those of Mr Crouse and the Commands of their Lordships the Postmaster General which is, briefly, so to order your concern that one Coachman may drive from London to Colchester & one from Colchester to London, and that there be a Coachman drive up and down nightly between Colchester and Ipswich.
　　Their Lordships desire this may be done the more immediately as they have had representations to them of the disagreeableness the present plan has on passengers, and I hope you will be assured that this would not be desired of you was it not that the general System requires such regulation. Mr Lawless will deliver this to you who has the Commands of the P.M.Gl. to see it so carried into effect.
T.H.

After this parting shot he leaves the conduct of affairs in the Office to his newly appointed deputy, Lawless. No doubt he intended to return as soon as he had seen that all was going well with the special coach. But the Court did not let him escape so easily. Contractors due to hold a meeting at Bagshot on August the 10th were told that Mr Hasker could not attend till the 17th 'in consequence of his being obliged to attend upon His Majesty longer than he expected'. So he had to conduct the usual business by remote control, Lawless and the clerks acting on daily instructions from Weymouth.

To Thomas Hasker Esq   Genl Post Office
                                        July 21 1796

Dear Sir

I beg leave to inform you that I saw Mr Boulton and gave him your Letter & had a long conversation with him on the subject, and used every means in my power to get him to agree with the directions given by Ld Chesterfield and yourself. I mentioned my being at Ld Chesterfield and with you and that it was his Lordship's direction that I should be on the road till everything was settled. After all this I am sorry to inform you that he positively refused to alter the Coachmen although I stated the terms of the Contract.

I also saw Mr Wilson who is perfectly agreeable but cannot make the alteration without Mr Boulton going with him in it. Under these circumstances I request that you will geve me some directions how to act, which shall be punctually obeyed.

                                        J.L. (Lawless)

This appeal having failed, Lawless was instructed to try to outflank the awkward Mr Boulton by getting the third joint chairman of the company, Mr Crouse, on their side.

To Mr Crouse, Norwich   Gen P. Office
                                        Aug 1st 1796

Sir

By desire of Mr Hasker I write to you concerning the Coachmen on the Norwich Road. Mr H's opinion is that there should be 4 coachmen from London to Colchester, that is 2 up and 2 down, and 2 from Colchester to Ipswich—and your Coachman remain the same; for at present there is nothing but Discontent among them. The state of the Coachmen at present are two from London to Inglestone [Ingatestone] and back and 4 from London to Ipswich, two up and down. Mr H. wishes to have your approbation which you think will be for the best, as the Coachmen between Inglestone and Ipswich complain that the Coachmen who comes and returns to London get all the profit, whilst they go double the length of

Ground and they cannot make a living. Messrs Waterhouse, Green, and Forster wishes the Coachmen to come to Colchester instead of Inglestone and return to London. Mr Hasker wishes the same and Mr Wilson, but Mr Boulton does not. A line directed to me at the Genl. Post Office will very much oblige Mr Hasker as I shall send it to him at Weymouth.

J.L.

This was by no means the only case of the kind whereby contractors seem to have humoured certain of their better coachmen. Hasker was strongly against it and always fought the arrangement till he got his own way—which he did in the present instance as will be seen (p. 200) though only after applying five hours' personal magnetism to Boulton. What T.H. meant by 'the disagreeableness the plan has on passengers' is best seen from a letter on the subject to a member of the public, though of a later date and on a different Mail.

Major General J. Davis

G.P.O.
Oct 13 1796

Sir

I have the honor of your letter, in answer to which I beg leave to observe that neither Coachman or Guard should claim anything of Vails (tips) as a right, having 10/6 per week each. But custom has too much prevailed in generally giving each a shilling at the end of the ground, but as a Curtisy not a right, and if they gain nothing it is the absolute order of the Office that they shall not use one word beyond Solicitation—this is particularly strong to the Guard, for indeed over the Coachman we have not much power; but if he drives less than 30 miles, as you first did, they should think themselves well content with 6d from each passenger.

I suppose that Jones, finding that you was so generous to the Coachman more than to himself, overpaying them, might add to his abusive Language, of which I understand he is apt to use too much. I have suspended him, the consequence of which will be a journey to Town to use Solicitations and make promises of good behaviour before he can be restored and, if you approve, I have not the least objection to his making you proper submission personally and to obtain leave of forgiveness from your hand. I am very much obliged by this information for the sake of punishing an impudent servant and to hang him up *in terorem* as a guide to others.

T.H.

Mr Hare   G.P.O.
Taunton   Oct 13 1796

Sir

On Tuesday the 16th of Aug. last, J. Davis, Major & Gen. took 4 Inside places and one outside place in the Exeter Mail, from Exeter to Bath. He complains of having been obliged to give fees to two Coachmen between Exeter and Taunton, and another Coachman and Guard from there to Bath. He also says that at Wells a Person wanted to go to Bath, that the Coachman sent him forward and at the end of the Town took him up. I give you this information to show how injurious it is to the Company to have so many Coachmen on so short a length of ground.

T.H.

The last part of this letter was a sly hint that one of the favoured coachmen was breaking his master's rules by the shocking practice of 'shouldering' or 'swallowing the passenger'. The man told to wait at the end of the town would not have been entered in the book of the coaching-office or the way-bill and his fare would be pocketed by the coachman—with a share for the guard, if compliant. *Shouldering* went on to the very end of the coaching days in spite of every means taken to prevent it. Connivance of a guard in this misdemeanour was always visited with dismissal, a coachman convicted of it was liable to seven years' transportation.

CHAPTER VIII

Letters to Mail-Coach Personnel and Others (2)

August to November 1796

BETWEEN the 1st of August and the 30th of November, when the last page in this volume was filled, there are three hundred and thirty-four letters dealing with all kinds of things, from matters of policy and discipline to the settlement of bills for the hire of post-chaises when coaches broke down beyond repair. The principal event recorded was the establishment of two Branch services from Birmingham, one to Walsall, the other to Lichfield. After taking great pains and making unusual concessions to get the former started the parties concerned in the contract fell out and Hasker takes a gloomy view of its prospects of survival. It does not figure in the time-bills for the following year, but it is shown in the fifth edition of Cary (1826) still 'inning' at the Castle, Birmingham and setting out at 10 A.M. as originally laid down by Hasker.

Mr Pickersgill's private bag is an interesting innovation which was destined to become an established service of the Post Office and one for which those who still use it must thank Hasker's enterprise and ingenuity. I don't suppose the P.M.G.s (taking the sea air once more) were given the least hint about it. The royal party returned from Weymouth a week earlier this year. The usual movement orders were issued on Sunday, September the 18th, to take effect early in the following week, the only variation being in the transport of luggage. The King (remembering the overturns) had commanded that no luggage was to be placed on the roof of any coach in which his household rode. Hasker had, accordingly, mobilised 'waggons and other conveyences' as relief transport. Charlton had been written to on the 14th—'Every-

*The Poole and Exeter
Mails loading at the
Gloucester Coffee
House with bags
brought from the
G.P.O. by mail-cart*

General Post-Office.

The Earl of CHESTERFIELD,
AND
The Earl of LEICESTER, } Postmaster-General

London to Bristol Time-Bill.

	Miles.	Time allowed.		
		H.	M.	

Dispatched from the General Post-Office, the   of   179
at **8**

Coach Nᵒ   sent out   { With a Time-Piece safe
{ Nᵒ   to

Arrived at the Gloucester Coffee-house, Piccadily, at

Willson ——	11	1	20	Arrived at Brentford at **9 20**
Fromont ——	46	5	25	Arrived at Thatcham at **2 45**
			20	To be at Thatcham by Forty-five Minutes past Two, were Twenty Minutes are allowed for Refreshment — To be off exactly by Five Minutes past Three o'Clock in the Morning
Porter ——	21½	2	40	Arrived at Marlbro' at **5 45** Delivered the Time-Piece safe to Coach Nᵒ gone forward To be at Marlbro' by Three Quarters past Five o'Clock in the Morning
	13	1	25	Arrived at Calne at **7 10**
				Arrived at Bath at
Dover ——	32	3	50	Arrived at the Post-Office, Bristol, the of 179 at **11** The Mail to be delivered at the Post-Office, Bristol, at Eleven o'Clock in the Morning
	123½	15	0	

Delivered the Time-Piece safe
Coach Nᵒ   arrived   { Nᵒ   to

THE Time of working each Stage is to be reckoned from the Coach's Arrival. Five Minutes for changing four Horses, is as much as is necessary, and as the Time whether more or less, is to be fetched up in the Course of the Stage, it is the Coachman's Duty to be as expeditious as possible, and to report the Horse-keepers if they are not always ready when the Coach arrives, and active in getting it off.

By Command of the Postmaster-General,

T. HASKER.

A time-bill of 1797

thing is yet smooth and I hope will continue so to the end.' He and Wilkins were sent down to supervise staff arrangements—'Take care they do not drive fast, make long stops, or get drunk.' This time a prompt settlement is made with the contractors. On September the 27th, Wilson of Lad Lane is handed a warrant for £560, and T.H. asks to be informed when all his sub-contractors have received their due shares.

In the course of October and November Hasker peppers the two principal contractors of the Liverpool and Hull Mail, Paterson and Howarth, with five letters in quick succession. Time-bill 33 shows that this Trans-Pennine coach was the busiest of all and travelled the worst road—so steep and so mud-foundered that for part of the way it was only officially timed to move at five miles an hour. The series begins 'You know the Mails must be delivered in Time or the whole correspondence of the Country is deranged. . . . No Coach pays so well as when it is well performed'. The last letter ends 'It is very disagreeable to me to be perpetually writing to you, which the Correspondence of the Country requires me to do, I hope you will not give me any further occasion; if you do, the next letter must be of a very serious nature'. The time-bill shows that Mr Paterson's coach has weathered the winter and (well or ill) is still being 'performed'.

The two Pennine crossings—that just referred to, and that of the Glasgow Mail between Catterick and Appleby—must have been formidable on mid-winter nights in 'seasonable' weather, but there is nothing to suggest in the three years covered by these letters that the Mails were seriously held up there. Those heavy four-horse vehicles with their tough crews seem to have managed better than the powerful motorised transport of today which, year by year, is shown in newspaper illustrations stranded by the drove on the Pennine roads.

Of the remaining letters, several relating to the affairs of the East Anglian and the Milford Mails are put together in this chapter, others throwing light on details of the system, in the next. But first, a note on the management of procrastinating passengers. The stage-coach travelled more slowly than the Mail, but stopped for meals where convenient to its patrons. The Mail stopped only where necessary for postal arrangements. Those who sacrificed comfort for speed had to put up with this. The Wisbeach Mail breakfasted at 3 A.M., the Glasgow lunched at 3.27, the Chester and Holyhead dined at midnight. On the Shrewsbury, only twenty minutes was allowed for breakfast after 12 hours 42 minutes' travel. Outside passengers would hardly have begun to thaw out in that time. It would be hard on all to abandon with alacrity the comforts of the inn for the renewed rigours of the road, and hard for the guard to risk a diminution of his tip by hustling them or the total loss of it by leaving them behind.

To Mail Guard White   Genl. P.Off
Copies to Wilson and   Aug 26.96
Boulton Ctrs.

Sir

· Stick to your bill and never mind what passengers say respecting waiting over time—is it not the fault of the Landlord to keep them so long? Some day when you have waited a considerable time, suppose 5 or 8 minutes longer than is allowed by the Bill, drive away and leave them behind, only take care that you have a witness that you called them out two or three times—then let them get forward how they can. Let the Innkeeper where you dine know that you have received this Letter.

T.H.

*   *   *   *

Private Bag

This is perhaps the first instance of the use of a private bag—an admirable facility still made available by the Post Office. Leeming lies between Boroughbridge and Catterick. It was passed by the Glasgow Mail at 1.37 A.M. going north, and 6.35 P.M. going south.

To Mr Pickersgille   Gen. P.Off
Leeminglane   August 26th 1796

Sir

The directions of the Mail Coaches being in my department, your Letter to Mr Freeling is therefore referred to me.

The gratuity you give for the conveying of your letter to and from B[orough] Bridge is very handsome and if you will continue [make] a box or an apperture in the door that the guard may put the bag into so that no delay may be occasioned on their going North, and lett your servant give the Bag to the guard going South, the moment the Coach arrives, without its stopping, it would be regular to your satisfaction.

When you have contrived a convenient place where the guard can Instantly leave the Bag of a morning please to favour me with the particulars and I will give the Guards such directions that appear necessary, and if afterwards you are disappointed give me a line.

T. H.

To Guards Henson and Harris

Genl P. Office
Sept 10 1796

Sir

You will for the future take care to convey Mr Pickersvill's [*sic*] bag to and from Leeming Lane every day and in the morning you will only have to get down and push the bag into the shutter of a window which is cut for that purpose. I have no doubt but that at Christmas Mr Pickersvill will sufficiently satisfy you for your Trouble.

H. N.

*   *   *   *

The Walsall Mail

Walsall, the oldest corporate town in Staffordshire (a borough by prescription), lay between two principal mail-routes. It was by-passed to the west by the Shrewsbury Mail and, to the east, by the Chester-Holyhead and the Liverpool Mails. It had an important industry in the very things on which all coaching depended—harness-making and saddlery—and felt itself deprived of due consideration by the Government under the new system of rapid communications. In the previous year it had 'memorialised' the Post Office, presenting a plan for diverting the Liverpool Mail. Hasker had given reasons (p. 126) why this should not be adopted. The short cut from Walsall to Stone, which he had surveyed and noted as a bad road, was still marked as such in Coltman's map of 1806. But new pressure had been brought to bear this time to serve Walsall from Birmingham by a branch Mail. Prominent among the new applicants was Waddell, owner of the Castle Inn, Birmingham, stage-coach proprietor, and mail-coach contractor on the end ground of the Bristol-Birmingham Mail. He seems to have been making overtures to Hasker for some time before official sanction was sought. T.H. was still doubtful of the wisdom of yielding. He knew it to be bad to open any new route so late in the year with the trials of winter so imminent and he was uncertain of securing co-operation from coachmasters already in business between the two places. Saverland was both Post Office Surveyor and Postmaster of Birmingham.

Wilkins   G.P. Office
Northampton   Sept 24 1796

Dear Sir

You will see part of your Instruction by Mr Waddell's letter. I think it will be the best way for the Coach to go twice a day—once from Birmingham at 10 o'clock after the arrival of the Bristol Mail and return from Walsall to be at Birmingham before two with London, Oxford, Coventry letters &c. Second Coach to leave Birmingham at one o'clock after the arrival of the Mail from London, Oxford &c and to return to Birmingham by four or half past with Letters for Bristol &c or, if but once a day, in the best manner they can. But I fear the Coaches must be going and coming at the same time from 12 to 2 o'clock. Mr Saverland will meet you there to finally settle it about the 8th of October, therefore this journey is only to see what can be done for the best in the Coach business—determine finally on nothing.

T.H.

Mr Waddle   G.P.O. Sept 24/96
Castle Inn, Birmingham

Dear Sir

It is determined by the P.M. Genl that a Mail Coach should run from Birmingham to Walsal and back every day and I have their Lordship's Commands to say that it will start 10th of October.

You know in my conversations with you I have always promised that you should have the housing of it or that it should dine at your house, and take up there, returning. I have directed Mr Wilkins to bring you this and to talk the matter over with you to see what you or the present Walsal Coachmaster can do most for the benefit of Correspondence and with your advantage.

T.H.

To Mr Wilkins
G.P. Office
Sept 26 1796

Dear Sir

I omitted to mention yesterday that perhaps it will be right for you to see the present Coachmasters between Birmingham and Walsal to see if they will take the concern in conjunction with Waddle. They perhaps may do it twice a day together, but observe it is only a penny a mile each way for once a day or in other words 1/6 per day, a uniform for the driver, or drivers, and Tolls clear. Hear all; determine on what is best in your own mind—but make no agreement till you see me and Mr Severland.

T. H.

Mr Waddle
G.P. Office
Oct 3 1796

Dear Sir

I received yours and shall adhere firmly to what I propos'd, the Coach must Inn at your house or you must work it. I have not yet seen Mr Perks; if I do not, will write you fully tomorrow.

Perks owned the principal inn at Walsall and was proprietor of stage-coaches which ran from there to the Saracen's Head in Birmingham but he was not in the mail connection, as Waddell was. The proposal was to adapt a coach belonging to one of these innkeepers to do the short journey as a diligence and with two unusual concessions— a coachman-guard and leave to carry four outside passengers.

Wilkins, Northampton
Gen Post Office
Oct 5th 96

Dear Sir

You may as well be off tomorrow or Friday for Birmingham. You will see what I have wrote to Mr Waddell which will, in fact, be your guide. The Time Bill should not be more than 1 hr. 20 mts., it being little more than 8 miles; this Mr Waddell will also sign. If he wishes to take 4 inside and 4 outside passengers let him, not more, and I should rather it was only two outsides.

T. H.

Mr Waddell, Birmingham   G.P.O.
                                                          5 Oct 96

Dear Sir

I was so full of business yesterday that I could not find time to write you in the way I wished so postponed it till today.

Mr Wilkins will be with you on friday or Saturday to see that you have made proper arrangements that you have a box under the seat of the Coachman to lock up or some other convenient lock-up place for the bag. You will also send me up the measure of your man that is to drive that he may have an uniform sent to him. He must do the duty of Guard as well [as] Coachman, and take the Oath of office, which Oath Mr Wilkins will bring with him. I do not know anything of Mr Perks, therefore you will agree with him to be joint contractor or without him, as you please. Mr Wilkins will give you a contract to sign which I will also sign, & get stamped when it reaches London.

If you cannot be ready by the 10th Inst., I do not see why you should not be allowed a week or fortnight longer to start.

                    T.H. (in his own handwriting).

Mr Wilkins   G.P. Off
                                                          7 Oct 1796

Dear Sir

Mr Perks is now with me and seems very reasonable respecting the short Mail Coach from Walsal to Birmingham. Therefore read my letter to Mr Waddle attentively and tell him it will be most for his interest to comply with Mr Perks's terms which are fair, and that I cannot expect Mr Perks's heavy business to be made subservient to the Mails except he wishes or agrees to it. In short, Perks is so fair that he must consent—it will keep him and us from perpetual trouble. Mr Saverland, I doubt not, will see the necessity of starting the Coach from Walsall not later than 11 and not sooner than 1 from Birmingham, otherwise there must be two Coaches and two sets of harness—in this Mr Freeling agrees.

                    T.H.

Mr Waddle   (Same date as above)

Sir

Mr Perks has been here and I wish you to join issue with him on the following terms as surely it will be most for your advantage. First, for him to bring his light Coach to your house and leave the heavy where it is, as certainly is fair.

He says if you are willing to convert to this he will book on the usual allowance of 2d per parcel, all to go by your concerns, and all passengers also. If you do not approve of this he will sell you his Coach and Horses, though I really think the former will be the best way.

Avoiding opposition is a very desirable end, and both to you and the G.P.Off; and this does that, and supplies your house and Mail Connections principally—and the others likewise.

Mr Perks will be able to work one Coach with the horses of the other, in short, to blend them together—you, on the other hand, will work it at great expense as your horses must sleep at Walsall every night.

T.H.

Mr Waddle of the Castle Inn, B'ham.   G. Post Office.
                                                 Oct 21 96

Dear Sir

I now consider you as the sole Contractor of the Walsall Mail Coach. I have got a letter sent from the Principal Surveyor's Office to Mr Jesson and the Inhabitants who solicited the Mail Coach to desire their support or that the Mail would fail, to their great inconvenience.

Respecting the Lichfield Mail Coach, as you & Mr Hare cannot come to Town I will in a few days send down Mr Wilkins—if their Lordships the Postmaster General determine from my report in favor of a Mail Coach.

Get what Coachman you please who, if you will send the measure will have the uniforms sent for him. Would it not be right to have the man you first proposed who is in London.

T.H.

Mr Wilkins
Genl Post Office
Oct 11th 1796

Sir

When you have finished at Birmingham I think you had better come to London. Every thing seems well settled there.

T.H.

But Hasker had reckoned without either of his hosts. One of the chronic difficulties he had always had to face was the jealousy of stage-coach proprietors for each other. If two were included in the same mail contract they always quarrelled about which inn the mail-coach should stop at. If the company were large and managed by a good chairman the Post Office might avoid getting involved in this competition, but if it were small they could hardly keep out of it. No doubt the crafty T.H. had argued that Waddell, at whose inn one Mail terminated and another stopped, if given the lion's share of the new contract, might be relied on to keep his partner quiet or conveniently get rid of him altogether, if troublesome. Then he would not continually have to write the kind of letter he was shortly going to pen to Mrs Shaw of Northampton 'I wish you would not let any private difference interfere but let your Coach breakfast there as usual', that is, at the inn of Mr Briggs, a co-partner in the Chester Mail. As an additional concession to the pushful host of the Castle Inn, T.H. had consented to establish another new branch to Lichfield for which Waddell had pressed and in which he would take a leading share.

To Wilkins, B'hm.
Oct 25, 96

Dear Sir

You will inform Mr Perks that he should have got our leave before he resigned and that the P.M.Gl. do expect that he will, in conjunction with Mr Waddell, fulfill his contract and, as by agreement, work the Mail Coach to Mr Waddell's only and one Coach beside, which was also agreed he should work to the Saracen's Head—if he was so attached to his old party that he could not give them up he should have so determined before he signed the Contract and have not let us into such an error but, being done, he must either work the Coach himself or give it up to Mr Waddell if he likes to take it on conditions that Mr P. drops his light Coach and only runs his heavy one—and if he does not fulfill his Contract or remove it on the above condition with the approbation of Mr Waddell, the P.M.Gl. will prosecute him.

Lichfield Coach

Mr Galwaltz   G.P.O. Oct 26 1796

Dear Sir

I rec'd yours and having such bad luck with the Walsall Coach puts us out of Heart with that to Litchfield. However, Mr Wilkins is at Birmingham and will see Mr Hare.

                                                            T.H.

To Wilkins, Birmingham   G.P.O. Oct 26/96

Dear Sir

As I have gone so far in the affair of the Litchfield & Birmingham Coach as to obtain the P.M.Gl's permission for its starting immediately we will go on with it—otherwise it would have been much better to have adhered strictly to Mr Palmer's plan never to start Mail Coaches after the 5th July—and this from some recent trouble I will remember in future.

Mr Freeling has written to Mr Saverland to meet you and fix the times of departure from Birmingham and from Litchfield—you will see by the Contract everything that is necessary and will make a Time Bill. Remember Messrs Waddell and Hare are to take Mr Hayward's horses at an appraisement.

                                                            T.H.

Affairs in East Anglia

It will be recalled that three members of the company which worked the Norwich (via Ipswich) Mail, Waterhouse, Green, and Forster, had complained that under the present arrangements their coachmen could not make a living. Hasker was trying to get this put right, but it was not the only difficulty on that route. The coach was constantly losing time and for this, Forster was blamed. He is determined to act towards this contractor in the drastic manner so often threatened and he takes Watson into his confidence. In the time-bills for 1797 Watson is shown as working a stage in both this and the Yarmouth Mail. In addition to these claims on Hasker's respect he was Crouse's right-hand man—

perhaps his son-in-law or near relation—and helped him in the management of his coaching business.

Mr Watson   Genl. Post. Off.
                                                            Sept 2nd 1796

D. Sir

Mr Forster does his duty in the Mail Coach very indifferently. Messrs Boulton & Wilson are willing to take it from him and Waterhouse would, he thinks have no objection to take it from them, if the accounts were settled and turned out to his expectation to the 13th Ult.; and W. & B. would wish him to have the stage as he is doing his business very well and, I do not doubt, thriving on it, but wishes to act with caution and therefore will not give his answer till he sees the accounts to the above time. This is therefore to request for this reason that they may be made out as soon as possible with conveniency, by Sunday if possible, for we have a meeting on Monday.

When the alteration takes place—the long desired alteration [p. 184]—I do not doubt but obtain, namely for Coachmen to drive from London to Colchester. Short Coachmen from Colchester to Ipswich not to ask [? for tips] except Passengers get out there.

I wrote to Mr Crouse on the subject of your extra Coach and rather wonder I have not heard in return—as my money has been kept at my Bankers to be promised for the Payment.

                                                            T.H.

Lawless, the deputy Superintendent, is told to take up matters with Forster. Guards have reported that his horses are not fit for the work. There is a short lull for the fruits of 'lenity' to show themselves, and then:

Mr Forster   G.P. Off.
                                                            Sept 22 1796

Dear Sir

Mr Lawless informed me when he saw you at Norwich that you intended to put more Horses on your ground and do the Business well—but instead of doing better you are doing worse. This morning your Horses lost 33 minutes up—it's the case every journey. If you do intend that I shall permit you to keep the ground you must keep time, for there can be no excuse at this present time.

                                                            T.H.

Postmaster   G.P. Off

Newmarket (Rowning, a contractor   Sept 23rd 1796
          See time-bill 17)

Dr Sir

    I am not at all surprized at your check being returned, Coachmasters having no character to lose don't mind such trifles. Your agreement is very plain and shall be kept. I am sorry for Mr Crouse's illness. I have wrote very pressing for him to come to Town when there will be a general meeting. If he does not come soon we must do without him. The 13/- was not enclosed for the man who cleans the arms.

                                 T.H.

This was the third application for that small sum due to Mr. Broadrib and part of his slender income (p. 124). The postmaster had stopped it from the guards' wages on July the 5th when Hasker first called for it. He had written again on September the 15th, 'It has slipped your memory, pray send it by return.'

On the 26th, Lawless is ordered to report at the Office and 'I hope you will come up by the Ipswich Mail that it may be in by 7 o'clock, which it has not been for a considerable time'.

T.H. writes again by the next post telling Lawless to talk to Waterhouse as well as Forster and to tell the latter that 'at this season, stinting the horses will be fatal to him'. He also writes to Guards Waters and Young (who had previously given information about the horses)—'Your Coach has been very late up at Colchester several nights lately... Show this letter to Mr Forster.'

On the 27th Lawless is written to again, 'See the enclosed bill. Tell Mr Forster to get fresh horses immediately and that I must see him in Town next Monday—shameful work—3 hrs. 32 mts coming over his 18 miles.' The time allowed between Ipswich and Colchester was 2 hrs 20 mins.

On the 28th (a Wednesday) Hasker convened a meeting in his office for the following Saturday of all concerned in the Norwich Mails (by command of their Lordships the Postmaster-General) and sent notices to Crouse, Rowning, Forster, Waterhouse, Green, Wilson, and Boulton. Crouse, being ill, could not attend, neither could Rowning or Forster. The last two were advised of the proceedings in the following letters. At the same time an odd appeal is sent to a Mr Andrew, 'a Brother Officer', meaning a retired Post Office official. The news it contains about the obnoxious Mr Roberts is revealing.

To Mr Forster, Ipswich   Gl Post Office
                                          Oct 2nd 1794

Dear Sir

At the meeting yesterday it was represented to Mr Wilson by the Commands of the Postmaster General that there was daily a great deal of time lost on your ground, beyond the extra time allowed you, and that in consequence thereof the delivery of Letters at Norwich and more so in London was retarded to the distress of Correspondence, the vexation of the inhabitants, and the injury of the revenue, and that he must either take the Stage himself, as by contract compelled, or find a fit person. He has found, and we have approved of Waterhouse, who has undertook to work it, beginning the next month's accounts, namely Sunday next, the 9th Instant. Mr Lawless will deliver you this and have some further talk with you & Mr Waterhouse will take your horses by arbitration (as is also the Custom) by the Command of their Lordships the Postmaster General.

I shall be sorry if you conceive this an injury to your Coach concerns, for nothing but the utmost necessity of a deranged Correspondence could have occasioned these decisive measures though you are not a Contractor.[1]

T.H.

Postmaster, Norwich   G.P.O. Oct 4/96

Dear Sir

I am much obliged by your communication and the manner of your showing it. I have had for some time past in various ways more trouble with the Norwich Coaches than all others.

Roberts has done himself no good and plagued me sufficiently. If he owed me a grudge he has took his revenge—but to the point— I have had a meeting, and after five hours conversation have brought Boulton to let the Coachmen be disposed of properly[2] and I hope Mr Forster's ground is transferred to better hands. But from the road via Ipswich being longer and the great detaintion there, you must not expect that Coach till about noon.

T.H.

[1] Only a sub-contractor.
[2] As described on pp. 184-5.

To Mr Andrew, Near Thetford.   G.P. Office

                                                      Oct 3 1796

Dear Sir

   As an old friend and a Brother Officer shall I entreat your interest
and aid to the support of Mr Willson's Mail Coach—by ordering
your game and other parcels to be sent by that conveyance instead
of by the Telegraph. The Mails were not taken from Mr Roberts,
as has been no doubt reported, but he gave them up voluntarily—
at only fourteen days notice and, as it is the wish of the P.M. Genl.
to give every encouragement to Contractors concerned with them
I hope you will have no objection to grant the favour I have requested. The conveyence is equally as expeditious or in fact more
so.

                               T.H.

   The rearrangement was put into force immediately and on October
the 4th Lawless was told to check all the arrivals and dispatches at
Ipswich of all coaches. Nothing further is heard of East Anglian
affairs till November the 16th when letters are sent to Boulton, Wilson,
and Watson to say 'The enclosed is a copy of a Bill sent me by Mr
Forster, which he claims to be due to him. I should think this can
only be settled by a meeting—if you can do it without I wish you
would'. To Watson he adds a postscript 'Mr Wilson and Mr Boulton
promised him he should be allowed for all the Ground he worked, and
it appears that Mr Roberts shared 10 miles for the same stage'. This
was evidently a factor in the Forster affair which Hasker had not
known. As Roberts quitted at a fortnight's notice, taking his horses
off all the stages he worked, this may have lost Forster his last chance
of gaining grace. It looks as though the thing had been kept dark
from interested motives and improved prospects for Waterhouse.
At any rate Hasker wrote to Forster at once in a mollified tone. He
said the account appeared to him very fair but would have to be
settled at a general meeting 'when I will do all I can to set it to rights,
though it is no part of my duty to interfere with contractors' private
accounts'. The mystery as to why Roberts was able to behave in
the way he did, and get away with it without being prosecuted for
breach of contract is cleared up in the footnote on p. 203. On the same
day T.H. was moved to send Crouse a reminder.

Mr Crouse   G.P. Off.

                                             Nov 16th 1796

Sir

   A few days since I informed you that I had paid your draft and
requested you would be so good as to send me up the Receipt.
I cannot get repaid without, and therefore must again beg you will
inclose it to me. My report to the P.M.G. is ready but I cannot
send it without the receipt.

                                             T.H.

But two days later he had to write in a different vein. Coldwell
was book-keeper at the Norwich coach-office, Roach, the postmaster
of Norwich.

Mr Coldwell   Gen. Post Office

Norwich   Novr 18/96

Sir

   I am obliged by your favor and must express my sorrow at the
account you give of Mr Crouse for whom I had a very great regard.
If he should yet be with you, assure him I will do everything I can
to accomodate his wishes. Mr Watson and yourself will of course
take care that everything is regular.

                                             T.H.

Mr Roach   Gen. Post Office

Norwich   Novr 18/96

Dr Sir

   I received your favor and have also had a letter from Mr Coldwell
respecting poor friend Crouse. I am very much concerned to hear
so bad an account of him. I can't say how you can, in the present
state of things be of any particular service, at the same time am
much obliged for your kind offer. But you may as well keep your
eyes and ears open.

                                             T.H.

But all must have been over when these letters arrived.

Watson   G.P.O.
Norwich   Nov 22/96

D. Sir

I have all your letters, and after condoling for the loss of a good
man who was the occasion of them, I have to observe that you was
perfectly right in sending up your Clerk to contradict the unac-
countable falsehoods that Mr Roberts propogated. It is always the
maxim of the Office to support their Mail Coach Contractors or
Proprietors, and they would not, without consulting them and
gaining their approbation, dispose of a concern to any person
however deserving, *much less to Mr Roberts whose conduct to the
Office was so unlike a man's of business that it cannot be forgot*, and
the only way he ever could be concerned again would be for all
concerned in our Mail Coaches to Norwich *to request it*, and that
would not be very palpable [? palatable] to the P.M.Gl. But
when all concerned do ask a favour for their mutual benefit, the
P.M.Gl. do consent however disagreeable it may be. But, as I said
before, this is very unlikely to happen, and this is the only way Mr
R. can again come in.[1]

I think you should desire the Executors to keep it secret what I
agreed to pay you and Mr Crouse for half your earnings—for as
he hires some stages, if Messrs Salisbury & Ratcliffe were to hear,
perhaps they might raise the price on the Executors which, in the
present state of things, should be avoided.

Respecting all the rest of the money matters your letters mentioned, it should in my opinion be settled at a meeting which must

---

[1] The Second Report of the Committee on Holyhead Roads and Harbour, 1810
gives Hasker's evidence on this point as follows. It throws more light.

'Mr Roberts of Fetter Lane, fourteen years ago, gave up a Coach to Yarmouth
and Norwich and another by Ipswich to Norwich, because the Postmaster General
would not agree to pay him sixpence per mile; he had not signed the contract and
never would: and it being a difficult road we thought it was better to let him have
it than to look for another; and not having signed he therefore gave it up at fourteen days notice. We got Mr Boulton of Charing Cross, and Mr Wilson of Lad
Lane, to furnish horses, with some little connexion they could get at those fourteen days notice, and they undertook the business. The consequence of which was
that Mr Roberts immediately opposed them down to Yarmouth; he did not
think it worth his while to go to Norwich; and directly where Mr Wilson and
Mr Boulton were most vulnerable, which was to Chester and Manchester, he
immediately set up coaches to go there, and the opposition has continued for
eight or ten years, and I do not know whether it is over now. Had they not been
strong contractors—the strongest party—they could not have stood.'

shortly take place, for then we take the opinion *of all concerned.* Always happy to hear from you, and wishing you great success, I remain—

I mean to desire Mr Willson to go down next week to counteract the false reports of Mr R.

I shall reserve your letters for Memorandums at the meeting whenever it may be.

T.H.

Final news of the Milford Mail

To Mr Nott (of Heath, Nott & Co, Carmarthen)   Gen P. Office

Sept 26 1796

Sir

You will see by the inclosed bill that one hour 35 minutes was lost upon your ground and that the Coach arrived too late at Bristol for the delivery. I think that instead of putting a seventh passenger on the Coach you should have thought of keeping time better, and before you engage further in Mail Coach business you should pay more attention to that you have got already.

T.H.

The allusion to further engagement in the mail-coach business recalls the Greville proposal and Hasker's letter to Nott of September the 10th (p. 167). On the same date as the above Charlton is written to and told 'You had better let me see you in Town as I want to send you to South Wales in a few days'. A powerful attempt is to be made to improve matters at New Passage. Hasker's claim to personal experience in crossings seems exaggerated, but gives an idea of the extent of his local knowledge and the frequency of former journeys over the mail-coach routes. The threat to move the Mail to 'the other passage' refers to Old Passage. This was from Aust in Gloucestershire to Beachley. After falling into disuse for many years it was reopened as a car-ferry in 1934.

To Charlton   G.P.O. Oct 10 1796

Dear Charlton

Mr Hasker desires you will go and stop two or three days at the passage and see if they can't cross sooner, and that there is no foul play.

H.N.

The guard insists on the right of the Royal Mail to make all other traffic give way

Late for the Mail

To Charlton
Genl Post Office
Oct 13th 1796

Dear Sir

Go over the water return with the Mail for three days or more if necessary, and be particular in dating the Bill as to wind and tide, number of waterman &c. Report to me (keeping a copy yourself) the exact time of the Coach's arrivals, the exact minute the boat departs and reaches the other side—and the exact minute the Coach departs. Inform the Proprietor of the Boats, Coachmen, &c that there are prodigious complaints at the detention in crossing which is often two hours lately and never less than one—tho I have crossed the passage a hundred times or upwards more than half of which passages have been made in 20 mts. Look to the Coaches and report everything separately and particularly.

T.H.

To Charlton
Genl Post Office
Oct 15 96

Dear Sir

Your report is very proper except in the way to Milford you do not say the dispatch of the Coach from Mr Haggarth. Let them all know we must have the utmost expedition at the passage—proprietors, watermen, Guards, Coachmen, &c are all lulled into security, as they think, because I have not been able to attend them. But they must awake or the Coach will go by the other passage.

T.H.

To Mr Bradley, Contractor
G.P.O.
Oct 31 1796

Dear Sir

I am directed by Mr Hasker to inform you that he would be very happy to grant you or any sett of Contractors as much indulgence as the nature of the duty, and even their own interests would permit. But to load the roof of the Coach with huge heavy Baskets would not only be setting a bad example to other Coaches but in a very short time no passenger would travel with it—such a thing as a turtle tied on the roof directed to any Gentleman once or twice a year might pass un-noticed but, for a Constancy, cannot be suffered.

H.N.

Bradley was chairman of the company. They were still using their old stage-coaches and Hasker had even had some difficulty in persuading them to fit them with locked mail-boxes. They did, however, carry the regular mail-guard.

Mr Charlton   G.P.O.
                                                              Nov 17 1796

Dr Sir

Say to Mr Kit Bradley & Mr Marmont that if their servants are suffered to go on so shamefully they will loose the Coach that road. Their Horses cannot be so bad, it must be the negligence of the Drivers. Trim the Guards who may keep better time if they will. You was right to go round by Carleon. Always see everything yourself. The Horse was proper at Newport Bridge, but how was it the person, Mr Morgan, on this side New Passage refused a Horse to the Guard, by which he was forced to take the Coach, and when the Passengers arrived they were forced to hire Chaises. Represent this to Mr Morgan, the Innkeeper there and if again repeated, the Mail will go by Aust Ferry.

                                   T.H.

Owing to a delay at Newport on the up Mail, due to the bridge over the Usk having been damaged, the guard appears to have taken the mails-bags forward on horseback, crossed the ferry, and demanded another horse at New Passage Inn. This being denied him (or the stable being empty), he went off all by himself, with his bags, in the waiting mail-coach, so that when the passengers and luggage arrived after the ferry-boat had made another crossing they had to shift for themselves.

C. Bradley (Severally)   G.P. Off
Marmont   Nov 19 1796

Sir

It is evident that you don't think the Mail Coach worth keeping by the manner you work it. The road being bad is not an excuse—they are not near so bad as they were 7 or 8 years ago. The real excuse is that you do not keep Horses enough to do it and have now brought it to arrive so late at each end that it can no longer be put up with. I shall therefore at the proper time give you notice to quit if I do not see an immediate ammendment.

                                   T.H.

Hasker sends a copy of this letter to Charlton and asks for a full report on the state of the road. 'If you find any part worse than it used to be I will have it surveyed and interdict (indict) it. When you reach Bristol and Bath, and all the way on the road, urge the Guards to keep time, the Proprietors &c. Say the arrivals were never so late— the Merchants never so vexed—and the bad weather hardly set in— what are we to expect when winter is in?' Two days later this is followed by another. 'Till Newport bridge is repaired you should propose to Mr Bradley to have a Coach placed on this side to forward the mail and passengers which would prevent a great delay. Passengers could walk over and luggage easily be conveyed.'

But all this galvanism does not seem to have produced the desired reactions. After containing himself for eight days he lets fly at every member of the Association.

Similar to all the Welsh Contractors   G.P. Office
Nov 29th 1796

Sir

    I received yours. Notwithstanding Charlton has been so long on your road the Coach is worked worse than ever. I never saw such a bill as come up today. I am out of all patience with this Coach and have a great mind to take the Mail from it immediately and send it the other road. I have sent Charlton down again, and if he does not succeed in getting it better done I shall attempt it no more.

    The roads may be very bad in some places, but surely not so bad as they were some years ago. I have no objection to indict the road but the Contractors do not seem inclined to do the duty well if even the roads were better. They all seem careless about it and expect the Coach to be worked with the same strength now as it is in summer. I am told there are very few horses, and those badly fed.

                       T.H.

The last page in the volume is now reached, but this is not quite the last word about the early Milford Mail that has come down to us. Time-bill 25 indicates that Hasker has, himself, made the journey again and has summed up the situation for 1797 in a single sentence. 'This Coach is worked so bad that it is almost sufficient employ for a Superintendant.'

CHAPTER IX

Miscellany

Breakdowns and roadside repairs

In his note on Time-bill 6, Hasker makes a passing remark about 'any trifling delay such as losing shoes, breaking a trace, &c, some of which happen every journey'. If that could be said of the Bristol Mail which, at that time, was the best found and ran over the best road of all the coaches, what can have been the case, night after night, of all the others? But news of these mishaps and more serious accidents never gets into the Letters unless there is some particular reason for mentioning them. A surgeon's bill for 'reducing a compound fractured leg of Thomas Hill, the Ipswich & Yarmouth Mail Coach Guard' calls for comment because it is larger than any other bill 'for a similar occasion' and 'I do not let the Postmasters, Surgeons, or Guards know that your Lordships usually pay such bills, thinking that if I did it would swell them to an extravagent amount'. About the event which caused the injury we are left in the dark. Or a reply to Freeling, who has asked why a bag was found unsealed, to say that the guard is not available, being 'detained in Town on the trial of the Coachman who drove over a boy in Bishopsgate Street'.

The coach carried a good outfit of tools and spares. The kit is thus listed in the Sheet of Instructions—

2 Trace chains	1 Wrench hammer	2 Gimlets	Nuts
1 Pole chain	1 Small wrench	1 Main bar	Worms
2 Tug chains	1 Small saw	Shackles	Screws
1 Hatchet	1 Drift pin	Bolts	Nails
1 Strong hammer	1 Large spike bit	Clips	Cord

At outlying depots, spare parts and also spare coaches were kept,

supplied by Vidler but placed under the care of a deputy superintendent. Murrell is written to on the 15th of September and told 'The
Season has hitherto been very favourable to us. You will therefore
make use of this time to lay up a stock of necessaries for the Winter,
as occurrences may point out their Want—Wheels, Axletrees, Springs,
&c, &c, &c.'

The most vulnerable part of the machine was the wheel. To have
added one to the list of spares carried on the coach would have increased
the weight a little but would surely have been worth while. It was
one of those obvious ideas which just did not occur either to them
or the early motorist until the more cumbersome device of the Stepney-
wheel had come and gone.

Wheels

Mr Vidler   G.P.O.
                                                     Sept 21st /96

Dr Sir

The sudden wet weather has an effect on wheels no doubt. The
near fore wheel of the Newmarket Coach and both fore wheels
of the Ipswich broke this morning. I must beg you will order
your people to pay particular attention to the wheels—and send
[them] out very perfect this night.

                                                     T.H.

(To the same, Nov 21)

The down Coach, No 33, was left at Rochester last night with
the off hind wheel broke. It broke 5 miles below there and was
dragged there. Exeter [mail-coach was] changed at Salisbury
[after] wheel broke. Shrewsbury ditto. Oxford ditto.

                                                     J. White.

Mr Baker   G.P.O.
(Foreman) the Mail Coach Manufactory   Oct 24 1796
Millbank

Dear Sir

In consequence of the off fore wheel of the Ipswich Coach
breaking this morning and the Guard being unacquainted with his

discipline, he will be sent to the Manufactory for a week to be taught. He had clips but did not know how to put them on.

J. W.

Springs

Mail Guard Shugden

G.P.O.
Sept 16th /96

Sir

How could it be possible for you to lose 2 hours 15 minutes in tying up a Spring, which has been frequently done by Durban on your road in 10 minutes. Have you got a long bar,[1] a rope, and a chain? I am not determined yet whether I shall suspend you for a month or order you up to the Mail Coach Manufactory to learn how to tie up springs.

T. H.

Axletrees

Mr Vidler

G.P.O.
Sept 14 1796

Sir

Pray be so good as to give particular orders that the Coach Axletrees are particularly examined, as several have broke lately, and I am informed that the Axletree of the Exeter Coach that broke on Saturday last had been in a suspicious state for some journeys.

T. H.

On October the 5th a clerk writes to Messrs Bradley and Nott, Contractors of the Milford Mail. 'So many accidents [have happened] lately to your Coaches by axletrees breaking that Mr Hasker has desired me to inform you that he thinks these axletrees that break are not properly welded and therefore break again directly, for which reason he recommends you to put new ones on and get the broken ones securely mended before they are made use of again.'

---

[1] It was suggested on p. 181 that this instrument was a crow-bar. It could hardly be confounded with the *main bar* in the list of spares to be carried. That was a wooden spar which hooked into the pole. A hook at either end linked into two shorter spars to which the traces of the leading pair were attached—the *leading bars*. If these horses were given to kicking, or did so in sudden fright, they were apt to shatter the main bar.

Perch-bolt (the pivot on which the fore-axle turned to steer the coach)

A complaint to Baker, the foreman or works-manager of Vidler's, that perch-bolts are not being properly inspected. Another one gone! 'the 4th which has broke of the Dover Coaches within these few weeks'.

Harness

There was a standing grievance that contractors kept their best harness for coaches which travelled by day, when its condition could be observed, and that the Mails, which travelled chiefly in the hours of darkness, were given the worst, causing many mishaps. Hasker's way with a persistent sinner was, after warning, to send him a good set of harness together with the bill. If that were not paid he would deduct the sum when settling the mileage account.

Mr Renham, Contractor.   G.P.O.
                                                         Sept 14 1796

Dr Sir

Some time since, hearing that your harness was in a very unfit state to do duty, I sent you a set, as is the custom of the Office, to supply Contractors whose harness and reins are bad, when they do not attend to representations from the Office. The Harness cost 14 guineas, but as they had been used a few times with the King's royal Weymouth you will only be charged £12—which sum please remit to me.

T.H.

Mr Chuck   G.P.O.
Ware   Sept 24/96

Sir

There is great complaints of your harness; it is so rotten that it is dangerous to travel with them. Pray be so good as to supply others, for if I have any further complaint I shall directly send you a new set down.

T.H.

Hasker had no authority to dictate to contractors what the design or detail of their harness should be, but was rightly anxious that they should use breechings which, by means of a strap round the horse's hind-quarters, helped him to take the strain when holding back on hills, which otherwise came entirely on his collar and shoulders. In William Felton's standard work on carriages of all sorts, published in 1796, there is no mention of a wheel-brake anywhere. This invention was introduced shortly afterwards, but not fitted to mail-coaches—Besant's still more advanced idea had never been followed up. Even in the improved design of 1836, when the Vidler family had lost its long-held monopoly, no brake was provided. Current opinion held the contrivance to be *dangerous*. Horses were trained to hold these heavy vehicles back on hills just not too steep to require the wheel to be skidded, and coachmen believed that they would be spoiled for the work if mollycoddled. But though breeching was an obvious amenity, it was hard to get contractors to use it. It added a little to the cost of purchase and was a little more trouble to take on and off at the changes. All Hasker could do was to issue a printed circular in tactful language. He probably sent this out from time to time, though only one sample is preserved. It is dated March 26, 1795, and was sent to all contractors.

Sir,

In consequence of the many Accidents that have happened in going down Hills, in a great measure for want of breechings, it is desired that, in future, you will be very particular in not suffering your Horses to go without.—I am, by Command of the Postmaster General,

Your very obedient servant

Thomas Hasker

Lamps

These burnt sperm oil supplied by the Post Office but charged against the contractors at 4s 6d a gallon. The lamps appear to have travelled a certain distance with the down Mails and then been changed, the first returning on the up Mails, for it is complained in one letter that it has been 'a practice for the lower Guards to work down the lamps belonging to the upper Guards, notwithstanding you each have a pair'. There was a lamp-cleaning room at the G.P.O. but at intermediate stages the contractors had to trim and clean the lamps. While apologising to a feminine contractor who has complained of the insolence of a guard, T.H. takes the opportunity of letting her know that he has heard of errors on the other side.

Mrs Clarke,   G.P. Off
Contractor,   8 Nov. 1796
Grantham

Dear Madam

I received yours. Ditchfield is in London but I have not seen
him yet. I shall certainly correct him for his impertinent behaviour
to you. It is his and every other Guard's instructions to behave
with civility. But perhaps something may be said for the feelings
of a Guard that hears the constant complaints of passengers against
bad lights and the disagreeable smell of stinking oil, especially when
through such things the passengers with hold the gratuity which the
Guards expect.

T.H.

In every way these primitive sperm oil lamps must have been a
fearful trial even when properly trimmed, and if one blew out on a
stormy night, how was it re-lit? The common (or Lucifer) match
was not yet available. The first improvement in the oil lamp was an
invention of Ami Argand made in 1784—the same year that the first
mail-coach ran. It had a circular wick with central tube for air induc-
tion; an adaptation was called Mile's Patent Coach Lamp. At some
time later, the Mile's lamp was adopted for the mail-coaches and a
printed leaflet on how to use it is among the collection of Instructions
relating to the year 1802. The lamps referred to in the early letters
may have been more primitive and less efficient. Guards taken to task
for driving without lights were probably only humouring the coachman who could do better without them. Guard Plouman was suspended for 'having no lamps with the coach when it drove against a
waggon . . . and lost 1 hour and 40 minutes'.

Parcels, perishable and poached

It must have been a refreshing novelty for Midland Birmingham
to be able to get fresh sea fish brought overnight from the source
of capture. No doubt they fetched a good price. These new fast
mail-coaches were godsends for the transportation of perishables and,
though it was strictly contrary to rule for the guards to carry parcels
of any kind, all the profits of which went to the contractors, their
conscience was never seared by this kind of transgression. It was a

sin that Hasker often winked at and was seldom hard on, though occasionally he had to take drastic steps, as contractors were continually complaining, and so were landowners, who found that their game was being disposed of through facilities previously unknown to local poachers. A few letters reveal what was going on.

To Guards (severally) Hopkins, Chandler, Merrik   G.P. Office
Sept 29th/96

Sir

I insist upon it that you do immediately pay 8/- for the two baskets of Fish you took from Bristol to Birmingham some time ago and which was enterd on the [way-] Bill but scratched out by yourself, also 1/8 for the Basket you took on Tuesday last—and remember that if I hear that you ever carry a Basket or parcel of your own that the carriage is not paid for again, you may depend on being discharged.

T.H.

Mr Waddell, Birmingham   G.P. Office
Sept 29th/96

Dear Sir

I have ordered Merrick to pay you 9/8, and if ever he is guilty of the like again that he shall be discharged.

T.H.

G.P.O. Oct 18/96

To the Superintendants

In consequence of several of the Mail Guards having been detected in carrying meat, vegetables, &c, &c, in their Mail Boxes, to the amount of 150 lbs weight at a time, the Superintendants are desired to take Opportunities to meet the Coaches in their District at places where they are least expected and search the Boxes to remedy this evil which is carried to too great a length.

The Superintendant will please to observe that Mr Hasker does not wish to be too hard on the Guards, such a thing as a Joint of Meat or a Couple of Fowls, or any other article for their own family in moderation he does not wish to debar them of the Previlege of carrying.

The Superintendant will report once a month on the above business.

T.H.

Separate letters to the Superintendants   G.P.O.
(Wilkins, Woolmer, Charlton, Murrell,   Oct 29 1796
Lawless)

Dear Sir

    Search as many Mail Boxes as you can and take away all Game not directed and anything also beyond a Joint for the Guard's family, and send to the chief Magistrate for them to dispose of to the poor of the parish, and every day, or as often as possible take an opportunity of meeting them unexpected and searching the Mail Boxes— there is many reasons for this—see the inclosed.

T.H.

Perhaps 'the inclosed' just mentioned was a copy of the following letter of even date, giving a dark but significant hint.

To Mail Guard H. Waters.   G.P.O.
                                                Oct 29 1796

Sir

    Some time since a Gentleman complained that a man waited for you on the road to sell game; that you took him up, and that he got on the roof of the Coach and bargained with you for the same, for which you paid him &c. The Gentleman told you of this at Scole Inn.

    Pray give me an account of this business by return of post.

T. H.

Scole Inn was a stop on the Norwich (via Ipswich) Mail. The house, built in 1655, remains one of the best-preserved old hostelries.

To W Woolmer Esq   G.P. Off
                                           Nov 14 1796

Dear Sir

    I just give you this line to say that I am informed that R Kelly and his son carry on a very extensive trade in game and fish, the son, acting as guard brings the articles up to Lancaster and the Father sells them there—will you look very closely into this business and not only prevent its continuance but punish according to the guilt.

T.H.

Mr Fagg, Contractor. G.P.O. 20 Oct. 1796

Dear Sir

You had better I think send Mr Pembrooke 3 Partridges—if you do not he is determined to enter an action against the Company —and if 3 Birds will prevent it I am sure your good sense will do it. Pray send me an answer what you do.

T.H.

The suggestion is evidently not for a gift but a replacement. Gifts of game birds were always made in even numbers—by the brace. It looks as if Mr Pembrooke had claimed from the contractor for a loss in transit and Fagg had tried to blame the guard, whom Hasker has questioned and exonerated. Hasker is clear in his own mind that the onus must be fixed on the coachman who had sole charge of all parcels, except in special cases. But in their correct delivery, the coachman must very often have had to depend on the good will of the guard, for he was frequently illiterate and unable to read the labels on his parcels.

Fagg was the owner of the Bell and Crown in Holborn and horsed the Poole Mail between London and Staines. There is no other allusion to the above mystery.

*　　*　　*　　*

Procedure of a guard's enlistment

'Mr Briggs, Mail Guard, Cambridge' is so addressed, so it may be presumed that he has passed the Hasker tests, been through the shops at the Manufactory at Millbank and been enrolled as a spare guard, but is only now to be fully-fledged. White writes to him on October the 15th (a Saturday) telling him that he is appointed. 'You will, return of post, send Mr Hasker the names, place of abode, and occupation of two Respectable Housekeepers (householders) to be your Bondmen. Do this immediately.' Having heard nothing by the following Wednesday, he writes again—

Sir

I wrote to you last Saturday to send up your bondsmen's names, but you have not thought proper to do it. I have Mr Hasker's orders to say if you do not do it immediately he will send down a man to take your place. Mr Lawless desired you to do this some time ago.

He writes again on the 24th—

I have sent your bond and sheet of Instructions to Mr Rose for him to get Mr Pearson to sign. You will then sign it yourself and take it to Bury for Mr Martin to sign. You will also take the copy of the Oath and get yourself sworn before a Magistrate at Bury, as you are there in the day. When this is done you must return the Bond, Oath, and Instructions to Mr Hasker and 7/- for the Stamp of the Bond. Let this be done immediately. You will keep the sheet of Instructions I send with this.

Mr Rose, Postmaster of Bury St Edmunds, is written to at the same time—

Dr Sir

Will you be so good as to get Mr Pearson to sign Inclosed Bond and make Briggs sign it and the sheet of Instructions. You will then give Briggs the Bond to be signed by the other Bondman at Bury. You will then be so good as [to] witness the signature of both bond and instructions. Send the Instructions to Mr Hasker.

Exemption from military service

Mail-guard J. Hopkins   G.P. Off

                                                         Nov 5 1796

Sir

Your situation as Guard do not exempt you from being drawn in the Militia, nor any other person in the Service of Government except in a Military Capacity—you had better pay a small sum to some club or society formed to furnish substitutes for such of the numbers that may be drawn; there are such societies in London and no doubt in Bristol also.

T.H.

Parishes had to provide a quota of militiamen as named by the county. The selection among able-bodied parishioners was then made by lot. If no substitute could be found, one could still buy oneself out for £10.

Suspension

This was Hasker's half-way corrective between fines and 'dismission'. We can follow the whole process in the following series of letters and note the care that was taken to establish a case against the accused.

To Mr Jackson, Postmaster,	Genl P Off
Exeter.	July 27 1796

Sir

You will please to put Cobley to work in the place of J. Hancock who I have Mr Hasker's orders to suspend for improper behaviour to a gentleman at Exeter and demanding 2/6 for his trunk, notwithstanding it had been freed by Mr Ware of Bridport and put into the Coachman's Boot.

J. White

To Mr Keele, Postmaster	Genl P Off
Salisbury	July 30 1796

Sir

You will please to suspend Jn Hancock's wages from last Monday till further Orders by direction of Mr Hasker. It is for improper behaviour to a gentleman at Exeter and for charging him 2/6 for the Carriage of a Portmanteau which had been freed by Mr Ware of Bridport.

J. White

To Guard Hancock	G.P. Off
	August 6 1796

Sir

I have represented to Mr Hasker the account of your transaction with the Gentleman as you stated it in your letter to me which he says is totally false, for in the first place the Gentleman did not come down with the Coach as you say but on Horseback and the portmanteau after being freed by a Contractor was put into the Coachman's Boot, so that you could have nothing to do with it at all, and Mr Hasker further says that your general Character all along the road is that of being a Drunken impudent fellow, and that you do not do your duty but send your bags by porters to the Office. He says that he feels for your family but it is your own fault that they are distressed. You ought to take care of your situation by doing your Duty properly, keeping yourself sober, and behaving with civility to everybody. I received the above Answer from Weymouth this morning where Mr Hasker is at present. He does not say how long you are to be suspended for.

H. N.

To Mr Forward   G.P. Off
of the Post Office   Aug 6 1796
Exeter

Sir

In consequence of a letter you wrote to Mr Hasker on behalf of Hancock he has desired me to acquaint you of the circumstances that induced him to suspend Hancock.

Mr Ware of Bridport had freed a portmanteau belonging to a gentleman that rode on Horseback and put it into the Boot under the Care of the Coachman. Hancock sent the portmanteau to the Gentleman's house at Exeter and demanded 2/6 which the Gentleman refused. He then went to the Gentleman himself and on being refused also he abused the Gentleman in a shamefull manner. Mr Hasker was also informed that he did not take his Bags himself to the Office but sent them by porters, and his general Character is that of a Drunken abusive fellow.

H. N.

To Mr Jackson, Postmaster   G.P.O. Aug 19/96
Exeter

Sir

On receipt of this restore Hancock to his situation again.

T. H.

P.S. Hancock thinks by having 5 children he may do his duty as shameful as he pleases, that he may act as improperly and cheat

everybody as he pleases—the 2/6 ought never to be passed over and
I shall always consider him a bad man.

T.H.

To Mail Guard Hancock G.P. Off
Aug 19 1796

Sir

Mr Hasker has this day ordered you to be restored to your place
again, and has desired me to inform you that if he has any complaints
again against you, either for neglect of duty or impertinence, or
extorsion to passengers, he will certainly discharge you if you had a
hundred children, therefore take care you deliver your bags yourself
at every Office and be content with what you earn fairly.

H.N.

Mail-carts

These, like the horse- and foot-posts, where still in use, would not
come under Hasker, and so are not mentioned. But those which
brought the bags from the G.P.O. to mail-coaches for the West of
England which started from Piccadilly were an exception. They were
driven by horses supplied by contractors and even that important
person, Mr Wilson of Lad Lane, was not exempt from Hasker's cen-
sure if he were late. They appear in the illustration facing p. 188.

To Mr Wilson Gen P Office
16 Sept 1796

Sir

The Exeter Mail waited a quarter of an Hour this morning at the
Gloucester Coffee house for the Cart, and being a West India Mail
was a great hinderance to the delivery. The Bristol Mail also waited
10 minutes for the return of the Cart. I hope you will give such
directions that it may not happen again. I fear the Horse is not fit
for this duty.

H.N.

CHAPTER X

Time-Bills of 1797

When I was first studying the Letters in the Record Room at St Martin's, Mr Devenport remarked that I might find more Hasker relics at the Post Office Museum. I said that I had never heard that the Post Office had a museum. Mr Devenport replied that the Post Office had nothing whatever to do with the Museum, that it was a private collection which had been amassed by an old Post Office man, and it was housed at Bruce Castle in Tottenham. The romantic ring of such a name in the purlieus of London I did not imagine would survive a personal visit. But I was mistaken.

After a longish journey by tube and trolley-bus I arrived at Bruce Castle—a truly astonishing building standing in its own grounds. It appeared to be a large 18th-century house with semi-octagonal projections at either end and a large clock-tower in three stages, surmounted by a cupola, rising over the porch in the middle. There was also a detached tower of narrow brick, obviously at least two hundred years older than anything else. Many readers will know Bruce Castle quite well, but I confess I had never heard of it and both its name and appearance caused me great surprise. I was to learn later that its name was indeed a link with Robert Bruce who held the manor in the 13th century. It was confiscated by Edward I when Robert set up as King of Scotland. The brick tower was part of a succeeding manor-house built at the time of Henry VIII and most of the remainder was another rebuild in 1720 by Lord Coleraine, whose arms remain in a large pediment on the north side.

When I reached the door of the Castle I found a notice to say that it was closed to the public. But presently I discovered a small side-entrance giving access to the heating-apparatus, which was still working.

Here I got an answer to my summons, and heard that, owing to the
building being pronounced unsafe, nobody but one or two members
of the Borough Library staff and the Curator was now allowed in.
He was away at lunch. Returning a little later, I met the presiding
genius, Mr Fenton, and explained the urgency of my mission. He
was most helpful. I signed a document saying that I entered the Castle
at my own risk and indemnified the Borough Council against damages
if it should collapse on top of me, and in I went.

The house contained part of the Borough public library, an old-
established local museum, and the Postal History Collection—which
I had come to see. This had been formed by W. V. Morton, who
was for some time Telephone Manager at Nottingham. Besides books,
pictures, models, and files of newspaper-cuttings, there were some
very substantial exhibits in the shape of full-sized pillar-boxes and an
antique *perambulator* for road measurement, which may have been
one of the very instruments used by Cary.

In 1920 Morton probably found his collection was taking up more
house-room than his family, and decided to sell it. It was on the
verge of being shipped to America, when the Union of Postal Workers
decided to buy it. One of their members was Chairman of the
Tottenham Libraries and Museums Committee, which had acquired
Bruce Castle. There was plenty of space in this roomy old house
and that alone might have suggested the place as a good home for
the Morton collection. But, by an odd coincidence, Bruce Castle
had an independent claim on it from quite a different Post Office
association. It had been acquired by the Hill family in 1827 as a
school with young Rowland Hill, later destined to be the greatest
of all postal reformers, as head-master. So here the collection came on
permanent loan.

Mr Fenton said that among the things upstairs was an oak chest
which he believed had been made for keeping a mail-guard's uniform
in. He took me to it and we had a look inside. The interior was
entirely papered with letters and my eye immediately caught the
signature 'Thomas Hasker'. Unfortunately these letters had been
badly mutilated by mischievous children so that only bits were legible.
It was clear from the remaining fragments that they were in the usual
Haskerian style and were by no means letters of congratulation. But
the guard must have been proud of them to have preserved them in
this manner. The most complete, however, was in a different tone;

it was the recommendation for a free pass for the guard's wife and family by the Milford Mail (now travelling the new Greville way). It was dated 1816, the year before Hasker's retirement. The letter reads—

> Mrs Farwell ... is wife of the Carmarthen Mail Coach [guard] who with her two children is proceeding into Wales and, if room, by your Coach. We shall be obliged by your permitting her to go free by any of your Coaches.
>
> | To the Gloster & | We are Gent. |
> | London Mail Coach | Your very Hbl |
> | Proprietors | Tho. Hasker |

Guard Folwell (as he spelt his name) was owner of the chest. On the lid was pasted his old Sheet of Instructions. This was also torn, but I could read one nice point which does not appear in the only complete Sheet of Instructions I have seen, which is of much later date. It reads—

> Only two outside passengers are allowed whose station must be one on the Box and one on the Roof ... [pret]ence of taking up a *Cadde* or Helper will never be admitted as an excuse for disregarding this order.

The cadde must have been some young fellow whom the guard allowed to ride on the coach in hilly country and relieve him of the tedious task of jumping up and down to skid and unskid the wheel: the name has survived on the golf-course. The sheet is dated 1805. It must have been very near that time that the number of outside passengers was increased to three, coinciding with the improved build of the coach, in which the body and box were combined in one unit. This removed the yawing gap which existed in the first patent coaches, which must have given a very unsafe perch to the passenger on the roof and caused his knees to work like concertina bellows as the body of the vehicle rocked on its springs. But, in the newer pattern, a safe rigid seat could be provided behind the coachman. Points in the Letters show that on the converted stage-coaches three outside passengers were already allowed and on the Walsall diligence Hasker was prepared to permit four.

The enforced exclusion of the public had made an opportunity for a reappraisal of the museum collections, postal and general, parts of which had been packed away since war days. Now, emerging in mixed assortments, they were dotted about like ornaments in the different rooms, creating a homely and intimate atmosphere impossible in the bondage of show-case and category—fossils, grave-goods of the Pharaohs, Victorian curiosities. They seemed to act as a fixative of time, obliterating such distinctions as 'past' and 'present'. To be allowed to wander in the rooms and corridors of this old house, where contemporaries of Palmer and Hasker had lived—and young Rowland Hill—whose walls had heard the rumble of the Glasgow Mails, passing regularly morning and evening, was a unique passport into the world I was trying to re-create.

We rummaged in the files of cuttings and documents for any further Haskerian relics but nothing turned up except some odd jottings which seemed to have been copied from a batch of mail-coach time-bills of the year 1797, but there was no indication as to whether these were in the Morton collection or not. No further trace was found in the document files, and the Record Room at the General Post Office knew nothing of their existence. So I returned home and started work on the Letters, which the G.P.O. had kindly allowed me to borrow. The more I studied these the more I felt how valuable that batch of time-bills would be if they could be brought to light. They would at least give the names of all the contractors who worked the Mails in the year after the letter-books ended and they would give other invaluable links.

In a very short time I heard from Bruce Castle that the wished-for discovery had been made. The time-bills had been bound, making a folio volume of 135 pages. I hurried off as soon as possible to examine this wonderful find. Within the front cover was the book-plate of Philip Stanhope 5th Earl of Chesterfield, and the familiar cypher 'Ch', with the date, 1797. In pencil was written 'I paid £20 for this —W. V. Morton'. All the bills, with six exceptions, bore Thomas Hasker's name in print at the foot. All times of arrival were filled in in red ink and, in the same medium and by the same hand, there were numerous annotations. It was a transcription of these notes which we had found among the document files and which had given us the clue to the existence of the volume.

More than once, in his letters, Hasker speaks of sending Lord

Chesterfield 'the arrivals', evidently meaning a current set of clean time-bills based on those returned by the guards. The set in question appears to have been presented to him at the end of March, 1797, and this was his last full year at the Post Office. He left in 1798 to become Master of the Horse, his place being taken by William Eden, 1st Baron Auckland. The happy thought must have struck him of having these bills properly bound in limp leather as a souvenir of his Post Office reign. Mr Morton must have had the good fortune to hear of their disposal out of the Chesterfield library and the courage and sound sense to pay the somewhat stiff price recorded. The principal writers on the subject of the mail-coaches, including Joyce, do not appear to have seen these time-bills, due to their long segregation in a private library.

The red ink annotations (now rendered in italic print) are in Hasker's own hand and they are obviously of a strictly confidential nature. One judges from the foregoing that when a coach is only a few minutes behind time the guard or contractor, or both, can expect to get a stiff letter from the Office the following day. The notes on the time-bills give an entirely different impression. They show that on nearly every route large allowances were made for the difficult conditions under which the staff had to work. The time-tables were made out in accordance with the contracts undertaken but when experience showed that it was quite impracticable, except under ideal conditions of weather, sunlight, and moonlight, to fulfil the 'arrivals' as laid down, a calculated latitude was given (but kept a strictly guarded Office secret). Rebukes and warnings would only come when the rot of slackness could be detected; they were then taken up sharp on schedule time and told (in a different sense from the present) to work to rule.

In the following pages I have given the substance of all these time-bills contained in the Chesterfield volume in a slightly simplified form to fit the page, with Hasker's notes in italic and a few by myself in ordinary fount. Only the detail for the down journeys is given in full. All points at which the time-piece was handed in to be checked or changed for another are marked 'T.P.' and halts specially planned for Post Office business are marked 'O.B.' Some of the bills are earlier forms, still in stock, and give spaces for marking the time on the local clock as well as the Mail time-piece. That this had to be done at all check-points is laid down in the earlier instructions, but in the

Chesterfield set local times are wanted only twice, and other things which the guards and postmasters would enter regularly don't appear.

Some readers will, I think, find these time-bills of interest in quite another way. Here are preserved the names of so many men who must have been great local characters in their day—for the contractors were mostly innkeepers. Certainly in the registers of their parish churches, perhaps graven in those walls, or on the old stones in the greensward surrounding them, their memories may be refreshed and the local historian given new matter for research. The epitaph of Lawrence of the White Lion at Shrewsbury who established 'the first mail coach to this town' (and is seen in Time-bill 8 to be horsing it from Shifnal) has already been mentioned. No doubt there are others awaiting discovery by the patient detective.

LIST OF THE TIME-BILLS

1 London to Dover
2   ,,   ,, Portsmouth
3   ,,   ,, Poole
4   ,,   ,, Exeter (via Salisbury & Dorchester)
4a ,,   ,,   ,,   ,,   ,, (with Lisbon mail)
5   ,,   ,,   ,, (via Marlborough & Bath)
6   ,,   ,, Bath & Bristol
7   ,,   ,, Worcester
8   ,,   ,, Shrewsbury
9   ,,   ,,   ,, (short bill to Birmingham)
10 ,,   ,, Chester & Holyhead
11 ,,   ,, Liverpool
12 ,,   ,, Carlisle
13 ,,   ,, Leeds
14 ,,   ,, Glasgow
15 ,,   ,, Edinburgh
16 ,,   ,, Wisbeach, Cambridge & Bury St Edmunds
17 ,,   ,, Norwich (via Newmarket)
18 ,,   ,,   ,, (via Ipswich)
19 ,,   ,, Yarmouth
20 ,,   ,, Weymouth (Royal Weymouth Mail)

Cross-post Mails

21 Canterbury and Margate
22 Portsmouth and Chichester
23 Southampton and Lymington
24 Weymouth and Dorchester
25 Bristol and Milford
26 Oxford and Bristol
27 Oxford and Gloucester
28 Hereford and Worcester
29 Ludlow and Worcester

30 Birmingham and Bristol
31 York and Scarborough
32 York and Whitby
33 Hull and Liverpool
34 Glasgow and Ayr

-----

35 London and Steyning, via Brighthelmstone (Brighton)
36 London and Hastings

D = distance in miles. T.A. = Time allowed. T.P. = Time-piece handed over for check or exchange. O.B. = Post Office business.

Hasker's notes are in italic. Down Mails given in detail. Up Mails summarised. Contractors' names appear below the 'ground' for which they were responsible, with mileage adjoining. The totals of time and distance do not always add up correctly which seems to show that these figures were based on earlier bills which were never amended in that respect.

London to Dover

	D.	T.A.		No. 1
			G.P.O. 8	P.M.
Ibberson				
& Co	32	4.30	Rochester 12.30	A.M.
,,	26½	3.40	Canterbury 4.10	,,
Miles	15½	2.20	Dover P.O. 6.30	,,
	74	10.30		

At Canterbury, going down, 20 minutes are allowed in Summer to sort the Camp Letters.

UP

Leaves Dover P.O. 6.30 P.M. Canterbury 8.50. *O.B. 20 mins* London 5.20 A.M.

At Canterbury, returning, 20 minutes are allowed to forward the Camp Letters.

London to Portsmouth

	D.	T.A.		No. 2
			G.P.O. 8	P.M.
Watson	36	5. 0	Mousehill 1	A.M.
Eames	18	2.30	Petersfield 3.30, *O.B. 15 mins*	,,
		15		
Bradley	18	2.30	Portsmouth 6.15	,,
	72	10.15		

At Petersfield 15 minutes are allowed to sort the short Letters.

UP

Leaves P.O. Portsmouth 8 P.M. (no waits). London 6 A.M.

London to Poole

	D.	T.A.		No. 3
			G.P.O. 8	P.M.
			Gloucester Coffee House—	
Fagg	21	2.30	Staines 10.30	,,
Williams	9½	1.10	Bagshot 11.40	,,
Grave	16	2. 0	Bentley Green 1.40	A.M.
Grave & Hobbs	15½	2. 0	Alresford 3.40 (T.P.)	,,
Rogers	12	1.30	Southampton 6.5, *Breakfast 25 mins*	,,
		25		
,,	20	2.25	Ringwood 8.55	,,
Whettel	17	2. 5	P.O. Poole 11	,,
	118½	15. 0		

Walking with the Bags at Southampton to and from the Office, and Office Business, cannot detain less than 35 or 40 minutes.

The Time Bill is made to arrive at 11 o'Clock, but 12 o'Clock ever was held the proper time of arrival.

This is a very quick Coach.

UP

Leaves P.O. Poole at 4 P.M. Southampton 8.30, *Supper 25 mins* (but see H's comment above). Alresford 11.20 (T.P.). London G.P.O. 7 A.M.

London to Exeter
(*via Salisbury and Dorchester*)

	D.	T.A.		No. 4
			G.P.O. 8	P.M.
			Gloucester Coffee-house, Piccadilly—	
Wilson	30½	3.55	Bagshot 11.55	,,
Demezy	20	2.30	Basingstoke 2.25	A.M.
W. Wilson	8½	1.10	Overton 3.35	,,
Weeks	28½	3.40	Salisbury 7.15 (T.P.), *Breakfast 20 mins*	,,
		30		
Shergold	10	1.20	Woodyeats 9.5	,,
Wood	12½	1.40	Blandford 10.45	,,

	D.	T.A.		No. 4
			G.P.O. 8	P.M.
Bryer	16	2.10	Dorchester 12.55, *Dinner 30 mins*	
		30		
Pine	9½	1.15	Honiton 6.40	,,
Land	16	2.10	P.O. Exeter 8.30	,,
	179	24.50		

UP

Leaves Exeter at 5 A.M. Honiton 7.10 *Breakfast 20 mins.* Blandford 2.50 P.M. *Dinner 30 mins.* Salisbury 6.20 (T.P.) *Supper 30 mins.* London G.P.O. 6 A.M.

They frequently wait [at Salisbury] for the Shaftsbury branch to come in before they can start for London—sometimes 30 or 40 minutes.

London to Exeter
(*Foreign Mail for Lisbon*)

	D.	T.A.		No. 4a
			G.P.O. 4	A.M.
Wilson	21	3.10	Staines 7.10	,,
White	9½	1.25	Bagshot 8.35, *Breakfast 30 mins*	,,
		30		
Demezy	20	3. 0	Basingstoke 12.5	P.M.
W. Wilson	8½	1.20	Overton 1.25	,,
		40	Andover—*Dinner 40 mins*	,,
Weeks	28½	4.30	Salisbury 6.35 (T.P.), *Tea 20 mins*	,,
		20		
Shergold	10	1.40	Woodyeats 8.35	,,
Wasse &				
Handy	12½	2. 0	Blandford 10.35, *Supper 30 mins*	,,
		30		
Bryer	16	2.20	Dorchester 1.25	A.M.
Warre	15	2.15	Bridport 3.40	,,
Ellard	12½	2. 0	Axminster 5.40	,,
Land	25½	4.10	P.O. Exeter 9.50	,,
	179	29.50		

This Coach carries the Lisbon Mail only once a week.

The mail was made up on Tuesday night, the coach leaving early on Wednesday morning. The bags were dispatched to Lisbon from

Falmouth 'generally on the Saturday Morning, if a Packet be in the Harbour.'[1] The coach appears to have been an auxiliary, that is, a stage-coach which carried the mail and a guard on that one particular journey in the week. It will be seen that it took five hours longer to make the journey than the regular Mail, its ordinary pace having been allowed for in the time-bill.

London to Exeter
(*via Bath & Taunton*)

	D.	T.A.		No. 5
			G.P.O. 8	P.M.
			Gloucester Coffee-house, Piccadilly—	
Wilson	11	1.20	Brentford 9.20	,,
Fromont	46	5.35	Thatcham 2.55, *Refreshment 20 mins*	A.M.
		20		
,,	21½	2.30	Marlbro 5.45	,,
,,	35	4.15	Bath 10 (T.P.), *Breakfast 30 mins*	,,
		30		
,,	19½	3. 0	Wells 1.30	P.M.
,,	—	—	Taunton 5.5., *Dinner 30 mins* (dist. and	
		30	time allowed omitted)	,,
Hare	43	5.30	White Ball 7.30	,,
Noseworthy	9½	1.10	Collumpton 8.40	,,
Thompson	12	2. 0	Exeter P.O. 10.40	,,
	196½	26.40		

This Bill is made to arrive at Exeter at 10.40, but it is a very fast Coach and in the best weather we do not expect to arrive before eleven.

UP

Leaves Exeter P.O. at 4 A.M. Taunton (time omitted) *Breakfast 20 mins.* Bath 3.45 P.M. *Dinner 30 mins* (T.P.). Marlbro 9 (T.P.) 'and off immediately'. Thatcham 11.45. *Refreshment 20 mins.* London G.P.O. 7 A.M.

This Bill is made to arrive in London at 6.40 at the General Post Office, but that is admitting the Mail from Trowbridge and Frome is at Melksham a quarter before 6, which so seldom happens that when the Coach could be there by that time they drive gently and do not attempt it, as they know

[1] Cary, 5th ed. (1812).

they are liable to wait so long—this can never be avoided when the branch fits in so very nice.

The Winter season this Coach is hurried up to Thatcham that the passengers may sup and the Coach be ready to set off, taking the Bristol Mail the moment it arrives. This saves ½ an hour, by which the Bristol passengers have time to sup, the mail being taken by the Bath Guard. The Bristol Guard is left to Guard his Coach to London, where it arrives ¾ of an hour after the other.

London to Bristol Time-Bill
(*Summer Bill*)
(see illustration facing p. 189)

	Miles	Time allowed		No. 6
			Dispatched from the General Post-Office (date) at 8 (P.M.) With a Time-Piece safe to Coach No sent out No	
			Arrived at the Gloucester Coffee-house, Piccadilly at	
Wilson	11	1.20	Arrived at Brentford at 9.20	
Fromont	46	5.25	Arrived at Thatcham at 2.45 To be at Thatcham at Forty-five Minutes past Two, w(h)ere Twenty Minutes are allowed for Refreshments—To be off exactly by Five minutes past Three o'Clock in the Morning	
Porter	21½	2.40	Arrived at Marlbro at 5.45 Delivered Time-Piece safe to Coach No gone forward To be at Marlbro' by Three Quarters past Five in the Morning	
	13	1.25	Arrived at Calne at 7.10	

	Miles	Time allowed			No. 6
			Arrived at Bath at		
Dover	32	3.50	Arrived at the Post-Office, Bristol the	of 179	
			at 11		
			The Mail to be delivered at the Post-Office,		
	123½	15. 0	Bristol, at Eleven o'Clock in the Morning		
				Delivered the Time-Piece safe to	
			Coach No	arrived No	to

The up Mail left Bristol at 4 P.M. and reached Thatcham at 11.55 P.M., where twenty minutes was again allowed for refreshment. London, 7 A.M.

DOWN

In winter the Time Bill is made to arrive at Bristol at ¾ past 11, but the Contractors never agreed to be there before 12. In summer they agreed to be there by eleven (great work) and which they generally are, allowing for a few minutes out of the London Office and 20 minutes difference in the clocks—and sometimes they even arrive before 11, which was the case this day, March 23rd, 1797 (when they) arrived at Bristol 10.50.

UP

In winter the Bill is made to arrive at ¾ past 7, but we do not expect it till 8, for their agreement is to work it up in 16 hours which, as the clocks are slowest at Bristol, will not bring it to London till about a ¼ or 20 mins after eight, and in summer about as much after seven, though we generally contrive to get them in by seven. Very great exertion—122 miles in 14 hours and ¾, and not less than 1 hour & ½ lost in changing Horses and supping exclusive of any trifling delay such as losing shoes, breaking a trace &c, some of which happen every journey.

London to Worcester

	D.	T.A.		No. 7
			G.P.O. 8	P.M.
Boulton	38	4.50	Henley 12.50	A.M.
Costor	23	2.55	Oxford 3.45 (T.P.)	
		30	Enstone. *Breakfast, 30 mins* (no time of arrival or distance given. This place is omitted altogether on the up bill. Probably Enstone had been given up in favour of Morton for breakfasting by 1797)	
Morris	27	3.35	Morton in Marsh 8.50	
Fieldhouse	30	4.10	Worcester 12 Noon	
	118	16. 0		

This bill has place for coachman's name.

In summer generally there by that time. In winter not expected till about one.

UP

Leaves Worcester P.O. at 3 P.M. At Oxford 10.45. *Supper 25 mi* and T.P. London 6.55 A.M.

Thongh the Bill is made to arrive at 6.55 it is not expected till 7, though we do all possible to get in before.

London to Shrewsbury

	D.	T.A.		No. 8
			G.P.O. 8	P.M.
Willan	18½	2.30	Uxbridge 10.30	
R. Allen	14	1.45	Wycombe 12.15	A.M.
J. Allen	26	3.27	Oxford 3.42 (T.P.)	,,
Beck	28½	3.40	Shipston 7.22	,,
Wright	11	1.20	Stratford on Avon 8.42,	
		20	*Breakfast 20 mins*	,,
Bark	12	1.30	Hockley Heath 10.32	,,
Babington	11	1.25	Birmingham 11.57 (T.P.)	,,
		1. 0	*Dinner, one hour*	,,

	D.	T.A.		No. 8
			G.P.O. 8	P.M.
Beck	14	2. 0	Wolverhampton 2.57	,,
Jones	12½	2. 0	Sheffnal 4.57	,,
Lawrence	18	2.50	Shrewsbury 7.47	,,
	165½	23.47		

This is a very fast Coach from London to Birmingham, and a very deep heavy road—therefore it is not expected to arrive at Birmingham before one o'clock in winter. With every exertion it could not be accomplished, which caused the Birmingham Bag to be sent the other way, namely, via Coventry to Birmingham.

Of course seeing the reason above, it cannot be expected at Shrewsbury till nine o'Clock in winter and sometimes later.

UP

Leaves P.O. Shrewsbury, at 7 A.M. At Birmingham 1.50. *Dinner, one hour* (T.P.). London, 6.50 A.M.

This Coach brings up the London Bag though it does not carry it down, as the Liverpool Coach which brings it down to Coventry is 18 miles further on its journey before the Bag sets out.

London to Birmingham
(*a short bill*)

	D.	T.A.		No. 9
			G.P.O. 8	P.M.
Wilson	26½	3.30	Redborne 11.30	,,
Parkins	27	3.35	Stoney Stratford 3.5 (T.P.)	A.M.
Soden	40	5.20	Coventry 8.25 'and off in 10 minutes'	
		10	disp. 8.35 by T.P. & Town Clock	,,
,,	20	2.30	Birmingham 11.5 by Time-piece.	
			by Town Clocks. (T.P.)	,,

A short bill for use of guards on the Shrewsbury Mail (No. 8).

In summer it generally arrives as the Bill specifies—a very great alteration this for Birmingham.

A Note appended on the short bills.

These short Bills have been in use about 3 years, which necessity pointed out by our wanting information of part of the Journey before the Bill returns, which in some cases is 4, 5, or 6 days—these short Bills return in two. There are six short Bills, namely Birmingham, Chester, Manchester, Leeds, Glasgow, and Edinburgh. By the Bill you will see how far they travel.

London to Holyhead

1st Day

	D.	T.A.		No. 10
			G.P.O. 8	P.M.
Boulton	12	1.30	Barnet 9.30	,,
Sweatman	11	1.30	St Alban's 11.0.	,,
Mrs Shaw	30½	4.27	Lathbury 3.27	A.M.
F. Shaw	14	1.58	Northampton 5.25 (T.P.), *Breakfast 30*	
		30	*mins*	,,
Briggs	15	2. 0	Welford 7.55	,,
Spencer	8	1. 5	Lutterworth 9.0. *Office Business 10 mins*	,,
		10		
Towle	11	1.30	Hinkley 10.40 (T.P.), *Office Bns. 10 mins*	,,
		10		
,,	8	1. 5	Atherstone 11.55	,,
Burton &				
Jarvis	15	2. 5	Litchfield 2.0, *Dinner 35 mins*	P.M.
		35		
Hanbury	9¾	1.15	Wolsey Bridge 3.50	,,
Hughes	7½	1. 0	Stafford. *Office Business and Tea 15 mins*	,,
,,	7	1. 0	Eccleshall 6.5	,,
Latham	21	3. 5	Namptwich 9.10	,,
Southern	10	1.20	Tarporley 10.30	,,
Paul	10	1.30	Chester 12 (T.P.), *Supper & O.B. One hour*	,,
		1. 0		

2nd Day

Smith	18	2.45	Holywell 3.45	A.M.
Potts	10½	1.50	St Asaph 5.35. *Breakfast 20 mins*	,,
		20		
Edwards	8	1.15	Abergele 7.10	,,

R

	D.	T.A.		No. 10
			G.O.P. 8	A.M.
Rous	11	1.50	Ferryside 9.0. *Half an hour for crossing*	,,
		30		
,,			Conway 9.30	
Archer &	17	2.50	Bangor Ferry-house 12.20	P.M.
W. Jackson			One hour for Crossing & Dinner	
			'Received from the Ferryman at—'	
J. Jackson	25	3.30	Post Office, Holyhead 4.50.	,,
	278¾	44.50		

This Coach should be first Coach at Northampton as it carries the Bye letters from Barnet and all intermediate Towns to be sorted at that Office. It generally is first.

The ferrys are generally crossed in the time allowed [i.e. at Conway and Bangor].

UP

Leaves Holyhead at 7 A.M. Dines at Conway 1.50 P.M. Chester 10.30 P.M. (T.P.) & Supper. *2nd day,* Stafford 6.25. Breakfast, 30 mins. Hinkley 12.40. (T.M.) & Dinner 30 mins. *3rd day,* London 4 A.M.

The Holyhead Time Bill is made to arrive at 4 o'Clock in the morning at the Gen Post Office. All the very long Coaches are made to arrive at a very early hour lest any breakdown or impediment should impede it at a great distance so long as to be too late for delivery. Liverpool, Manchester, Leeds, Glasgow, & Edinbro are of the same Class.

As Boulton is named as first contractor out of London the Mail must at that time have started from the Golden Cross, Charing Cross and not The Swan with Two Necks.

London to Liverpool

	D.	T.A.		No. 11
			G.P.O. 8	P.M.
Wilson	26½	3.30	Redbourne 11.30	,,
Parkins	27	3.35	Stoney Stratford 3.5 (T.P.)	A.M.
Soden	40	5.20	Coventry 8.25, *Breakfast, 30 mins*	,,
		30		
,,	12	1.50	Coleshill 10.45 (T.P.)	,,

	D.	T.A.		No. 11
			G.P.O. 8	A.M.
Burton &	15	2. 0	Litchfield 12.45 (T. & C.), *Dinner, 35 mins*	,,
Dale		35		
Hanbury	9¾	1.15	Wolsey Bridge 2.35	P.M.
Lillyman	12	1.35	Stone 4.10 (T. & C.), *Refreshment 15 mins*	,,
		15		
,,		10	Newcastle, *10 mins allowed*	
Massey	21½	2.50	Congleton 7.25 (T.P.)	P.M.
Wilkinson	14	2. 0	Knutsford 9.25	,,
Bowman	12	1.40	Warrington 11.5	,,
Simpson	18	2.30	Liverpool 1.35	A.M.
	207¾	29.35		

Entries for comparing time-piece with local time 'By Time-Piece' and 'By Clock' only appear in this bill and in No. 15. Shown as (T. & C.)'.

Considering the road, it is a fast Coach to Coventry to carry the Birmingham Bag.

Generally a delay here (Lichfield) of 20, 30, or 40 mts occasioned by the letters coming in late from Birmingham—though that I prevented early last week by bringing the letters earlier from Bristol than ever by one hour. This alteration commenced the 20th March, 1797.

The time allowed for tea at Stone is to accomodate the ride from Wolverhampton which is generally waited for 30 or 40 mts. From these delays the Coach seldom arrives at Liverpool till near 3 o'clock.

UP

Leaves Liverpool at 10 P.M. Stone 7.5 A.M. Breakfast 25 min (T. & C.). Lichfield 10.15, Ref. 20 m. Coventry 2.25 P.M. Dinner, 30 mins. Stoney Stratford 8.40, Supper 25 mins. London 4.20. Timepiece 'delivered safe' at Congleton and Coleshill.

This Coach is made by Time Bill to arrive at G.P.O. by 4.20 but the Contractors and the upper Guards is told that when they get within a few stages of London—if they are early—they may take more time than the Bill expresses, as it will enable their Horses to go faster down—which speed is wanted with the Birmingham Bag.

London to Carlisle

	D.	T.A.		No. 12
			G.P.O. 8	P.M.
Wilson	27	3.35	Redburne 11.35	,,
Goode	8	1. 5	Dunstable 12.40	A.M.
Levi	33	4.40	Northampton 5.20 (T.P.), *Breakfast 30 m*	,,
		30		
Benton	32	4.20	Leicester 10.10 (T.P.)	,,
Holland	28	3.45	Derby 1.55, *Dinner 30 mins*	P.M.
		30		
Wallis &				
Houghton	13	1.45	Ashbourne 4.10 (T.P.)	,,
Hargrave	15	2.10	Leek 6.20, *Refreshment 15 m*	,,
		15		
Goodwin	13	1.45	Macclesfield 8.20	,,
Pickford	20	2.35	Manchester 10.55 (T.P.)	,,
		4. 5	'To depart precisely at Three o'Clock in the Morning'	A.M.
Paterson	11	1.50	Hulton Lane 4.50	,,
Middlehurst	11	1.40	Chorley 6.30	,,
Cooper	10	1.25	Preston 7.55, *O.B. 30 mins*	,,
		30		
,,	22	3.10	Lancaster 11.35, *O.B. 10 mins* (T.P.)	,,
		10		
Rigg	11	1.25	Burton 1.10	P.M.
Masterson	11	1.25	Kendal 2.35, *Dinner 40 mins*	,,
		40		
Gibson	15	2.30	Shap 5.45	,,
Buchanan	11	1.30	Penrith 7.15	,,
Wilson &				
Fairbairne	18	2.45	P.O. Carlisle 10	,,
	309	50. 0		

Generally at Manchester in Summer by the Time the Bill specifies, 10.55; in Winter about an hour later.

The Coach for the North does not leave this place till 3 o'Clock—for if they did they would be too early at Chorley and pass by before the letters are brought in by ride from Warrington, which are brought to that Town by Liverpool Mail Coach, including the Birmingham, Chester Bags, & the great Correspondence from the Westward.

Generally at Carlisle in Summer at the time the Bill states; in winter about an hour later.

UP

Leaves Carlisle at 3.30 A.M. Shap 7.45. *Breakfast 20 mins.* Kendal 10.35. *O.B. 10 mins.* Lancaster 1.35 P.M. (T.P.). *Dinner & O.B. 40 mins.* Preston 5.25, *Tea 20 mins.* Manchester 10.45 P.M. 'Where till Two in the Morning is allowed for Supper, Office Business, &c' (T.P.). Ashborne 8.35 A.M. (T.P.). Derby 10.20, *25 mins* (a halt in which there would be a chance for breakfast, but this is not specified, which suggests that if the coach were late in, time would not be officially allowed for it but the coach would leave on time at 10.45). Leicester 2.30 P.M. *Dinner 30 mins* (T.P.). Northampton 7.20 (T.P.). *Supper 30 mins.* G.P.O., London 5.10 A.M.

Sometimes delayed at Penrith for the Whitehaven ride but generally in summer arrives at Manchester before eleven. From which place it does not start till two, see Bill.

London to Leeds

	D.	T.A.		No. 13
			G.P.O. 8	P.M.
Willan	19	2.20	Colney 10.20	,,
Parkin	16	2.15	Dunstable 12.35	A.M.
Levi	32½	4.40	Northampton 5.15 (T.P.), *Breakfast 30*	
		30	*mins*	,,
Bruce	43	6. 0	Loughborough 11.45	,,
Gray	15	2. 0	Nottingham 1.45 (T.P.), *Dinner 30 mins*	P.M.
		30		
,,	14	2.10	Mansfield 4.35	,,
Lovett	12	1.50	Chesterfield 6.25	,,
,,			Sheffield 8.5, *Supper 30 mins*	,,
Peach	26½	4. 0	Barnesley 10.55	,,
Hick	20	3. 0	P.O. Leeds 1.55 'by Timepiece' & by	
			Clocks 'and the Mail Coach from York	
	198	29.45	at by Clocks.'	,,

In summer we generally contrive to get this Coach to Leeds by 2 o'Clock. The time it ought to arrive at winter the Road has been so bad we sometimes could hardly get it there by four; in which case a Horse is ready and sets off after the Cross Coach with the Bradford, & Halifax London Bags—this perhaps happens 6, 8, or 10 times in a Year.

UP

Leaves Leeds P.O. at 10.5 P.M. Nottingham 9.10 A.M. (T.P.) leaves at 10.15 'by Clocks' (here given a preference over Time-Piece, see note below). The printed bill only allows half an hour, the amendment gives *65 minutes*, time for the best breakfast on the road. (T.P.) Leicester 2 P.M. *Dinner 30 mins.* Northampton 7 P.M. (T.P.) *Refreshment 20 mins.* G.P.O., London 4.50 A.M.

That the time may be regular, to accomodate the Town of Nottingham, let them arrive ever so early they do not leave it 10.15 by Town Clocks.

London to Glasgow

1st Day

	D.	T.A.		No. 14
			G.P.O. 8	P.M.
Willan	10	1.15	Whetstone 9.15	,,
Dyson	14½	1.50	Brickwall 11.5	,,
Barker	14½	1.47	Baldock 12.52	A.M.
Thorn & Walker	18	2. 0	Eaton 2.52 (T.P.)	,,
Sibley & Holmes	13	1.35	Alconbury Hill 4.27	,,
Sibley	7	0.50	Stilton 5.17	,,
Cook	14	1.45 30	Stamford 7.2, *Breakfast 30 mins*	,,
Sturtle	21	2.50	Grantham 10.22 (T.P.)	,,
Clark	14	1.50	Newark 12.12	P.M.
Tomlinson	13	1.45	Tuxford 1.57	,,
Clark	10½	1.30 40	Barnaby Moor 3.27, *Dinner 40 mins*	,,
Forster	14	1.45	Doncaster 5.52	,,
Hall	15	2. 5 30	Ferrybridge 7.57 by T.P., by Clocks (T.P.), *Supper 30 mins*	,,
Denton & Parker	16¾	2.10	Wetherby 10.37	,,

2nd Day

Smith & Fretwell	12	1.30	Boroughbridge 12.7	A.M.
Fretwell	12	1.30	Leeming Lane 1.37	,,
Clark	11	1.20	Catterick Bridge 2.57	,,

	D.	T.A.		No. 14
			G.P.O. 8	A.M.
Farguson &				
Thompson	14	1.40	Greta Bridge 4.37 (T.P.)	,,
Thompson	9½	1.30	Spittal (Inn) 6.7, *Breakfast 25 mins*	,,
		25		
Fryar	17½	2.15	Appleby 8.47	,,
Buchanan	14	1.55	Penrith 10.42	,,
Fairbairne				
& Wilson	18	2.20	Carlisle 1.2 (T.P.), *O.B. 1 hour*	P.M.
		1. 0	Dispatched 2.2	
Wilson	10	1.15	Longtown 3.17	,,
Black	14	1.55	Ecclefeckan 5.12	,,
Scott	11	1.20	Dinwoodie Green 6.32	,,
Carruthers	11	1.20	Moffat 7.52 (T.P.), *Refreshment 25 mins*	,,
		25		
James Rae	19	2.50	Abingtown 11.7	,,

3rd Day

	D.	T.A.		
Gillespie	23½	3.40	Laverock Hall 2.47	A.M.
Bain	14½	2.10	P.O. Glasgow 4.57	,,
	405¾	57. 0		

UP

Leaves Glasgow 3 P.M. Moffat 11.40 (T.P.) *Supper 25 mins.* *2nd Day* Carlisle 5.55 A.M. *Breakfast 1 hour* (T.P.). Penrith 9.15. *O.B. 10 mins.* Appleby 11.20. *Dinner 30 mins.* Greta Bridge 3.35 P.M. (T.P.). Boroughbridge 8.5. *Supper 35 mins.* *3rd Day* Ferrybridge 12.15 A.M. (T.P.) by T.P. by Clocks. Barnaby Moor 4.20. *Breakfast 30 mins.* Grantham 10.20 (T.P.). Stamford 1.20. *Dinner 45 mins* 'To wait till 4 o'Clock for the York Coach'. Eaton 8.40 (T.P.). *4th Day.* London 4.15 A.M. The time taken is given as 59 hrs, 15 mins—two and a quarter hours longer than on the down journey.

DOWN MAIL

The Glasgow Mail Coach is very fast—9 miles an hour part of the road, as the road is farthest, in order to be at Ferrybridge before the York, which it generally is. This Coach is pretty fast all the way to Carlisle, full 8 miles an hour. Below Carlisle on some of the stages we do pretty well, on other we don't go above 6 miles an hour from two causes, no completion & very bad road—seldom arrive there (Glasgow) before 7—in winter often not till 9—but full as well as promised for, tho the Bill is so made out, it was not expected to be there near so soon. It must also be at Stamford before the

*York, or the few letters from the Baldock would not be put into the Bye
Bags which the York carries.*

UP MAIL

*If the Mail from Glasgow does not arrive by eight o'Clock in the morning
(at Carlisle), the Carlisle Coach is dispatched for Ferrybridge; and if the
Bags from Glasgow arrive a little time after they are sent after by Horse.
This has not happened above five times since the Coach run.*

*Though the Bill is made out to be so early as 1.20 at Stamford we do not
expect them there till between 2 & 3. They have to dine and the York Mail
generally arrives by ½ past 3 for which it carry the bye letters up the Baldock
road. Should it not come by 4 (very seldom the case) it sets out without them.*

London to Edinburgh

1st Day

	D.	T.A.		No. 15
			G.P.O. 8	P.M.
Willan	13	1.40	Waltham Cross 9.40	,,
Dyson	10	1.15	Ware 10.55, O.B. 15 mins	,,
		15		
Chuck & Daintry	17½	2.20	Royston 1.30	A.M.
			10 minutes allowed to take out Lord Hardwick's letters.[1]	
Ubsdy	6	0.45	Arrington 2.15	,,
Griffits	15	1.55	Huntingdon 4.10 (T.P.), *Breakfast 30 mins*	,,
Sibley	12	1.30	Stilton 6.10	,,
Cook	14	1.45	Stamford 7.53, O.B. 15 mins	,,
		15	*To sort short letters.*	
Sturtle	11	1.30	Witham Common 9.40	,,
,,			Grantham 10.50 (T.P.)	
Clarke	24	3.10	Newark 12.50, O.B. 40 mins	P.M.
		40		
Thompson & Tomlinson	23	3. 0	Barnaby Moor 4.30	,,
Stanuel	14	1.45	Doncaster 6.15 (T.P.), *Refreshment 15 mins*	,,
		15		

[1] Lord Hardwick's house, Wimpole Hall, at Arrington.

	D.	T.A.		No. 15
			G.P.O. 8	P.M.
Woodcock	15	2. 0	Ferrybridge 8.40 By T.P. ...	
			By Clocks ...	,,
Denton	12	1.35	Tadcaster 10.15	,,
Hartley	9½	1.20	P.O. York (T.P.)11.35, *Supper & O.B.*	,,
			1 hour	

2nd Day

	D.	T.A.		
Hartley &				
Pulleyn	17	2.15	Thormanby 2.50	A.M.
Bulmer &				
Hirst	15	2. 5	Northallerton 4.55 (T.P.), O.B. *10 mins*	,,
		10		
Smith	16	2. 5	Darlington 7.10, *Breakfast 20 mins*	,,
Trenham	9	1.15	Rushyford 8.45	,,
Wrangham	9	1.10	Durham 9.55, O.B. *15 mins*	,,
		15		
		30	Newcastle (times and distance not given) (T.P.), *Dinner 30 mins*	
Hall	29½	4. 0	Morpeth 2.40	P.M.
Nelson	10	1.20	Felton 4	,,
Wilson	9½	1.20	Alnwick 5.20	,,
M'Donnel	14½	2. 0	Belford 7.20	,,
Dixon	15½	2.10	Berwick 9.30 (T.P.), *Supper 30 mins*	,,
		30		
Hume	11¼	1.50	Press 11.50	,,

3rd Day

	D.	T.A.		
Lorimer	15	2.10	Dunbar 2.0	A.M.
Clark	11	1.30	Haddington 3.30	,,
Drysdale	18½	2.30	G.P.O. Edinburgh 6.0	,,
	396	57.50		

UP

Leaves Edinburgh 3.45 P.M. Berwick 11.45 (T.P.). *Supper 30 mins. 2nd Day*. Newcastle 9.5 (T.P.). *Breakfast 30 mins.* Durham 12 noon *O.B. 15 mins.* Darlington 2.15 P.M. *O.B. 15 mins.* Northallerton 5.5. *Dinner 30 mins* (T.P.). York 9.50 (T.P.) 'where 2 Hours & 10 Min are allowed for Supper, Office Business, &c. To be off at 12 o'Clock.' *3rd Day.* Ferrybridge 2.55 A.M. by T.P. and by Clocks. Doncaster 4.55 (T.P.) *Breakfast 30 mins.* Newark 10.10 *O.B. 10 mins.* Grantham (no time given) (T.P.) *Dinner & O.B. 40 mins.* Huntingdon 7.20 (T.P.) *Supper & O.B. 40 mins.* Royston 10.50 *O.B. 10 mins.*

4th Day. Ware 1.20 A.M. *O.B. 15 mins.* G.P.O. London 4.25 A.M. The up journey is timed 25 minutes longer than the down.

Down Mail

At Huntingdon have sometimes to wait for the cross mail from Cambridge which was the first cause of using short Bills. Till then we did not know for six days of the situation, which was almost too late to correct it.

Generally arrives at Edinbro at the time the Bill states in summer & in winter not above an hour later, except there was some extraordinary impediment.

Up Mail

If the Coach [does] not arrive from Edinbro by 12 o'Clock the Mail Coach sets off from there for London with the Newcastle Bag.

This Coach is got to York as early as possible, there being so much Office business and so many dispatches as well as arrivals.

To arrive at York at night	H. m.	To leave York at night	H. m.
From *Scarbro & Whitby*	8.45	For *Borobridge* at	9.30
,, *Hull*	9. 0	,, *Scarbro & Whitby*★	12.30
,, *Newcastle*	9.50	,, *Hull*★	12.30
,, *Liverpool*	10. 0	,, *Newcastle*★	12.30
,, *London*	11.30	,, *London*	12. 0
,, *He(l)msly*	8.30	,, *Liverpool*	12.30
Three days a week.			
,, *Borobridge*	11.20	*Those marked with a star depend on the arrival from London.*	

London to Wisbeach

No. 16

	D.	T.A.		P.M.
			G.P.O. 8	
Bolton	13	1.40	Waltham Cross 9.40	,,
Dyson	9	1.10	Ware 10.50	,,
Chuck &				
Daintry	7½	2.20	Royston 1.10	A.M.
Whitechurch	14½	1.50	Cambridge 3 (T.P.), *Breakfast 20 mins*	,,
	20			

	D.	T.A.		No. 16
			G.P.O. 8	A.M.
Barron	12	1.50	St. Ives 5.10, O.B. *10 mins*	,,
		10		
Smith	12	1.50	Chatteris 7.10	,,
Smith &				
Laughton	19½	3. 0	Wisbeach 10.10	,,
	97½	14. 0		

This is not a very fast Coach as they have plenty of time to answer their letters before 4 o'Clock in the afternoon for so small a town as Wisbeach.

UP

Leaves Wisbeach at 4 P.M. St Ives 8.45, *10 mins* O.B. Cambridge 10.45 (T.P.) *Supper 25 mins.* London G.P.O. 6 A.M.

Cambridge to Bury
(A branch of the above)

	D.	T.A.	
			Cambridge 3.20 A.M. '20 minutes after the arrival of the London Mail Coach'
			Newmarket—
Rowning, Yardley, & Edwards	27½	4.0	Bury 7.20 A.M.

Returned

Bury 6.30 P.M.
Newmarket—

Rowning,
Yardley, &   Cambridge 10.30 P.M.
Edwards

London to Norwich (via Newmarket)

	D.	T.A.		No. 17
			G.P.O. 8	P.M.
Boulton	11	1.25	Bald Stag 9.25	,,
Stokes	20	2.35	Hockerill 12	Midnight
Boulton	12	1.35	Bournbridge 2.25	A.M.
Rowning	12	1.35	Newmarket 4 (T.P.)	,,

	D.	T.A.		No. 17
			G.P.O. 8	P.M.
Crouse	20	2.40	Thetford 6.40, *Breakfast 30 mins*	A.M.
		30		
„	29	3.35	Norwich 10.45	„
	112	14.45		

This Coach thro the summer generally arrives at Norwich before 11, in winter very seldom so late as ¾ past—so that they have very good time till half past 4 to answer their letters.

UP

Leaves Norwich at 4.30 P.M. Thetford 8, *Supper 30 mins.* Newmarket 11.10 (T.P.). London 7 A.M.

London to Norwich (via Ipswich)

	D.	T.A.		No. 18
			G.P.O. 8	P.M.
Wilson & Boulton	38½	4.55	Witham 12.55	A.M.
Waterhouse	13½	1.45	Colchester 2.40 (T.P.)	„
„	18½	2.20	Ipswich 5.10, *Breakfast 30 mins*	„
		30		
Watson	24	3. 0	Scole Inn 8.40	„
Crouse	20	2.30	Norwich 11.10	„
	114½	15. 0		

The great quantity of business to be done at Ipswich, both down and up, will detain the Coach with the best exertions 45 Minutes, sometimes 55, that we do not expect them this road at Norwich much before 12—nor is it of great consequence as the other road—as the London Bag is carried that way, namely, by Newmarket.

UP

Leaves Norwich at 4 P.M. Ipswich 9.30, *Supper 30 mins.* Colchester 12.20 A.M. (T.P.). G.P.O. London 7 A.M.

This Coach leaves Norwich at 4, having more miles to travel and a worse road than the one via Newmarket.

London to Yarmouth
(*Auxiliary Coach*)

	D.	T.A.		No. 19
			London 6	P.M.
Boulton &				
Wilson	38½	6.10	Witham 12.10, *20 mins allowed for Supper*	A.M.
			between London and Witham	
Waterhouse	32	4.50	Ipswich 5 A.M. *Breakfast 30 mins* (T.P.)	
		30		
King	24	3. 5	Yoxford 8.35	A.M.
Watson	29	3.30	P.O. Yarmouth 12.5	P.M.
	123½	18. 5	Coachman's name——	

This is not a Mail Coach till it takes the Bags at Ipswich, & with the 15–20 or 25 minutes that the Office business takes at that.

We do not expect to reach Yarmouth in the best weather above 15 or 20 minutes before one. In winter the Inhabitants cannot answer their letters, and they were made fully to understand before the Coach started that except four months of the summer they must expect it.

UP

Leaves Yarmouth at 2.30 P.M. (space for coachman's name again). Ipswich, 9.5. *Supper 30 mins* (T.P.). London G.P.O. 8.35 A.M.

A Mail Coach returning no further than Ipswich.

A time-piece only between Yarmouth and Ipswich? Being a stage-coach between London and Ipswich, it takes two hours longer for the journey than the Mail.

London to Weymouth
(*the Royal Weymouth Mail*)

	D.	T.A.		No. 20
			G.P.O. 3 G. & C.	P.M.
			The Horse Guards 3.20	
	22	2.45	Egham 5.45 (T.P.) G. & C.	,,
T. Willson	8	1.15	Bagshot 7	,,

	D.	T.A.		No. 20
			G.P.O. 8 G. & C.	P.M.
Demezy	20	2.15	Basingstoke 9.15	,,
W. Willson	18½	2.15	Andover 11.30 (T.P.) G. & C.	,,
Weeks	17½	2.15	Salisbury 1.45	A.M.
Shergold	10½	1.15	Woodyeats 3	,,
Wood	12½	1.30	Blandford 4.30 (T.P.) G. & C.	,,
Bryer	11	1.25	Piddletown 5.55	,,
Warr	13	1.38	Weymouth 7.33 C.	,,

G. & C.—spaces for names of Guard and Coachman.

This Coach is only for the Season His Majesty is at Weymouth.

Does not do duty but carry His Majesty's dispatches and the Weymouth Bag.

UP

Leaves Weymouth at 4 P.M. Egham 7. Horse Guards 9.30. G.P.O. 10 A.M. No intervals shown for meals or office duty. Time Piece changed (or checked) at Blandford, Andover, and Egham. Spaces for names of Guards and Coachmen as on the down bill.

Not a break down or overturn for two Years. The worst accident that has happened has been a broken pole.

Canterbury and Margate

	D.	T.A.		No. 21
			Canterbury 4.30 A.M.	
			20 Minutes after the Mail Coach from London.	
Benson	17	2.45	Arrive at Margate 7.15 A.M.	
			Return	
			Margate 5 P.M.	
Benson	17	2.45	Arrive at Canterbury 7.45	
			in Time for the Mail Coach going to London	

Only in the Season, about 18 or 20 weeks.

No time-piece mentioned and time-bill not signed by Hasker or anyone else.

Portsmouth to Chichester

	D.	T.A.		No. 22
			Portsmouth P.O. 9	A.M.
Bradley	—	—	Corsham—	,,
,,	9	1.15	Havant 10.15	,,
Kemp	9	1.15	Chichester 11.30	,,
	18	2.30		

This short Coach would have set out sooner but for the Bye letters from the Bristol Branch which it takes up at Corsham, which ride is a very short one and in the night.

			Return	
			Chichester P.O. 4	P.M.
Kemp	9	1.15	Havant 5.15	,,
Bradley			Corsham—	,,
,,	9	1.15	Portsmouth 6.30	,,
	18	2.30		

No time-piece mentioned. Subscribed 'Send these Bills daily to Mr Hasker, General Post Office' and 'The Bristol Mail at' with no time given.

Southampton to Lymington

This is a unique specimen. It is smaller than the others and has an ornamental border with a large royal coat of arms on top and is headed 'FOR *His* MAJESTY'S *Special Service*'. Hasker explains by saying—'*I have not a new bill. They are being printed in the Country*'. It is the only one which bears an exact date. Quoted verbatim.

	D.	T.A.		No. 23
			'Dispatched from the Post-Office, *South-ampton*, the Mail for Lymington the 25 Day of March, 1797 at 5 m. p. 7 o'Clock in the Morning'	
			A. Beare Postmistress	
Mr Rogers	18	2.30	'Received the Mail from *Southampton* at Lymington at 35 m. p. ten o'Clock in the Morning'	
			A. Shepard Postmaster	

251

| | D. | T.A. | | No. 23 |

Returned

'Dispatched from the Post-Office, *Lymington*, the Mail for *Southampton*, the 26 Day of March, 1797 at Five o'Clock in the Afternoon'

A. Shepard   Postmaster

Mr Rogers   18   2.30   'Received from Southampton the Mail from Lymington, at ½ p. 7 o'Clock in the Afternoon.'

A. Beare   Postmistress

The Lymington Mail Coach is a branch from the Pool at Southampton and serves that town and Lyndhurst remarkably well.

Weymouth and Dorchester

| | D. | T.A. | | No. 24 |

Weymouth 10.30 A.M.

De la Motte   8   1.20   Dorchester 11.50   „

The Mail from London   *Generally   about ½ past 12, Noon*

The Mail from Exeter

Return

Dorchester 12.55   P.M.

Weymouth 2.15   „

The shortest Mail Coach there is. A branch just for Weymouth.

The bill is subscribed 'Return these Bills daily to T. Hasker, Esq; General Post Office'. No time-piece mentioned. No general footnote.

Bristol to Milford

| | D. | T.A. | | No. 25 |

P.O. Bristol 12.15 Noon, 30 minutes after the arrival of the London Mail.

Carr   10   1.20   Arrived at the New Passage at 1.35

Tide. 3 hours ebb

	D.	T.A.		No. 25
			Wind. N.E.	
			Number of Passengers in the Mail Coach, and no other Person but such as are Passengers are to be permitted to go in the Mail Boat, by Command of the Postmaster General.—	
		1. 0	Number of Watermen with the Boat 6	
		30	Arrived across the Passage at 2.35. *Dinner 30 mins*	
Bradley	27	4.20	Cardiff 7.25, *Supper 30 mins*	
		30		
,,	12	1.55	Cowbridge 10.35	
,,	18	2.50	Tybach 1.25 A.M.	
Marmont	16	2.25	Swansea 3.50, *Breakfast 30 mins* (T.P.)	
		30		
Nott	27	4.35	Carmarthen 9, *Refreshment 30 mins*	
		30		
,,	32	5.15	Haverfordwest 2.45	
Owen	9	1.20	Milford 4.5 P.M.	
	151	27.0		

Packet sailed at—

(The bill shows a particular state of wind and tide so must represent a specific occasion, perhaps a journey by Hasker. If so, he should be rebuked for having omitted to note the number of passengers on the boat and the time of the sailing of the Packet for Waterford.)

This passage is three miles wide at High Water and I have often crossed it in 20 minutes, but sometimes, when the Wind blows strong with the Tide, it cannot be crossed in less than two hours & ½. In these cases they are obliged to row about 3 miles up the River and cross to Chapel Rock, for which purpose the Proprietors of the Mail Coach engage with the Proprietors of the Passage to furnish six watermen.

UP

Leaves Milford at 9 o'clock with Irish Mail. Carmarthen 3.35 P.M. *Dinner 35 mins.* Swansea 8.40 P.M. (T.P.). Cardiff 4.20 A.M., *Breakfast 30 mins.* New Passage 9.10, Tide 2 hours flood, wind S.S.W. Arrived across Passage 10.40, 5 passengers, 6 watermen, 1½ *hours allowed for crossing and refreshment* (no margin for the latter in this case). Bristol 12 noon.

This Coach starts at nine o'Clock in Summer and eight in Winter, except a packet is in sight, in which case they stay for the Mail. This Coach is worked so bad that it is almost sufficient employ for a Superintendant. Not a patent Coach.

Oxford to Bristol

	D.	T.A.		No. 26
			P.O. Oxford 5	A.M.
Costar	37	5.20	Cirencester 10.20, *Breakfast 30 mins*	,,
		30		
Pickwick	33	4.50	Bath 3.40, *Dinner 30 mins*	P.M.
		30		
,,	13	1.50	Bristol 6	,,
	83	13. 0		

This is not a patent Coach and never has given any trouble. This shows the difference of Coachmasters—it never, I may say arrives at Bristol later than 6, nor at Oxford later than 10—seldom so late.

Bristol to Oxford

Leaves P.O. Bristol at 7.30 A.M. Bath 9.30 O.B. *30 mins.* Cirencester 3 P.M. *Dinner & O.B. 1 hour.* Oxford 9. 30 P.M.

On the return journey (only) Fairford and Farringdon are shown on the time-bill. A time-piece was carried.

Oxford to Gloucester

	D.	T.A.		No. 27
			Oxford 3.55	A.M.
			10 Minutes after the arrival of the Worcester Mail from London	
Costar	11½	1.30	Witney 5.25	,,
Stephens	7¼	55	Burford 6.20, *Breakfast 20 mins*	,,
		20		
James Heath	9	1.15	Northleach 7.55	,,
Moses Heath	12¾	1.55	Cheltenham 9.50	,,
John Heath	9½	1.35	Gloucester 11.25	,,
	50	7.20		

*This Coach does not start from Oxford quite so soon as the Bill expresses
—but frequently it is at Gloucester by 12 Noon.*

Gloucester to Oxford

Leaves Gloucester at 3 P.M. Arrives at Oxford 10.30 P.M. No halts shown but
20 minutes more allowed over the whole journey. An error in addition on the
time-bill makes the time the same as the outward journey.

*This Coach has not been too late for the Worcester Mail but once in four
years, which time it has run; though it is only directed to arrive there 15
Mts before the Worcester, which brings its mail on to London.* (The up
Worcester Mail is due at Oxford at 10.45, leaving for London at 11.10.)

Palmer said that in his absence in 1787 Bonnor had turned out the
contractors of this coach as they had refused to use one of his Besant
models. Apparently no one would then take the service on until
Hasker got it re-started on April the 5th, 1794.

Hereford and Worcester

	D.	T.A.		No. 28
			Hereford P.O. 7	A.M.
Mr Mason	16	2.40	Ledbury 9.40	,,
			Sent away at 9.55	,,
	16	2.40	Worcester 12.35	P.M.
			Returned	
			Worcester P.O. 12.40	,,
	16	2.40	Ledbury 3.20	,,
			Sent away at 3.35	,,
	16	2.40	Hereford 6.15	,,

This Coach is only 3 days a week.

This bill is another unique specimen. It is called not a 'Time-bill'
but a 'Way-bill' and must have been designed for duty for both when
it was still a horse-post 'ride'—before the coach or its predecessor,
the diligence, started running. In that time the service was worked
by 'Postmaster, Hereford' still printed on the bill. It is footed 'Return
each Way-Bill (by the first Post) to

S. Woodcock
Surveyor, *Glocester.*'
and has the following instead of the usual footnote—

'N.B. This Mail must be conveyed at the Rate of Six Miles in the Hour at least, and the Way-Bill truly and exactly dated at each Stage. Every Deputy or Contractor will be responsible (at their Peril) for the regular Performance of their Riding Duty. And if any Post-Boy or Rider, carrying this Mail, is found loitering on the Road, he will be committed to the House of Correction, and confined to hard Labour for one Month.'

It is here in use as a time-bill and not a way-bill but no time-piece appears to have been issued.

Ludlow and Worcester

	D.	T.A.		No. 29
			P.O. Ludlow 7	A.M.
Dukes	9	1.20	Tetbury 8.20	,,
Knowles	23	3.40	Worcester 12	,,
	32	5.0		
			Returned	
			P.O. Worcester 2	P.M.
Knowles	23	3.40	Tetbury 5.40	,,
Dukes	9	1.20	P.O. Ludlow 7	

This Coach is only three times a week.

A time-piece was carried.

Birmingham and Bristol

	D.	T.A.		No. 30
			P.O. Birmingham 5	P.M.
Waddel	14	1.45	Bromsgrove 6.45	,,
Healey	13	1.40	Worcester 8.25, *Supper 20 mins*	,,
		20		
Davis	16	2.30	Tewkesbury 11.15	,,
Philpott	11	1.40	Gloucester 12.55, *O.D. 10 m.*	A.M.
		10	N.B. The Wooten Bag to be left at Cambridge Inn.	
Sydney	16	2.20	Newport 3.25	,,
Weeks	18	2.30	Bristol 5.55	,,
	88	12.53		

This Coach does a great deal of duty and carries the great Cross Mail. It never, till my last journey on that road, during the month of March 1797, arrived at Bristol till seven o'Clock, or at Birmingham till nine, though the bill is made out to arrive a full hour earlier each way. I knew it would be of the greatest service to the Letters going Northward, save time at Litchfield and give an earlier delivery at Birmingham; but till this journey never could induce the Contractors to keep time.

UP

Leaves Bristol at 7 P.M. Newport 9.30 *Supper 20 mins.* 'N.B. The Wooten Bag to be left at Cambridge Inn.' Worcester 4.30 A.M. *O.B. 10 mins.* Birmingham 8 A.M.

York to Scarborough

	D.	T.A.		Nos. 31 & 32
			York 12.20. (60 mins after the arrival of all mails)	A.M.
Batty & Pulleyn	10½	1.25	Spittal Beck 1.45	,,
Yacker & Weatherhead	7½	1.15 20	Malton 3, *O.B. 20 mins*	,,
Marfleet, Dale, & Prudence	22 40	3.30 6.30	Scarborough 6.50	,,
			Returned	
			From Scarborough 2	P.M.
Marfield, Dale, & Prudence	22	3.30	Malton 5.45 Mail received from Whitby at— Received Mail from Bridlington at	,, ,, ,,
		15	*Tea 15 mins*	
Yacker & Weatherhead	7½	1.15	Spittal Beck 7.15	,,
Batty & Pulleyn	10½ 40	1.25 6.40	York 8.40	,,

*This Mail Coach is four times a week to & from York & Scarboro &
three time a week to and from York & Whitby. The other days, to each
place the mail is carried by horse to complete the 7 days a week. The Malton
& Scarboro roads divide at Malton.*

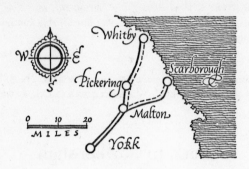

*The double black line; every day Coach to Malton. The single black
line: 4 times a week to Scarboro. The single black line; 3 times a week to
Whitby. The red line [here shown as a dotted line]; as described—the
ride.*

York to Whitby

The same contractors as above. Leaves York at the same time. Pickering
4.50 A.M. Scarborough 8.20 A.M.

Leaves Whitby 12, Noon. Malton 5.30. Awaits the mail from Scarborough
and Bridlington. *Tea 15 mins.* York 8.25 P.M.

Hull and Liverpool

1st Day

	D.	T.A.		No. 33
			Hull P.O. 3.15	P.M.
Baker	12	1.45	Bishop Burton 5	,,
Heard	15	2.15	Barnaby Moor 7.15	,,
Hartley	12	1.40	York 8.55 (T.P.), *Refreshments &c 3 hrs*	,,
		3. 0		

2nd Day

	D.	T.A.		
Backhouse				
& Pulleyn	10	1.15	Tadcaster 1.15	A.M.
Hartley	14	2.15	Leeds 3.30 (T.P.), *P.B. 15 mins*	,,
		15		

	D.	T.A.		No. 33
Hindle	18	3.25	Halifax 7.10, *Breakfast 30 mins*	A.M.
		30		
Howarth	12	2.30	Littleborough 10	,,
Paterson	16	2.25	Manchester 12.20 (T.P.), *Dinner 1 hr*	P.M.
		1.0		
,,	19	2.30	Warrington 4	,,
Bowman	18	2.30	Liverpool 6.30	,,
	146	27.15		

There is not a Coach in the Kingdom that does more duty than this throughout. From Hull it brings the Bye Letters for the North, West, and South, and the London Bags thro Beverly &c to York. At York it takes all the Correspondence from the North for Leeds &c &c; at Bramham Moor for the Glasgow Coach; at Leeds it receives the London Bags for Bradford, Halifax &c, and goes on to Manchester and Liverpool with the great Bye cross Correspondence—and visa versi returning. At Warrington it leaves the Chester and Irish letters and, in its way to York, returning, takes them up again, waiting till ¼ past 6 if its not in.

Liverpool to Hull

Leaves P.O. Liverpool 3.30 A.M. Manchester 8.30 (T.P.) *Breakfast 45 mins.* Halifax 2 P.M. *Dinner 45 mins.* Leeds 6.25 *Tea 20 mins* (T.P.). York 10.10 P.M. (T.P.). No regular times given for wait, but note 'Left at 12 (midnight) with London mail'. The Mail from London, if running to time is due at 11.35.

Some part of this road [i.e. between Halifax and Leeds, across the Pennines] is so very deep with clay that it cannot be performed at more than 5 miles an hour—but it so happens that the correspondence will admit it.

Glasgow and Ayr

	D.	T.A.		No. 34
			P.O. Glasgow 9	A.M.
Buchanan &				
Corson	22½	4.0	Kilmarnock 1	P.M.
Dun	12½	2.0	Ayr 3	P.M.
			Return	
			Ayr 8	A.M.
Dun	12½	2.0	Kilmarnock 10	,,
Corson &				
Buchanan	22½	4.0	Glasgow 2	P.M.

259

A smaller sized bill, very plain. There is a space for the guard's name, departing and returning, but there is no time-piece mentioned and nothing at all on the foot of the bill to indicate who it is to be forwarded to.

London and Steyning

(Through Croydon, Godstone, East Grinstead, Uckfield, Lewes, Brighthelmstone, and Shoreham)

	D.	T.A.		*No. 35*
			G.P.O. 8	P.M.
Holding, of the Borough	31	5.10	East Grinstead 1.10, *O.B. 15 mins*	A.M.
		15		
Dunstone, of Lewes	29	4.50	Brighthelmstone 6.15	,,
Steer, of Steyning	13	2.10	Steyning 8.25	,,
	73	12.25		

The Mail to Arundel at
The Mail to Worthing at

UP

Leaves Steyning P.O. 5 P.M. East Grinstead 12 A.M. *O.B. 15 mins.* London G.P.O. 5.25 A.M.

'This Time to be punctually observed, that the Mail may be in London, at Twenty-five Minutes past Five o'Clock in the Morning.',

No time-piece is mentioned as being sent out on this bill. At each stage a blank left for 'Postmaster' to sign. The bill is signed by B. J. Bartlett, Surveyor, G.P.O.

Brighthelmstone (written Bristelmestune in Domesday Book) was altered to Brighton early in the 19th century.

London and Hastings

(Thro' Bromley, Sevenoaks, Tunbridge, Lamberhurst, and Battle)

	D.	T.A.		*No. 36*
			G.P.O. 8	P.M.
Holding of the Borough	10	1.40	Bromley 9.40	,,

	D.	T.A.		
			G.P.O. 8	*No. 36*
				P.M.
Holding of				
the Borough	14	2.20	Sevenoaks 12	A.M.
			And the Mail from Hastings at—	
Sprange of				
Tunbridge	17	2.50	Lamberhurst 2.50 *O.B. 1 hour*	,,
		1. 0		
Sharpe of				
Lamberhurst	16	2.40	Battle 6.30, *O.B. 10 mins*	,,
		10		
Lidwell of				
Battle	8	1.20	Hastings 8	,,
	65	12.12		

'This Time must be punctually observed, that the Mail may be at Hastings at Eight o'Clock in the Morning.'

			Returned	
			Hastings P.O. 4	P.M.
Lidwell, of				
Battle	8	1.20	Battle 5.20, *O.B. 10 mins*	,,
		10		
Sharpe, of				
Lamberhurst	16	2.40	Lamberhurst 8.10, *O.B. 1 hour*	,,
		1. 0	The Mail from Rye at o'Clock	
			The Mail from Tenterden at o'Clock	
Sprange, of				
Tunbridge	17	2.50	Sevenoaks 12	A.M.
			The Down Mail from London at o'Clock	
Holding of				
the Borough	14	2.20	Bromley 2.20	A.M.
,,	10	1.40	London G.P.O. 4	,,
	65	12. 0		

'This Time must be punctually observed that the Mail may be delivered at the General Post-Office, at Four o'Clock in the Morning.'

As in the Steyning bill, no time-piece mentioned, a blank for postmaster's signature at each stage, the word 'Received' at each stop instead of 'Arrived'. Bill signed by B. J. Bartlett, Surveyor, G.P.O.

CHAPTER XI

Instructions and Circulars, 1792 to 1817

THERE are two bound volumes of these covering the years 1792 to 1840 when most of the mail-coaches had been run off the roads by the railways. The following selection is only made from the years of Hasker's reign, which ended in 1817. The remainder are very similar, the succeeding Superintendents reiterating complaints about the same faults which Hasker had so often found. They were also worded on his model, though the individual touch of the old master is just missed. The last but one in the complete series, dated 1840, has a familiar ring—

> Complaints having been made by Mail Contractors that their Trade is seriously interfered with by Mail Guards carrying Parcels &c. I am commanded to acquaint them that they are strictly prohibited, under pain of dismissal from carrying Parcels of any description on their own account, *whether they have the permission of the Contractor or not*, for so doing.
>
> If therefore, after this Notice, any Guard shall carry Parcels, he will do so with a full knowledge of the consequences that will follow such a proceeding.

All these papers, with a few exceptions, are printed notices, most of them in the form of circular letters sent out to postmasters, contractors, or guards. Some are notices of lost mail-bags or luggage with rewards offered for their recovery, or notices of the kind mentioned on p. 59, where an offender against the rule of giving way for the Mail is made to sign a public apology which is then exhibited in the window of every post office in the kingdom, a painless form of the pillory that was doubtless more effectual than a local prosecution.

For many years after Palmer's plan had come into existence no mail-coach appears to have been held up by highwaymen, though there had been occasional robberies from the mail-box, either by forcing the lock at a propitious moment on a dark and stormy night when the guard and coachman were helping to put a new team to at a change, or simply through the guard neglecting to lock it. But after 1800 this complete immunity ceased. New tacticians came on the road who found it easy to hold up the coach by placing obstructions in its way. Felled trees were used coupled by harrows and ploughs to cripple the poor horses. Notices then became frequent stating where the hold-up took place and offering large rewards for information leading to the detection of the felons. In these it is only stated that an attempt had been made to hold up the Mail, never that it had been actually stopped or robbed, though it is known from the files of the press that there were several successes for the robbers and also that on some occasions the guard used his blunderbuss effectively.

The first circulars were issued in 1792 when Palmer had left the Post Office under the order of suspension. In June his name had been deleted from the new establishment, but Hasker did not yet sign with his full new rank of Surveyor and Superintendent. These printed circulars, notices, and open forms (with appropriate gaps for filling in) are not so intimate as the letters or the confidential notes on the time-bills but they keep us in touch with the Superintendent and his management of the 'concern' for the remaining twenty years of his reign.

To the GUARDS   G.P.O. Aug 29 1792
When any accident happens, write what it was on the time-bill, at the very next Stage, and the next Day give a more particular description of it, by Letter to me—how it happened, the Cause, what was broke, and what Damage done;—mind and do not neglect this.

Thomas Hasker
Superintendant of Mails

To the GUARDS   G.P.O. Jan 4th 1793
Sir,
    I am commanded by the Postmaster-General to desire you will be particularly active at changing and stopping Places—and to use every Exertion to keep the Coach to Time at this inclement

season, or give a Reason why;—but take Care that Reason is a sufficient One or you will be punished.

Yours &c
Thomas Hasker

If Snow is not on the Ground, it is expected you will see the Duty is performed in Time.

To the Guards   G.P.O. July 23 1794
Sir,

Notwithstanding the Instructions given to the Mail Guards, so many Faults are continually committed, and so much negligence exists, that several have been dismissed, and others suspended during the last Week; it may fairly be supposed that they never have read their Instructions, if they have, they have forgot or lost them.

This is therefore to inform them that if they do not obey such Directions thoroughly, which they have sworn they would, they will be dismissed and prosecuted; the Duty is very plain, and any Guard can do it if he will.

Thomas Hasker
Superintendant of Mails

If you have lost your Sheet of Instructions apply to this Office for a fresh one.

G.P.O. April 3d 1795

ANOTHER WARNING TO MAIL-GUARDS

I am very sorry to be under the Necessity of addressing the Mail Guards on such a subject; but though every Direction and Inspection is given them, and they are fully informed of the Punishments that must follow if they do not do their Duty, yet, notwithstanding this, and every Admonition given in every way that can be devised, four Guards, that were looked upon as very good ones, have in the course of the last Week, been guilty of such Misconduct as obliges their Discharge; for the Public, who trust their Lives and Property in the Conduct of the Office, can never be expected to suffer such neglect to pass unnoticed.

The four Guards discharged are,—

J. RAPER, for leaving his Mail-Box unlocked at Ferrybridge, while the Mail was therein.

WILLIAM JOBLIN, for going to the Office at York, drunk, to fetch his Mail, though barely able to stand; and for abusing the Post-Master, &c.

W. BARKER, for bringing the Mail on the outside of the Mail-Box, and on the Roof, and converting the Mail-box to another use.

W. FIELD, for going from London to Newmarket without Fire-arms.

T. Hasker.

CONTRACTOR'S POWERS TO INSPECT

To the Guards   May 19th, 1795

Many Proprietors having complained that the Guards carry Fish, Poultry, and other parcels, on their own account, in the Mail Box, they are hereby ordered always to permit the Contractors to examine it; and if any such Parcels are found, the Proprietors may use their Pleasure in disposing of them.

THOMAS HASKER
Surveyor and Superintendant of Mails.

CLOCK TIME (a printed form)   General Post-Office
179

SIR,

By the Bill of this Day, you have omitted writing down the Guards Names and Number of the Coach. I must beg you be very particular in dating the Bills, also by Time Piece and Town Clocks both.

Your most obedient Servant
THOMAS HASKER
Surveyor and Superintendant of Mails

Postmaster

CIRCULAR

General Post-Office
February 10th, 1798

SIR,

I Have the Honor of the Commands of the Postmaster General, to make known to you, that should you retire from the Public Line and quit your Inn, you must not expect to continue in the Mail Coach Concern; for so many Innholders are quitting their Inns, and retaining Possession of their Coaches, that will be the cause of bringing forward very formidable Oppositions by those Persons who have taken such Inns.

Their Lordships are obliged to give this Order from some Occurrences that have recently happened.

I am,
SIR,
Your most humble Servant,
THOMAS HASKER
Surveyor and Superintendant of Mails

(addressed to Mail-
Coach Contractors)

PUNCTUALITY (printed form to Mail Guards)   General Post-Office
February 8, 1799.

SIR,

THE late heavy Fall of Snow having occasioned great Irregularity in the Mail Coach System, I have the Commands of my Lords the Postmaster-General to direct, as the Roads are now open, that you do not delay longer in Towns than the Time allowed by the Time Bill; that you do not stop at Inn or Alehouses, but that you use all your Time on the Road to the End of *your* Journey,—and that you give Orders to Horsekeepers to have the Horses ready harnessed at the Time the Coach ought to arrive, and should they not, that you assist them as much as your other Duty will allow. And that you do every Thing in your Power to get your Coach regular. A proper Notice will be taken of your Conduct.

THOMAS HASKER
Surveyor & Supt. of M.C.

LOST VEHICLES (printed form)   General Post-Office
April 27th, 1799

SIR,

Several Mail Coaches being still missing that were obstructed in the Snow since the 1st of February last, this is to desire you will immediately represent to me an Account of all spare patent Mail

Coaches that are in the Stage where you travel over, whether they are regular Stationed Mail Coaches, or Extra spare Coaches, and the exact Place where they are, either in *Barn*, *Field*, *Yard* or *Coach-house*, and the Condition they are in, and if they have Seats, Rugs, and Windows complete.

THOMAS HASKER.

To Mail Guards   Surveyor and Superintendant of Mail Coaches.

PUNCTUALITY   General Post-Office
                                                    Nov 13, 1799

SIR,

YOU are desired to use every Endeavour to keep Time on the Ground you are Guard to, and if there is any Error in the Horses, Coachmen, or Harness, civilly represent it to the Proprietor to whom they belong.—You will also write me a Letter informing me of the Condition your Horses and Harness are in on every Stage, and if a good willing Coachman, and state why you cannot keep Time, that I may directly apply to the Contractors if necessary.

Your's, &c.

Mail Guard   T. Hasker.

Surveyor and Superintendant of Mail Coaches

To the GUARDS

You are desired to leave two or three of the enclosed Bills at every Village you pass through in your journey, and request they may be posted up in some conspicuous Place;—leave a bill or two also at the Houses you stop to Water at; you need not leave them at the Post-Offices, as they will be sent there.

Your's, &c.

THOMAS HASKER.

(enclosure to above)

Caution to Waggoners (a Government publication issued March 20, 1800). Possibly this is the 'Bill' referred to in the foregoing instruction).

It gives a limitation on the number of horses which may be used with specified breadth of tyre on Turnpike roads. Ref. Act 13 George III, C. 84.

Breadth of wheels				No. of Horses				
Four-Wheel Carriages	9	inches		8 Horses and no more.				
,, ,, ,,	6	,,		6	,,	,,	,,	,,
Less than	6	,,		4	,,	,,	,,	,,
Two-Wheel Carriages	9	,,		5	,,	,,	,,	,,
,, ,, ,,	6	,,		4	,,	,,	,,	,,
Less than	6	,,		3	,,	,,	,,	,,

And the Wheels to roll on a *Flat* Surface

UNAUTHORISED DRINKS, PASSENGERS, AND   General Post-Office 1800
PARCELS.

SIR

STOPPING at Alehouses on the Road between Stage and Stage, under Pretence of watering Horses, but in Reality to drink, have been found very detrimental to the Service; I have, in Conjunction with many Principal Mail Coach Contractors, determined to anihilate so shameful a Practice, and I have my Lords the Postmaster-General's Commands to send the enclosed Letter to all the Guards, and this to you, desiring you will immediately give full Directions to your Coachmen not to go into, or even stop at such Houses—it is only done (under Pretence of Necessity) to carry on bad Commerce, to the Injury of yourselves, by illegal Practices of taking up Passengers and Parcels which are never accounted for.

I am
SIR,

To Mail   Your most humble Servant,
Contractors   T. Hasker.

'ADDITIONAL MILEAGE'—A BONUS?   General Post Office
(printed form to Contractors)

SIR

I am commanded by the Postmaster General to inform you that the Time lost on your Ground, between   and   by the Mail Coach, as it was on its way to   was Minutes; and I am further directed to desire you will immediately give some Orders that Time may be kept, for it is only to such as

keep Time and do their Duty well, the additional Mileage can be
given.

> I am
> By Command of the Postmaster General,
> Your most humble Servant,

To the Mail Guards

In addition to your instructions I need not add one word if you
would perform your duty therein set down, and which you solemnly
undertake; but however, at a time when every minute should be
used on the road, and not one wasted at Calling Houses, I have the
commands of my Lords, the Postmaster General, to direct you, at
the peril of your situation, and with an assurance that you shall
forfeit it if found out that you do not quit your Coach to go into
any Public House, or stop at any place on the road, but where you
have letters to leave, or real coach business to perform, as from the
dearness of corn and the weakness of horses no time must be wasted;
see to this, and if coachmen will stop, write me of their misconduct.
Read the instructions sent herewith.

> T. Hasker.

General Post-Office
6th February, 1800.

(Circular to all concerned)   General Post-Office
                                       February   1801

SIR

I send you the enclosed, being the Case and Punishment of a
Coachman who received Money for Passengers for his Master's
Use, and feloniously witheld it; for which offence he is condemned
to Transportation for Seven Years.

The Intent of this is to prevent such Crimes in Coachmen and
Guards for the future, as a Committee of Proprietors in *London*
are entering into an Association to prosecute all such Offenders.

> I am,
> SIR,
> Your's &c.

(enclosure)

Warning notice re JOHN SPERINK, coachman of the Banbury
coach (employed by Thomas Fagg) who pocketed part of the fares

of passengers after leaving the Bell and Crown Inn, Holborn. Prosecuted at the Old Bailey. Sentenced to be transported for seven years.

'Guards by dividing any of the money which a coachman may secrete or keep back from his master, are liable to punishment as if they had themselves taken it.'

To the Guards

MANY Proprietors having complained that the Guards carry Fish, Poultry, and other Parcels, on their own Account, in the Mail Box: They are hereby ordered always to permit the Contractors to examine it, and if any Parcels are found the Proprietors are desired to take them to their own use, or send them to a Poor House, Hospital, or to some charitable Purpose, immediately informing me of the Delinquent.

THOMAS HASKER
Surveyor and Superintendant of Mail Coaches.

January 1st 1802

To the Mail Guards
(a repetition of circular for February 6th with postscript)
N.B. I repeat this letter in consequence of recent circumstances, particularly the Bristol Mail Coach Horses running from the Magpye, Hounslow Heath, with the Coach, while the servants were in the Ale-house drinking.

To MAIL COACHMEN and GUARDS
A further warning against carrying 'any Game, Fish, Fowl, Package or Parcels whatsoever clandestinely'. A warrant is out against a guard of the Bristol Mail (absconded) who had received stolen poultry. 1st January 1803

CAUTION to all DRAYMEN and CARMEN
(Public apology)

I, WILLIAM PARKINS, Drayman to Messrs. Sharpe, Lucas & Co. did on Wednesday Evening, the 24th Day of November, entangle the Horses of the Exeter Mail Coach, and did not stop when called upon, by which means the Pole, Splinter Bar, and

Traces were broken, and the Lives of the Coachman and Passengers much endangered; for this a Prosecution was commenced against me, but upon me acknowledging my Fault, thus publicly begging Pardon, and in further Consideration of my Wife and Family, the Prosecutor, Mr *John Vidler*, has agreed to withdraw the same, my Master being Security for my paying the Expenses.

(Sign'd)   WILLIAM PARKINS

Witness,

(Sign'd)   T. Daniel, Mail Coach Factory
Millbank, Novr. 25th, 1802.

Warning in Hasker's handwriting about guards 'seen about the Town for the purpose of dealing buying selling or trafficking after the Coach has arrived two hours or until after 6 o'clock in the evening'.

Memo in Hasker's handwriting.

T. Kitchen

Is fined 5 Guineas for suffering a man to ride on the roof of the Mail Coach on Thursday last. If he had not owned the truth he would have been dismissed. Which he may be now if he had rather than pay the Fine for the Fund.

General Post Office   February 5th 1803

GENERAL POST-OFFICE
March 10th 1803

SIR,

FOR some Time past, under the Excuse of former Dearness of Provender and various others, the Contractors have frequently booked two Outside Passengers and carried extra Luggage; but their Lordships the Postmaster-General, having granted a Half-penny per Mile, in addition to the Penny already given for carrying the Mail by Patent Mail Coaches, they do expect in future that no extra Passengers may be booked or carried, nor any Luggage tied on the Roof of such Patent Mail Coaches, and are resolved to dismiss or prosecute for any such Breach of Contract.

I am, Sir

Your most humble Servant,

To Mail Contractors   Thomas Hasker.

To the MAIL GUARDS

GENERAL POST-OFFICE
April 23rd, 1803

IN consequence of late Disasters, and Information of further intended Depredations,[1] (as you was informed on the Bills the 20th Instant) you are again directed never to lose sight of your Mail Box, but when obliged so to do on your Way to and from the Post-Offices.—This is a further warning to you; but read your Instructions, and attend thoroughly thereto.

THOs. HASKER.

P.S. Four Mail Guards are turned from the Service this Week, for taking up People on their Mail Box or quitting it, namely, G. Jackman, T. Smith, R. Carter and C. Tompkins.

(in handwriting) The Guards are desired to be particularly careful to see that their Sacks are always tied, that the Bags contained therein may not drop out.

General Post Office
May 23rd 1803

Letter from John Hughes of the Stamp Office re taxing of coach horses. Dated 11 July 1798.

To the Mail Guards

GENERAL POST-OFFICE
June 14th, 1803.

HALF my Time is employed in receiving and answering Letters of Complaint from Passengers respecting the improper Conduct and impertinent Language of Guards. I am very sorry to dismiss sober honest Men, but I must have Civility also, and when you behave impertinently to Passengers, they find out some other Error to couple their Complaint with, that nothing less than Dismission can succeed. This plainly shows how circumspect Guards should be in their Behaviour, and I must insist that you conduct yourself so properly in all your Words and Actions as to prevent Complaints.

Yours, &c.

T. HASKER.

[1] Handwritten note by H 'information is received that several robberies similar to that of the Chester Mail Coach will be attempted'.

To the Guards (in handwriting)   General Post Office
                                                  October 22 1803

A Complaint has been made by the Lord Mayor to Mr Freeling
of the Mail Guards blowing their Horns of a Sunday going through
the Streets during the time of Divine Service. You will take notice
if any Guard is known to blow his Horn coming in of a Sunday
Morning or going out in the Evening they will be fined severely
for it.

Tho. Hasker

(In H's handwriting)

Mr Hasker was obliged to leave Town or would have delivered
the purport of the underwritten to the Guards.

Gentlemen,

I am very sorry to order in all the Guards to witness a dismissal
of one old in the Service but so imperious is the duty that
was he my Brother he must be dismissed. Indeed I do not think
there is a Guard who hears this but will say a Man who goes into
an Alehouse stays to drink (and at Brentford) at the dusk of Morning
leaving his Mail Box unlocked Deserves to loose his situation.
And he is dismissed accordingly. And I am sure I need not tell
you to avoid such misconduct—to read your instructions and mind
them. I am the more sorry for this as guards who have been some
time in the service are fit for no other duty.

(Circular)   *To the Guards*

YOU know the Bags, whether General, Bye, or Short, you
ought to receive and deliver in your Duty.

If you do not receive them, or if any Impediment happens, or
Error occurs, to vary the regular Progress thereof, inform me,
saying where the Bag was from or going to, and specify the Day
and Date, with every Particular, by the first Post.

Your's &c.

General Post-Office   THOs. HASKER.

April 20, 1804

(Bill)   GENERAL POST OFFICE, 16th June 1804

SOME evil-disposed Persons, having on the Night of the 5th Instant, placed in the Middle of the Turnpike Road, near Welwyn Green, a Gate, and have set up at the entrance of Welwyn Lane two other Gates a-cross the Road, evidently for the purpose of impeding the Passage of the Mail Coaches and other Carriages, and of injuring the Persons of the Passengers and the Property of the Masters.

Whoever will give Information, so that one or more of the Persons concerned in this Outrage may be discovered and brought to Justice, shall receive a Reward of

TWENTY POUNDS.

By Command of His Majesty's Postmaster-General
Francis Freeling
Secretary.

Caution to Carters

WHEREAS I *Edward Monk*, Servant to James Smith, of Pendlebury, near Manchester, Farmer, did, on Tuesday the Twenty-fourth Day of July last, misconduct myself in the driving of my Master's Cart on the Pendleton Road, by not only driving furiously in the Cart, but damaging the York and Liverpool

MAIL COACH,

and endangering the lives of the Passengers: for which

The CONDUCTOR

of the Mails has directed a Prosecution against me, but on Condition of this my public Submission, and paying the Expenses attending it, all Proceedings have been discontinued: and I thank the CONDUCTOR and the Gentlemen whose lives I endangered, for their very great Lenity shown me; and I trust this will operate as a Caution to all Carters or Persons who may have the Care of Carts and other Carriages, to behave themselves peaceably and properly on the King's Highway. Witness my Hand the Second Day of August, 1804.

Signed in the Presence of	the Mark of
James Hankin, Clerk to Mr	X
Redhead, Attorney at Law,	EDWARD MONK
Manchester	

To the Mail Guards

GENERAL POST-OFFICE
November 7th, 1804.

MAIL GUARDS are fully apprised of their Duty by every Direction and Instruction given them; they are also fully informed of the Punishment that must overtake them, if they are found out in breaking or neglecting it; but so many Guards have of late, in defiance of every Admonition, been guilty of great Misconduct, that it has been determined on to dismiss some, fully hoping that such a Step will act as an Example to the Remainder; but should it not, for any Breach of their Instructions, they will be dismissed.

The Guards discharged are,

COX, for having taken up a parcel at Bristol to deliver at Tetbury, with the Carriage paid, which Parcel was found in his Mail Box.

FAGAN, for carrying Fish and not paying the Carriage; it was taken from the Mail Box,

BATES, for suffering a Passenger above the Number; the pay of whom and the other Outside, the Proprietors say would not have been brought to an Account but being inspected; and for other Breaches of Faith,

MOFFATT, for being drunk, forgetting his Bags, and having to go back for them, by Order of the Duke of Montrose.

KELLY, for Drunkenness, leaving his Bags wrong, and disobedience of Orders.

PAINTER for Smuggling.

(Circular)

To the Mail-Coach Proprietors.

General Post-Office,
Sept. 4th, 1804.

SIR,

In case of any Application from the Postmaster of your Town for Assistance to forward any Expresses on the Government Service, *in the Event of any urgent Necessity*, My Lords the Postmaster-General assure themselves that you will readily and cheerfully afford such Assistance to the utmost of your Power.

I am, Sir,

Your most humble Servant,

THOMAS HASKER.

(Circular)   General Post-Office,
                                                MARCH 18th, 1805
SIR,

   IT has been represented and proved by Mr Willan, that the
Guard of the York-Mail brought up, on his own Account, either
gratis or for pay to himself, several Passengers, from Huntingdon
to London,—This is to give Notice, that the Guards are expressly
forbid by their Instructions, not only to intermeddle with the
affairs of the Coach, which evidently belongs to the Coachmasters
and their Servants, and with which the Guards can have no business,
but are directed and swear to give Notice if the Coachman take up
any Passengers that they do not account for to their Masters.

                          I am,

                             Sir,

To the Mail-Coach   Your most humble Servant,
Contractors.   THOs HASKER.

Regulations for carriages during the funeral procession of Lord
Nelson. Issued at the Mansion House, Friday, Jan. 3 1806

                                     GENERAL POST-OFFICE
                                          April 5, 1805.
SIR,

   I AM desired by my Lords the Postmaster-General to represent
their Commands, that you will examine the Mail Box as often as
possible, to see that the Guards do not carry any Parcels, Packages,
or Goods, on their own Account, and any Article in their Possession,
that they do not properly account for, take away and dispose of it
as you think best, by giving it to any Workhouse, Hospital, or
other charitable Institution, afterwards informing me of the Particulars.

                          I am,

                             SIR,

To all Contractors   Your most humble Servant,
                                     THOMAS HASKER.
SIR,

   I REQUEST to know how many *Horses* you have lost by Death,

or rendered unfit for any Service in the Mails or other Stage Coaches since the 5th of April last Year.

I am, Sir,

Your most humble Servant,

To Contractors   THOMAS HASKER.

(Circular)

GENERAL POST OFFICE
Edinburgh, 14th April 1806.

WHEREAS Information has been received, that early this Morning His Majesty's Mail Coach was obstructed in coming out of Dumfries by some evil-disposed Person or Persons having maliciously placed Boughs or Branches of Trees across the Turnpike Road, by which the conveyance of the Mail was much retarded, and the lives of the Passengers endangered;

A Reward of TWENTY POUNDS Sterling is hereby offered to any Person who will give such Information as will lead to the Discovery of the Person or Persons guilty of this atrocious Offence, to be paid upon Conviction.

By Order of the Postmasters General,

WILLIAM KERR, Secretary

To the Guards (in handwriting, not signed).

Three Irishmen are in Custody for Highway Robbery. One of them has confessed and declared that their purpose in going out was to rob the Mail Coach—their first step was to watch an opportunity and fire at the Guard which it is supposed might have been easily obtained as they are so frequently off their guard. They had Pistols found on them. It is therefore necessary in addition to your former instructions to direct that you are particularly vigilant & watchful, that you keep a quick eye to every Person stirring and that best possible condition and ready for instant Duty.

23rd March 1802 G.P.O.

LOST,

ON Monday night the 24th of February last, from the Mail Coach, between Haverfordwest and Milford, a large Canvas Parcel, containing Wearing Apparel, Bedding, Table Cloths, and Military Articles for an Officer going abroad. If the Finder will bring it, or any Part of it, to Mr Rees, of Haverfordwest, he will receive FIVE POUNDS for his Trouble. (torn)

GENERAL POST-OFFICE
June 29 1807

SIR

I send you a circular letter as forwarded to the Proprietors at the extremity of the Roads, and as this improper mode of loading the Mail Coaches has become too general to suffer it to continue, you will, with Civility, prevent all Attempts of the Proprietors to infringe on their Contract by such Practice; and, in Cases where it may be persisted in, inform me.

Yours, &c

Mail Guards (circular   THOMAS HASKER.
alluded to, missing)

GENERAL POST OFFICE
December 5th, 1811.

SIR

AT this Season and particularly this Year, when in consequence of the warm Autumn, and wet Weather, the Horses are very weak, and Roads very heavy, it is incumbent on you to use every possible exertion at Changing Places, and where Stoppages are made at Post Offices or otherwise; so that even if a minute can be saved in changing Horses, or going to and from the Offices, or where the Coachmen may necessarily stop, (for they must not be permitted to stop otherwise) by these and such Exertions (the Means of obtaining which occur every journey) it is expected the Mails will be kept more regular to Time than they have been some Days past.—On any Occurrence where you cannot keep Time, you are expected to write me particulars.

I am

Yours, &c.

Mail Guards   T. HASKER.

To the Mail Guards

General Post-Office
July 10th 1815

SIR

I have the Commands of my Lords the Postmaster General to inform you, that a Mail Coach and Horses were seized the 8th ultimo for having a Tub containing Smuggled Spirits regularly Booked but not Permitted. It being in a Box and sent as Parcel by the Coach, the Guard could not have anything to do with it, except he saw it; in which case it was his duty to have noticed to the Proprietors the dangerous risk they were likely to incur. But the intent of this is, to caution you against carrying any thing; and to remind you that you will find in your Printed Instructions sent Annually, that you are not to carry on any account whatever, for any person or yourself, any Parcel, Packet, or other Thing in your Mail Box or on the outside of the Coach. In short, read your Instructions, and abide by them; to which you are frequently directed to attend.

Yours &c
T. Hasker.

To the Mail Coach Proprietors   General Post-Office
                                                                                 July 10th, 1815

SIR

The Aberdeen and Edinborough Mail Coach and Horses having been seized on the 8th of last Month, for conveying, as Luggage, a Cask of Whiskey, which was discovered by an Officer of the Customs at North Queensferry. I have it in Commands from my Lords the Postmaster General to make the same known to you by a Circular Letter. The Commissioners of Customs having decided, that blame was attached to the Proprietors in not examining the Package by shaking, or otherwise, to endeavour to ascertain its contents, as in all cases the parties conveying illegal traffic make themselves responsible, they have, at the request of the Office, consented to release the Carriage and Horses, on the Proprietors paying all expenses, and remunerating the Seizing Officer.

As by Contract you are bound to save harmless the Postmaster General from all Forfeitures, Penalties, and Demands, which may happen by reason of any neglect or transgression with the Mail Coach, it becomes the more necessary to give you this as a caution for your future government.

I am
SIR
Your obedient Servant
T. Hasker.

General Post-Office
November 30th, 1815

WHEREAS some evil-disposed Persons late on the night or early on the Morning of the 19th November Instant, placed across the Turnpike Road, in different places, between Northwich and Warrington, Eight or Ten Gates and a Door; and within about a Mile of the Town of Warrington, a Broad Wheeled Cart across the centre of the Road, evidently with a view to cause destruction to His Majesty's Mail Coach, and to endanger the Lives of the Passengers, Coachman, and Guard, which was happily prevented by the Driver discovering the same in time to avoid them.

His Majesty's Postmaster-General, for discovering and bringing to Justice such attrocious Offenders, do hereby offer a REWARD of

FIFTY POUNDS

to any Person who shall discover the Offender or Offenders, so that one or more of them may be convicted of the Offence.

And in case any one of the Offenders will discover the Persons guilty of the same, he will be paid the same Reward, and be admitted an Evidence for the Crown.

By Command of the Postmaster-General
F. FREELING
Secretary.

TO THE MAIL GUARDS   General Post-Office
July 1816

As many accidents have happened by the improper loading of the Fire Arms, although the Guards have positive orders not to fire them wantonly, it is deemed proper to state to them—That the Top of the Powder Horn is a sufficient charge for the Blunderbuss, with ten or twelve shot the size of a pea,—That for the Pistols two-thirds of such a charge is proper,—That they must be particular to ram the charge well that air may not be confined between or beyond the charge,—And that they keep their Arms clean, and never loaded above a week.

If these rules are strictly observed, the like accidents will be avoided.

THOMAS HASKER

This is rather a puzzle. Perhaps the accidents happened at the weekly re-loading. The quickest and safest way of doing this would be to shoot off the old charge. If the weapons had been over-loaded there might be trouble.

The next, intended for circulation among the guards, is a slip of paper in Hasker's handwriting and the last document on which his signature appears.

If any Illness or Accident occasioned by Duty befalls a Guard, He must apply to me or any Clerk in this department, who will give him an order to Mr Heather or Mr Atkinson, as may be nearest to his abode, to obtain assistance.

Jany 15th 1817   T. Hasker.

CHAPTER XII

Palmer's Last Man

THAT last circular just quoted is perhaps the most revealing of all the Hasker papers. It shows that T.H. had managed to institute an arrangement whereby his guards could receive medical attention quickly and without having to pay for it. Formerly, they had first to settle their doctor's bill and then forward it to headquarters where it still could not be paid without the sanction of the P.M.G., so that the guard might be kept out of pocket for a long time or never get the money at all. Though Hasker growled menacingly all the while at the splendid *corps d'élite* he had dragooned he was exceedingly proud of them and looked after their interests well.

Hasker had seen the 'concern' through right from the very beginning into the period of its first consistent improvement. This was due to a number of factors which were not present when mail-coaches began running. The two main changes which were rapidly taking place were in the condition of the roads and the breed of horses. MacAdam had done much to improve the roads managed by the Turnpike Trusts. Telford had been busily occupied in the North, and in 1810 he came to Wales to carry out a survey for the Holyhead Road Commissioners, sponsored by the Government. He began work on this great undertaking in 1815. Some improvement in time and distance had been made ten years earlier, largely owing to the enterprise of Lawrence of the White Lion at Shrewsbury who (to quote from his epitaph again) had not only attracted the first mail-coach to his home town but was also instrumental in 'opening the great road through Wales between the United Kingdoms' (a reference to the recent Union with Ireland, though the Post Offices were not yet re-united). This road, made by a number of Turnpike Trusts, had been boldly thrust through the wild Pass of Nant Ffrancon at a thousand feet above sea-level. A great deal of it was bad and dangerous, and that going through the Pass, where the coachman must drive in darkness, was unwalled. But the Conway ferry (a much dreaded passage) was avoided by this route, and one mail-coach was allowed to use it. Now, however, the Irish Members of Parliament, who had for so long sat comfortably in Dublin, had to go to Westminster, and the accidents they met with travelling on this coach were largely responsible for the agitation which forced the Government to employ Telford. It was in 1817 that the Commissioners decided to eliminate the Bangor ferry as well and instructed Telford to prepare plans for a bridge over the Menai Straits.

Just at that juncture, Hasker handed over the reins to his successor, Charles Johnson. When Telford had completed his task on the Irish road, all the way between London and Holyhead, Hasker's ideal could surely be said to have been reached. The time for the Holyhead Mail (including stops) was shortened from 44 hours, 50 minutes, to 26 hours 55 minutes, the actual running-time being an average of 10 miles 1 furlong, an hour, between London and Holyhead, which meant speeding much faster at intervals to keep this up.

By this time, too, horse-breeders had made a speciality of the coach-horse. It was founded on the animal which had long been reared on the Cleveland Hills in Yorkshire. This Cleveland horse, given a fair dash of bloodstock, produced a mettlesome beast of good stamina, capable of keeping up the pace at a long swinging trot on moderately even ground, and springing hills at a gallop.

Reliability was already an established tradition and the saying 'Right as the Mail' which, as I have said, I can remember hearing, must have come into use about then. As the road surfaces and quality in horseflesh steadily improved, time-bills were speeded up, and a new generation of coachmen drove the Mails. The bulky man much given to the bottle became gradually extinct. Many of the younger men were spare, active fellows and teetotallers. Skill in driving, with a minimum use of the whip, had become a matter of pride, and the best coachmen were known 'down the road' as 'artists'.

But the Royal Mail was not, by any means, left alone in its new-found glories. The veteran stage-coach was emulating it in all respects. The great days of the coaching era were really just beginning when Hasker, whose tireless efforts had set the standards, if not the pace, retired. Only now did writer and artist begin to see in public coaching matter worthy of record, and only when the great days were gone did the principal authors on the subject write from recollection. They treated it then as a theme of high romance—and so indeed it was. A lingering glow from this ardour makes an annual showing on Christmas cards. But the man who provided the sinews for that glamour is quite forgotten.

John Vidler, who still held the contract for the supply of all mail-coaches, died in 1826, leaving to his daughter, Elizabeth 'all my right and interest in the Mail Coach factory at Millbank'. She had married one Edward Parrott and the firm was now called Vidler and Parrott. Apparently the new bearer of the family name was a younger brother, George Moore Vidler, and he had the say in the policy of the firm when the contract at last came to an end on January the 5th, 1836. In the previous summer, a sudden storm had blown up between a House of Commons Commission of Inquiry and the Post Office, in which Vidler's contract came under heavy fire, and the Commission decided not only that it must not be renewed but that, when put out to public tender, Vidler must be prohibited from bidding. The decision was made in the middle of July and Vidler was told about it. The Post Office, which had not been allowed a say in the matter, was completely taken aback. If the coaches should be withdrawn on the date when the contract expired, how could they possibly be replaced by the successful bidder? Even if the matter were decided immediately, there could barely be time to build and equip such a large number of vehicles. The system had now been extended to the very ends of our earth—from Penzance to Wick—and Vidler's coaches were estimated to travel three thousand miles a day.

They had to go cap in hand to the outraged contractor and beg him to allow them an extension of time. This he refused to do—not by a single minute. Freeling was still Secretary to the Post Office, and now a baronet. He was the last of Palmer's original team and had always held his old chief's memory in loyal affection. He had supported Hasker enthusiastically, for his interest in the mail-coaches had never flagged. Indignant as he was at the maladroit interference of the Commission, he was determined not to stand by and do nothing about the threatened crash of the whole system. He was then in his seventy-second year and nearly worn out by a long and harassing career. But he mustered all his powers and executed a feat equal to

Palmer's boldest stroke. When January the 5th came and Vidler's coaches departed, one and all, for the Millbank Factory, new coaches were waiting ready at every point to 'keep the Duty regular'. From Penzance to Wick not a post was lost. Not only were these vehicles new, they were made according to the latest design, in which mathematician and scientist had worked closely with the coach-builder.

Freed of the old shackles of patent rights and building contract, the mail-coach reached its final stage of perfection, a state also achieved by its emulator the stage-coach which now equalled it in speed and (in several cases) in regularity of timing. It is about this year, 1836, that most has been written and engraved of the coaching era, and it was on Christmas Day in that year that the phenomenal snowstorm swept the land, in which every mail-coach foundered, giving rise to further publicity in print and painting. This time is called the heyday of coaching, but the railway-rot had already set in which was to turn all but one or two mail-coaches off the road within a single decade.

There are excellent accounts of this time by men who knew it when they were young, keen gentlemen-coachmen, accustomed to bribe the professional men to let them drive—even the sacred Mail. From them we hear much about the contractors who horsed these later Mails and, like the coachmen, were of a much superior type to those with whom Hasker had to deal. But among the older names I only find two survivals—the Faggs of the Bell and Crown, Holborn, and Maria Fromont, a daughter or granddaughter of the man who was the butt of so many Haskerian threats. She still kept the King's Head at Thatcham and ran a considerable coaching business and also a large farm. Fromont, himself, had evidently been a great character and independent—so was she. To customers who complained, she had a neater way than the ordinary of making a commonplace observation and would say that 'she didn't care if she could only see them once'.[1]

The railways came and the coaches went, but not the tradition of time-keeping to schedule or the glamour of carrying the Royal Mail. When the transition was first made, the guard of a mail-train was still a Post Office man and rode on a perch near the roof of the mail-van. But the name had long been copied on the stage-coaches, though in that case the man was only a footman and not armed and, so, not

[1] Stanley Harris, *The Coaching Age*, 1885.

guarding. The railway adopted it for the man in charge of the train. Right down into the first quarter of the twentieth century these railway guards wore 'baldricks' with a small pouch attached. I have often asked them what this pouch was for, but they never could tell—certainly they never used it, and I think it was just a smart bit of uniform like a bugler's cords, but derived from the pouch worn by the mail-guard to carry his time-piece in. When the mail-van became a travelling post office, the mail-guard descended from the roof and rode as an 'inside', now dignified with the name of superintendent. He took the time-piece with him. There it is to this day! Every night a time-piece is sent down from the G.P.O. in London and handed 'safe' to the superintendent[1] of a T.P.O.[2] who fills in a time-bill as the train makes its journey. At the end he 'delivers the time-piece safe' to an emissary of the local postmaster. I have been secretly told that it is their wrist-watches, checked by radio time, that they rely on and they don't look at the time-piece from one end of the journey to the other. But that rather enhances than diminishes one's wonder at the force which started so persistent a ritual.

[1] Now called *inspector*.
[2] Travelling Post Office.

A SHORT BIBLIOGRAPHY

Down the Road, C. T. S. Birch Reynardson	1875
Annals of the Road, Captain Malet (in which 'Nimrod's' essays on driving and coaching are included)	1875
Coaching, with Anecdotes of the Road (mainly relating to stage-coaches), Lord William Pitt Lennox	1875
Road Scrapings, M. E. Haworth	1882
Old Coaching Days, Stanley Harris	1882
The Coaching Age, Stanley Harris	1885
Highways and Horses, Athol Maudslay	1888
An Old Coachman's Chatter, Edward Corbett	1890
Coaching Days and Coaching Ways, W. Outram Tristram	1893
A Manuel of Coaching, Farman Rogers	1900
John Palmer, Charles R. Clear	1955
Stage-coach and Mail in Days of Yore, C. G. Harper	1903
The History of the Post Office, Herbert Joyce	1893
The British Post Office, Howard Robinson	1947
The Royal Mail to Ireland, Edward Watson	1917

The printed Reports of Select Committees of the House of Commons (1810–1815) on the Holyhead Road and Mail-coach exemptions contain evidence by Thomas Hasker in characteristic style, also by John Vidler and several contractors, including the only survivor of the original men, John Willan of the Bull and Mouth. The Report of the Select Committee on Railroad Communications (1837–1838) vividly illustrates the enormous difficulties the Post Office had to face at that time. Their position was reversed. Instead of dictating terms to coachmasters who were in competition with each other, they were, themselves, dictated to by a single powerful monopoly. Post Office guards still travelled on a high perch at roof level on the railway-coach, as much exposed to the weather as before, but a rude travelling post office was already in the experimental stage. Time-bills are given which show that although greater speed was obtained punctuality was seldom achieved owing to the constant breakdown of locomotives, obstruction by head-winds and by side-winds 'which drives the flanches of the wheels against the rails' and many other 'impediments'. But the tradition of absolute punctuality, deeply implanted by T. H., asserted itself in due course and that watchword of the Mail was emulated by all concerned on the railway.

INDEX

Aberdeen, 169–70, 183–4

Abergavenny, 72, 164

Abergele, 237

Abingtown, 243

Accidents, and breakdowns, 51, 53, 56, 78, 87–8, 91, 96–7, 99, 168, 173, 181, 208–11, 250

Alconbury Hill, 78, 79, 99–100, 114, 141, 142, 242

Allen, C. (Oxford guard), 94

Allen, Philip, 19

Allen, Ralph, and 'farming' of bye- and cross-posts, 11–13, 14, 16, 19, 21–2, 65, 73, 83

Alnwick, 245

Alresford, 230

Alton, 128, 129

Andover, 178, 180, 231, 250

Andrews, Mr (near Thetford), 199, 201

Annan, 150

Apology, public, for obstructing mail- coach, 57, 262, 270–1, 274

Appleby, 189, 243

Argand, Ami, 213

Aris, the (guard), 158

Arrington, 244

Ashbourne, 240, 241

Ashby, J. (Congleton guard), 173

Ashby de la Zouch, 127

Atherstone, 127, 237

Auckland, William Eden, 1st Baron, 225

Aust-Beachley ferry, 73 n., 204, 206

Axle-box, safety, 43–4

Axle tree, 45, 210

Axminster, 45, 231

Ayr, 259

Bagshot, 36, 132, 179, 181, 184, 230, 231, 249

Baker, Mr (Vidler's foreman), 209, 211

Baldock, 242, 244

Band-brake, 43, 44

Bangor, 238, 283

Bank-notes, cutting in half, 15

Banning, Mr (assistant Deputy P.M., Liverpool), 173–4, 175–7

Barker, W. (guard), 265

Barnaby Moor, 242, 243, 244, 258

Barnet, 114, 141, 237, 238

Barnsley, 241

Basingstoke, 230, 231, 250

Bates, Mr (guard), 275

Bath, 10–11, 13, 14, 17, 22, 35, 71, 75, 83, 187, 232, 234; cross-post to Oxford, 12, 254; stage-coach to London, 15, 17, 170; Palmer its M.P., 37; Mr Pickwick of, 170

Bath Mail, 109–10

Battle, 261

Beattock Summit, 106

Belford, 245

Benson, 25, 63–4, 67–8

Bentley Green, 230

Berwick-on-Tweed, 129, 130, 245

Besant, John, coach-builder, 23, 29, 30, 41, 42–4, 45, 46, 100–1, 255

Biggleswade, 114

Birmingham, 19, 44, 55, 126–7, 235, 236, 237, 256–7; branch services from, 188, 191–7; fish carried to, 213–14

Bishop Burton, 258

Black Book, 56, 94–5

Blandford, 84, 133, 172, 180, 181, 230, 231, 250

Bonnor, Charles (Deputy Comptroller General), 22–3, 24–6, 29–31, 34–8, 39, 40, 46, 47, 49, 63, 64, 66, 68, 79, 92, 255

Boroughbridge, 190, 242, 243, 246

Boulton, Matthew, 44–5

Boulton, Mr (of Golden Cross, Char- ing Cross), 152, 155–6, 157, 161, 182, 184, 185–6, 198, 199–201, 203 n., 238

Bournbridge, 247

Box, coachman's, 42, 45, 46, 95, 223

Bradford and Nott (contractors), 210

Bradley, Christopher (contractor), 205–6, 207
Braithwaite, David (clerk to P.M.G.), 32, 81
Bramham Moor cross-roads, 140–3, 259
Brecknock (Brecon), 70, 71, 72, 164, 165, 166–7
Breechings, 83, 84, 211–12
Brentford, 232, 233, 273
Brickwall, 242
Bridgend, 103
Bridlington, 257, 258
Bridport, 180, 231
Briggs, Mr (Cambridge guard), 216–17
Brighton, 58, 260
Bristol, 11, 12, 22, 29, 55, 70, 71, 75, 126, 204, 234, 252, 254, 256–7; cross-post to Exeter, 12; stage-coach to London, 15, 17; first mail-coach from, 17, 19; Deputy Superintendent at, 49
Bristol Mail, 62, 69, 70–1, 75–6, 93, 159, 192, 208, 220, 233, 239, 270
Bristol Road, 14; first mail-coach on, 17–18, 20, 69, 116
Broadrib, William, 124, 132, 149, 199
Broadwake, 114
Bromley, 260, 261
Bromsgrove, 256
Brown, Johanna ('Mrs John Besant'), 102–3
Bruce, Mr (Leicester contractor), 120
Bruce Castle, Post Office Museum at, 221–5
Bryer, Mrs (contractor), 180
Bugden, 100
Bull and Mouth (coaching-inn), 124
Bunbury, Sir Charles, 150–1
Burford, 254
Burney, Fanny, 28, 83
Burton-in-Kendal, 240
Burton-on-Trent, 127
Bury St Edmunds, 150–1, 217, 247
Bye-letters, 12–13, 18, 20, 114, 177 n., 238, 251, 259
Byng, Hon. John, 58–9, 100

Cadde (helper), 62 n., 223
Calais, 80
Calne, 94, 233

Cambridge, 104, 142, 151, 246, 247
Camden, John Jeffreys Pratt, Baron, 15, 16, 34, 36
Canterbury, 80, 229, 250
Cardiff, 70, 71, 109, 253
Carlisle, 78, 79, 89–90, 100, 118, 150, 243; Deputy Superintendent at, 49, 90, 104, 105; Deputy Postmaster at, 63; second coach to, 100, 113–15
Carlisle Mail, 130, 131, 145, 240–1
Carmarthen, 71, 72, 164–9, 253
Carter, John (first mail-guard), 54, 69–70, 74–5, 98, 107–8, 116–17
Carteret, Lord, 16, 23, 28
Cary, John (map-maker), 2–3, 7, 37, 65, 66–7, 97, 188
Castle Inn, Birmingham, 191, 193, 195, 196
Catterick, 189, 190, 242
Chandler, Mr (guard), 214
Charlton (Deputy Supt. of Mail-Coaches), 49, 84, 85, 136–7, 140, 179, 188, 204–5, 206–7, 215
Chatham, 58
Chatteris, 247
Check-points, 48, 225
Chelmsford, 150
Cheltenham, 70, 254; special mail-coach for royal visit, 25–6, 29, 63, 64, 82
Chester, 12, 19, 149, 203 n., 237, 238
Chester Mail, 4, 103, 189, 191, 196, 272 n.
Chesterfield, 241
Chesterfield, Philip Stanhope, 5th Earl of (Postmaster-General), 28, 31, 32, 35, 36, 49, 185; Hasker's correspondence with, 60–159, 224–6
Chichester, 251
Chorley, 240
Chuck, Mr (Ware contractor), 211
Cirencester, 104, 254
City of Dublin Steam Packet Company, 4, 5–6
Clarendon, Lord, 23
Clarke, Mrs (Grantham contractor), 213
Coachmen, 42, 53, 87, 91; uniforms for, 25, 171–2, 194, 195; box for, 42, 45, 46, 95, 223; relationship with guard, 51, 54, 55, 95–6, 216, 276; hard-drinking, 54, 283; 'ground'

of, 61; and overturning, 87, 91, 99; tips for, 184, 186–7; difficulty in making living, 186, 197; coachman-guard, 193, 194; new generation of, 283, 285

Coal, tax on, 18

Colchester, 110, 155, 161, 162, 163, 184, 185–6, 198, 199, 248

Coldwell, Mr (Norwich book-keeper), 202

Coleshill, 238, 239

Colney, 241

Commissioners of the Peace, 112–13

Congleton, 239

Contractors: 'ground' of, 41, 61; inn-keepers or, 42, 89–90, 178, 193, 226, 265–6; as distinct from proprietors, 61; 'voluntary' contributions from, 63; notice to quit, 119–20, 124, 126; subsidising of, 155–7, 161, 182; Hasker's criticism and prodding of, 161, 163–4, 167–9, 189, 206–7, 211; instructions to, 179–80, 192–204, 268, 271; power to inspect mail-box, 265, 270, 276

Conway, 238

Cook, Thomas (coachman), 87, 91, 99

Cooper, Mr (Preston postmaster), 96, 120–1, 139–40

Cork, Merchants of, 71, 164, 168

Corn, scarcity of, 130–2

Corsham, 251

Counties, indictment of, 112, 153–4

Country letters, 11, 12

Coupling reins, 52

Coventry, 236, 238, 239

Cowbridge, 253

Cox, Mr (guard), 275

Cross-post letters, 12–13, 18, 19, 20, 77, 88 n., 149, 250–62

Crouse, Mr (Norwich contractor), 152, 155, 182, 184, 185, 190, 198, 199, 201–2, 203

Cullompton, 119, 232

Cuxhaven, 148, 151, 162

Danders, Mrs (office cleaner), 88

Darlington, 245

Davies, Ashton, 6

Davis, Major General J., 186–7

De Quincey, Thomas, 1, 2, 3, 9, 46–7, 87

Dead letters, 88

Delivery times of, 20; delay owing to checks on pricing, 33–4, 35; delay on Norwich Mail, 200

Demezy, Mr (contractor), 121, 133–4, 158, 172, 179

Derby, 240, 241; deputy postmaster at, 63

Devenport, G. W. P., 221

Dibbin, Mr (Thatcham postmaster), 171

Dickens, Charles, 170

Diligence, 255; Portpatrick, 89, 115–16, 150; Walsall, 127; Wisbeach-Cambridge, 151

Dinwoodie Green, 243

Dispatch, times of, 20; delays in, 143–4

Donaghadee, 28, 89

Doncaster, 117, 242, 244, 245

Dorchester, 137, 231, 252

Dover, 19, 58, 148, 172, 229

Dover Mail, 80–1, 97–8, 148, 211

Drunkenness, 54, 69, 107, 116, 265, 268, 269, 270, 273, 275

Drysdale, Mr (Edinburgh innkeeper), 169–70, 184

Dublin, 5, 89, 90

Dumfries, 28, 90, 105, 150, 277

Dunbar, 245

Dundee, 183

Dunhill, Mr (Doncaster postmaster), 117

Dunstable, 240, 241

Durham, 245

East Grinstead, 260

East India Company, 110

Eaton, 242, 243

Ecclefeckan, 243

Eccleshall, 237

Edinburgh, 77, 145, 169, 170, 183–4, 237

Edinburgh Mail, 110, 111, 114, 142, 169, 244–6

Edwards, Mr (surveyor), 150, 169–70

Egham, 120–1, 134–5, 139–40, 180, 249, 250

Emanuel William, (Oxford guard), 94

English Mail-Coach, The (De Quincey), 1, 46–7

Enstone, 235

Exeter, 19, 45, 110, 126, 187, 218, 231, 232; cross-post to Bristol, 12

Exeter Mail, 44–5, 65, 88, 108, 110, 134, 139, 158, 178, 209, 220, 270

Express post, 162, 163, 275

Fagan, Mr (guard), 275

Fagg, Thomas (contractor), 216, 269, 285

Fairford, 254

Falmouth, 29, 148, 232

Faringdon, 254

Felton, 245

Fennel, Mr (guard), 171

Fenton, F. (curator, Bruce Castle), 222

Ferries, 73, 159, 164, 204–6, 238, 252–3, 283

Ferrybridge, 79, 105, 108, 115, 117, 142, 242, 243, 244, 245, 264

Field, W. (guard), 265

Firearms, 20, 41, 58, 124, 263; cleaning of, 124, 149, 199; issued to horse-posts, 149, 151 n.; misuse of, 173–5, 280–1; dismissed for not carrying, 265; loading of, 280–1

Flushing, 80, 81

Foot-posts, 220

Foreign mail, 29, 77, 80, 98, 107, 110, 148, 151–2, 162–3, 231–2

Forster, Mr (Norwich contractor), 184, 186, 197–200, 201

Franking, 123

Freeling, Sir Francis, 71, 92, 107, 121, 122, 190, 208; as Resident Surveyor, 22, 27, 28, 29, 36, 37, 40, 112, 114; as Secretary, 63, 102, 105, 165, 197, 273, 280, 284; arms horse-posts, 149, 151 n.

Fromont, Mr (of King's Head, Thatcham), 17, 76, 119, 122, 123, 171, 285

Fromont, Maria, 76, 285

Funeral expenses, 50, 117

Galloway, 28, 89, 150

General Post Office, 7–8, 11, 17, 58, 179, 212, 286; early closing of, 20; late mails from, 143–4

George III, King, special coach service for, 25, 26, 27, 63, 82–8, 125, 133, 134–5, 178–81, 188

Glasgow, 37, 90, 100, 106, 108, 113,

237, 259; riding-post from Edinburgh, 79, 169; and road repairs, 144–6

Glasgow Mail, 114, 141–2, 145, 189, 242–4

Gloucester, 70, 71–2, 73, 164, 165, 254–5, 256; deputy postmaster at, 63

Gloucester Coffee House, 58, 69, 79, 123–4, 220, 230, 232, 233

Gloucester Lodge (near Windsor) 133; (at Weymouth), 83, 133 n., 180

Golden Cross, Charing Cross, 156 n., 170, 238

Gosport, 128

Grantham, 242, 243, 244, 245

Great North Road, 14, 19, 74, 78, 100, 114

Green, Mr (Norwich contractor), 186, 197, 199

Greta Bridge, 243

Greville, Hon. Charles Francis, 74, 158–9, 164–7, 182–3, 204

'Ground', distance travelled by guard, 53, 56, 61–2

Guppy, John (coachman), 99

Hackney, toll-gate, 82

Haddington, 245

Halifax, 259

Hamboro (Hamburg) Mail, 98, 148, 151–2, 162–4

Hamilton, Sir William, 74, 159

Hammersmith toll-gate, 81

Hampack, Captain Colin, 157

Hancock, John (guard), 218–20

Hardwick, Lord, 244

Hare, Mr (Taunton contractor), 119, 120, 124–5, 178, 187

Harewood, 141

Harness, 83, 84, 211–12

Harris, Stanley (quoted), 58, 285

Harris, Mr (guard), 191

Harwich, 80, 81, 98, 151, 153

Hasker, Thomas, 2, 3, 25, 45, 53; at trial of Cary, 3, 67; his correspondence, 7–9, 17, 19, 49, 60, et seq.; appointed Superintendent of Mail-Coaches, 22; and Palmer's mail-coach plan, 29, 39, 47; promoted Surveyor and Superintendent of the Mail Coaches, 36–7, 39–40;

allowed five Deputies, 49; high standards, 55–6, 216–17; his task and methods, 59, 60; his spelling, 61; gingering up of contractors, 64–5, 119–20, 160, 197–204, 206–7; tactics with 'Memorialists', 70–3, 78–9, 126–9, 149–52; humanity, 88, 102–3, 107, 117, 281, 282; appeals for salary increases to staff, 105–6, 138–9, 154; reserves right to appoint own men, 118–19, 182–3; subsidised contractors, 155–7, 161, 182; plans expansion of service, 169–70, 183–4; instructions and circulars, 262–81; retires, 283

Hastings, 260–1
Hatfield, 79, 114
Havant, 251
Haverfordwest, 253, 277
Hawkins, Thomas (guard), 94
Heath, Nott and Co. (coachmasters), 166, 167, 168, 204
Hedge, Mr (Yarmouth contractor), 163–4
Henley, 235
Henson, Mr (guard), 191
Hereford, 255
Hertford, 113–14
Highways Act (1555), 112
Hill, Rowland, 222, 224
Hill, Thomas (guard), 208
Hinckley, 237, 238
Hockerill, 247
Hockley Heath, 235
Hoddesden, 114
Holmes, Mr (of Alconbury Hill), 99–100, 114
Holyhead, 19, 238
Holyhead Mail, 3, 4, 48, 189, 283
Holywell, 237
Honiton, 231
Hopkins, J. (guard), 214, 217
Horn-blowing, banned during divine service, 273
Horse-posts (riding-posts), 16, 18, 19, 20, 79, 220, 255; arming of, 149, 151 n.
Horses: hiring of, under relay system, 13–14, 17; changing of, 16, 52–3, 234, 278; harness of, 83–4, 211–12; underfeeding of, 102, 144; tax on, 116, 272; provender for, 130–1, 144,

269; extra, for Royal Weymouth Mail, 178–81; taken by appraisement, 197; taken by arbitration, 200; breed of, 282, 283
Howarth, Mr (contractor), 189
Hubberston, 74
Hull, cross-post to Liverpool, 77, 258–9
Hulton Lane, 240
Huntingdon, 78, 100, 111, 114, 142, 244, 245, 246

Ice, removal of, 117–18
Indictment of parishes and counties, 112, 113, 126, 153
Inglestone (Ingatestone), 185, 186
Inland Post Office, 23, 39; senior clerks of (Presidents), 108, 109, 110, 144
Innkeepers, 14, 17, 42, 62, 89–90, 99, 100, 114, 120, 158–9, 165, 170, 178, 183, 193, 226, 265–6
Inverbervie, 183
Ipswich, 155, 162, 164, 184, 185, 198, 199, 200, 203 n., 248, 249
Ipswich Mail, 110, 113, 150, 161, 199, 209
Ireland, 4–6, 25, 28, 30, 71, 72, 88–90
Irish Day Express, 5
Irish Mail, 3–6
Irish Post Office, 89, 282

Jackson, the (Exeter postmaster), 218, 219
Jeffs, John (guard), 104
Joblin, William (guard), 265
Jockey Club, 150
Johnson, Charles, 283
Johnson, Mr (Gravesend postmaster), 107
Johnson, Mr (Manchester guard), 177
Joyce, Herbert (quoted), 32, 34, 57, 73, 147

Kelly, J. (Lancaster guard), 177, 215, 275; R., 215
Kendal, 240, 241
Kew, 83, 84, 179
Kiddal Lane End, 141
Kilmarnock, 259
King's Messengers, 85–6, 125, 131
Kingstown, 5
Kitchen, T. (guard), 271
Knutsford, 149, 239

Lamberhurst, 261
Lamps and oil, 41, 52, 140, 173, 212–13
Lancaster, 177, 215, 240, 241
Lathbury, 237
Lathom, Mr (Ware contractor), 120
Laverock Hall, 243
Lawless, J. (Deputy Supt. of Mail-
    Coaches), 49, 179, 184–5, 198, 199,
    200, 215, 216
Lawrence, Robert of Shrewsbury, 58,
    226, 282
Lawrence Kirk, 183
Leading-bar, 52, 210 n.
Ledbury, 255
Leeds, 19, 141, 142, 237, 258, 259
Leeds Mail, 130, 131, 153, 241–2
Leek, 240
Leeming Lane, 190, 191, 242
Leicester, 120, 240, 241, 242
Leicester, George Townshend, Earl of,
    joint Postmaster-General, 2, 49;
    Hasker's correspondence with, 60,
    et seq.
Letter Carriers, 111
Levi, Mr (contractor), 130–1
Lichfield, 188, 195, 196, 197, 237, 239,
    257
Lisbon, 148, 231–2
Littleborough, 259
Liverpool, 19, 76, 239; cross-post to
    Hull, 77, 258–9; Postmaster of,
    174–7
Liverpool Mail, 4, 126–7, 140, 141, 191,
    240, 274
Livery, 46–7, 57
Llandilo, 72, 164
Llandovery, 72, 164, 166
Lock-release, 43, 44
London, Midland and Scottish Rail-
    way, 6
London and North-Western Railway,
    4–5
London Tavern, 20, 33, 35
Long bar, 181, 210
Long coach, 134, 135
Longfellow, Mr (coach-proprietor),
    165–6, 168
Longman, Messrs (publishers), 66, 67
Longtown, 243
Loughborough, 241
Ludlow, 256
Lutterworth, 237

Lymington, 251–2
Lyndhurst, 252

MacAdam, John Loudoun, 282
Macclesfield, 119, 240
Mail-boats—see Packets.
Mail-box, 42, 45, 50, 78–9, 272; lock-
    ing of, 50, 55, 78, 94, 95, 206, 264,
    273; immunity from search, 55; in-
    creased size, 78, 135; contractors
    allowed to search, 265, 270, 276
Mail-cart, one-horse, 19–20, 21, 220
Mail-coaches: tokens, motto on, 3;
    frailty of, 23; early patents, 23, 29,
    40, 41, 42–7, 77, 102, 103, 123, 133;
    Millbank manufactory, 30, 41, 51,
    118, 209, 210, 216, 284; new, 45,
    123, 133, 134–5, 212, 285; livery of,
    46–7, 135; maintenance and servic-
    ing, 47, 119, 138, 208–11; gear of,
    52–3; roof-loading on, 55, 78, 122,
    188, 205, 265, 271; priority over
    civilian traffic, 57–8, 96–7; weight
    of, 78, 121, 133, 134; weight of
    mail carried, 78, 123; stage-coaches
    as auxiliary, 128, 162, 193, 232;
    repairs to, 208–11; spare parts,
    208–9; absence of brakes, 212;
    improved design of 1836, 212, 285;
    lost, 266–7, 285
Mail-coach services: Palmer's propo-
    sals, 7, 8–9, 15, 16–17, 21; first (from
    Bristol), 17–18, 20, 69, 116; speed
    of, 18, 20, 22, 112, 283, 285; subse-
    quent programme, 19; dislocation
    caused by, 20–1; charges for—see
    Mileage Rates, Postage; organisa-
    tion, 39–40, 47–9, 56, 59; by branch
    diligence, 127, 193; economies in
    Scottish, 146–7; express, 162–3, 275;
    routes of, 229–61; improvements in,
    282–6; time-bills of:
        Birmingham and Bristol, 75, 159,
            191, 256–7
        Bristol to Milford, 19, 70, 109,
            119, 189, 204–7, 252–4; (second
            service), 164–8, 223
        Bristol and Portsmouth, 19
        Canterbury and Margate, 250
        Carlisle and Portpatrick, 88, 89,
            115, 130, 160
        Glasgow and Ayr, 259–60

Hereford and Worcester, 255-6
Hull and Liverpool (via York), 76, 140, 175-7, 189, 258-9
Lichfield and Birmingham, 195-7
London to Bath and Bristol, 17, 29, 75, 76, 81, 93, 109, 116, 119, 220, 233-4
London to Birmingham, 236-7
London to Carlisle, 90, 100, 113-14, 130, 240-1
London to Chester and Holyhead, 19, 103, 189, 191, 196, 237-8
London to Dover, 19, 80, 107, 229; (foreign), 80, 97, 107, 116
London to Edinburgh (via York), 77, 78, 104, 110, 111, 114, 141, 169, 244-6
London to Exeter (via Bath), 75, 76, 81, 119, 232-3; (Lisbon Mail), 148, 231-2; (via Salisbury), 19, 65, 81, 88, 108, 134, 137, 158, 220, 230-1
London to Glasgow, 89 n., 90, 100, 106, 113-14, 118, 145, 189, 190, 224, 242-4
London and Hastings, 260-1
London to Leeds, 19, 130, 153, 241-2
London to Liverpool, 19, 126, 191, 238-9
London to Norwich (via Ipswich), 82, 111, 113, 155, 162-3, 182, 184, 185, 197, 248; (via Newmarket), 19, 82, 105, 155, 182, 247-8
London to Poole, 81, 128, 216, 230
London to Portsmouth, 19, 29, 81, 125, 128, 229
London to Shrewsbury, 19, 81, 127, 189, 191, 235-6
London and Steyning, 260
London to Wisbeach, Cambridge and Bury, 105, 151, 189, 246-7
London to Worcester, 94, 235
London to Yarmouth (auxiliary), 162, 197, 249
Ludlow and Worcester, 94, 256
Oxford to Bristol, 75, 103, 126, 170, 254
Oxford to Gloucester, 41, 254-5
Portsmouth to Chichester, 251

Royal Weymouth (London to Weymouth), 65, 77, 82, 88, 91, 92, 99, 120, 125, 131, 132-40, 158, 172, 178-81, 188, 249-50
Southampton to Lymington, 251-2
Walsall and Birmingham, 191-7
Weymouth and Dorchester, 137, 252
York to Scarborough and Whitby, 138, 257-8.
See also Bath Mail; Bristol Mail, etc.
Mail-coach Stone, 168
Mail-guards, 19, 42, 206, 210; first (on Bristol Road), 19, 69-70, 98, 107-8, 116-17; unofficial, 20; duties of, 50-1; pay, 50, 58, 92, 117; training, 51-3, 56; trials and temptations, 53-5; 'wangles' of, 54-5, 213-16, 270; enlistment of, 56, 182-3, 216-17; extra, 56, 58, 107; uniform, 58-9, 172; 'ground' of, 61-2; pay for extra duty, 92; discipline, 94-5, 118; instructions to, 94-5, 190, 191, 223, 239, 263-5, 266-81; awards for valour, 103-4; relieved of cleaning firearms, 124; tips for, 130; firearms misused by, 173-5, 280-1; coachman-guard, 193, 194; suspended for having no lamps, 213; not exempt from military service, 217; suspended for overcharging, 218-20; free pass for wives of, 223; warnings to, 264-5, 269, 275; passengers' complaints of, 272-3; medical attention for, 281, 282
Mail-trains, 285-6
Main-bar, 52, 210 n.
Malton, 138, 257, 258
Manchester, 19, 105, 119, 120, 149, 177, 203 n., 237, 240, 241, 259; Deputy Superintendent at, 49, 174
Mansfield, 241
Margate, 250
Marlborough, 17, 19, 69, 94, 107, 108, 116, 178, 232, 233
Marmont, Mr (of Pyle), 168-9, 206
Mathews, J. (guard), 126
Meals, stops for, 54, 189-90, 230 et seq.
Melksham, 232
Menai Straits, 283
Mercury (stage-coach), 139

Merrick, Mr (guard), 214
Middlewich, 127
Mile: statute and Post Office, 65-6, 97
Mile End toll-gate, 82
Mileage rates, 28, 41, 66, 67, 79, 88-9, 97, 115, 129, 134, 145, 150, 151, 155-6, 161, 170, 183, 193
Mileage warrants, 149, 182, 268-9
Miles' Patent Coach Lamp, 213
Milford Haven, 19, 70-1, 73-4, 205, 253
Milford Mail, 19, 70-4, 109, 189, 204-7, 252-4
Military service, exemption from, 77, 217
Millbank, Vidler's coach factory at, 30, 41, 51, 118, 209, 210, 216, 284
Moffat, 243
Moffatt, Mr (guard), 275
Monk, Edward (carter), 274
Monmouth, 70, 72
Montrose, 183
Moreton-in-Marsh, 235
Morpeth, 245
Morton, W. V., 222, 224, 225
Mousehill, 229
Muirkirk, 90
Murrell, Mr (Deputy Supt. of Mail-Coaches), 49, 174, 209, 215

Nant Ffrancon Pass, 283
Nantwich, 237
Nayland, 110
Needle, Mr (? Gloucester Coffee House porter), 122, 123-4
Nelson, Lord, 276
Nettlebed, 70
New Itinerary of the Great Roads of England and Wales (Cary), 2-3, 7, 37, 65, 66, 97, 188
New Passage ferry, 73, 159, 164, 204-6, 252-3
Newark, 242, 244, 245
Newbury, 75, 77
Newcastle-on-Tyne, 104, 108, 245
Newcastle-under-Lyme, 128, 239
Newmarket Heath, 104, 151, 155, 247, 248
Newport (Mon.), 206, 207, 256
Nicholas, H. (clerk), 49, 85, 86, 109, 135, 138, 154, 161, 218-19
Nicholas, Mrs, 92-3

Nicholls, S. (Manchester guard), 172
Northallerton, 245
Northampton, 48, 49, 82, 92, 237, 238, 240, 241, 242; road repair, 153
Northleach, 254
Northwich, 127, 280
Norwich, 19, 111, 155, 156, 198, 200, 202, 203 n.; Deputy Superintendent at, 49
Norwich Mail, 19, 105, 113, 161, 162-3, 182, 197-204, 215, 247-8
Noseworthy, Mr (Cullompton contractor), 119
Nottingham, 241, 242

Ogilby, John (map-maker), 65-6, 113
Old North Road, 77, 100, 114
Old Passage ferry, 204, 205
Oliphant, Robert (Deputy P.M.G.), 27-8
Omnibus, forerunner of, 135
Ostend, 80
Overtaking, 96-7
Overton, 230, 231
Oxford, 70, 71, 104, 209, 235, 255; cross-post to Bath, 12, 254

Packets and packet-stations: Dover, 80-1, 98, 148; Falmouth, 110, 148, 232; Harwich, 81, 151, 153; Holy-head, 4-6; Milford Haven, 73, 165; Portpatrick, 28, 89; Yarmouth, 148, 151, 157, 162
Painter, Mr (guard), 275
Palmer, John, 1-2, 7, 50, 62, 63, 73, 74, 138, 255; theatrical interests, 10-11, 16, 22; his scheme for mail-coaches, 15-17, 34, 112, 284; opposition to, 19-20, 28-9; becomes Surveyor and Comptroller General, 21-2; clash with Walsingham, 25-6, 28, 33, 82, 88, 117; tries to reform Scottish post, 27-8; intrigue against, 29-32, 35-6; suspended, 34; dismissed, 36-7, 39; on patent-coach contract, 40-1; and schedule time, 47-8; shortens stages, 66; introduces pension scheme, 117
Parcels, 82; carried by stage-coach, 15; illicit traffic in, 54-5, 121-3, 213-16, 265, 268, 275, 276, 278-9; perishable, 55, 213-16, 265, 270,

275; on Royal Weymouth Mail, 82, 85; decrease in, 152; prohibited, 262

Parishes, indictment of, 112

Parkin, Anthony (Solicitor to Post Office), 63, 111, 112, 113, 126

Parkins, William (drayman), 270–1

Parrott, Edward, 284

Passengers, 15, 54, 58, 152; 'outside', 42, 53, 189, 193, 223, 271; unlimited on stage-coach, 42; complain of delay, 144; complain of being forced to tip, 186–7; 'swallowing' of, 187; fares withheld by coachmen, 187, 269–70, 276; procrastinating, 189–90; surplus and unauthorised, 268, 271, 272, 275, 276; complain of guards' conduct, 272

Paterson, Mr (contractor), 189

Patterson, David, 2, 37, 66

Peach, Mr (Leeds contractor), 126

Pendleton, S. (Liverpool guard), 94

Penrith, 240, 243

Pension, 50, 117

Perambulator, 3, 65, 222

Perch, 45, 52; Perch-bolt, 211

Perishables, transport of, 55, 213–16, 265, 270

Perks, Mr (Walsall coachmaster), 193, 194–5, 196

Petersfield, 229

Pickering, 258

Pickergill, Mr, private bag, 188, 190–1

Pickford, Mr (contractor), 119, 120

Pickwick, Moses (coachmaker), 170–1

Piddletown (now Puddletown), 84, 178, 179, 180, 250

Pitt, William, 15–17, 18–19, 29, 30, 33, 34–5, 36, 147, 149

Plouman, Mr (guard), 213

Plymouth, 29

Pole-chains, 52

Poole, 128, 230

Portland, 3rd Duke of, 125

Portpatrick, 28, 88–90, 115–16, 150

Portsmouth, 19, 29, 46 n., 125, 128, 129, 229, 251

Postage: evasion of, 14, 15, 121–3; increased rate, 18, 21, 28–9, 66–7, 88, 97; basis of, 28–9, 66, 88–90, 97, 145, 170, 183; surcharge for Scotland, 146

Post-boys, 12, 14, 15, 39, 66, 89 n., 111; arming of, 149

Post-chaise, 11, 51, 75, 89, 90

Post-houses, 13–14, 17; stages between, 66

Postmasters, 172; and bye-letters, 12; and early mail system, 13–14, 18; deputy, 33, 42, 62, 63–4; innkeepers as, 42; and time-piece checks, 48; poorly paid, 63–4, 68; and false time-bills, 137–8

Postmasters-General: and appointment of staff, 21–2; duality of post, 23; appointment a sinecure, 31–2; Hasker's letters to, 60–159

Post Office: and road survey, 2–3, 37, 66–7, 97; reluctant to adopt Palmer's scheme, 8–9, 16, 17–18, 19–21, 32; and 'farming' of bye- and cross-post letters, 11–13; Palmer's appointment in, 21–2; irregularities in, 24, 25, 29–31; Palmer dismissed from, 36–7, 263; Hasker's work in, 36 *et seq.*; standard mile of, 65–6; uniform of, 68–9, 79, 171–2; Surveyors of, 111–12, 172, 192; and indictments, 112, 126, 153; not responsible for road repairs, 145, 146; cuts Scottish mail services, 146

Post Office Act (1711), 21, 33

Post Office Act (1765), 14

Prepayment, 33

Presidents (Inland Office senior clerks), 108, 109, 110, 144

Press, 245

Press gang, 76–7

Preston, 240, 241

Pricing, checks on, 33

Princess Royal (stage-coach), 100, 113

Priority, over civilian traffic, 57–8, 96–7

Private bag, 188, 190–1

Proprietors: as distinct from contractors, 61; circulars to, 275, 278, 279

Provender, 130–2, 144

Punctuality, 47, 86, 266–7, 278, 288

Quarter Days, 120

Raglan, 72

Raper, John (guard), 117, 264

Redbourne, 236, 238, 240

Rees, John (guard), 103
Relay system, 13–14
Renham, Mr (contractor), 211
Repairs, 56, 181, 208–10
Reynolds, Richard, 18 n.
Rider (mail-girl), 14 n., 256
Riding posts—*see* Horse-posts.
Ringwood, 230
Roach, Mr (Norwich postmaster), 202
Roads: measurement of, 3, 13, 37, 65–6, 67, 97, 222; state of, 104–5, 106, 108, 109, 110–13, 117, 127, 144–5, 154, 206–7, 259; upkeep of, 112–13, 145–6, 153–4; improvements in, 282–3
Robberies, 15, 16, 93–6, 149, 263, 272, 277; attempted, 277, 280
Roberts, Mr (Yarmouth sub-contractor), 152–3, 155–7, 161, 199, 200–1, 203
Rochester, 209, 229
Rockcliff, 103
Roller-bolts, 52
Rose, Mr (Bury St Edmunds postmaster), 217
Ross-on-Wye, 72, 164
Rowning, Mr (Newmarket contractor), 199
Royal monopoly, 14, 57
Royston, 77, 244, 245, 246
Rushyford, 245

St Albans, 237
St Asaph, 237
St Ives (Hunts), 247
St Martin's le Grand, 7, 221
Saddle-pads, 52
Salisbury, 65, 88, 92, 158, 178, 180, 209, 230, 231, 250
Sandbach, 127
Sandwich, Lord, 99–100, 114, 115
Sanquhar, 90
Saracen's Head inn, Birmingham, 193, 196
Sargeant, William, 68
Scarborough, 138, 257, 258
Scole Inn, 215, 248
Scotland, 25; postal reforms in, 27–8; turnpikes, 82, 146; hard weather in, 104, 106, 108, 129–30; road development in, 146; surcharge on postage, 146

Seaman, R. (Yarmouth postmaster), 152
Sevenoaks, 261
Severn estuary, 73, 164
Shaftesbury, 231
Shap, 240
Sheffield, 241
Shelburne, Lord, 15, 16
Shergold, Mr (Salisbury contractor), 180
Sheridan, R. B., 16 n.
Shifnal, 226, 236
Shipston-on-Stour, 235
Shoreditch toll-gate, 82
'Shouldering' practice, 187
Shrewsbury, 19, 58, 226, 236, 280
Shrewsbury Mail, 58, 81, 127, 189, 191, 209, 226
Shrubles, Mr (Benson postmaster), 63–4, 68, 125
Shugden, Mr (guard), 210
Sibley, Mr (of Bell, Stilton), 114, 115
Sick-benefit, 50, 117
Sluys, 80, 81
Smallberry ('Smallboro') Green, 81, 82
Smuggling, 55, 77, 153, 278–9
Snowstorm, phenomenal (Christmas Day, 1836), 285
South Wales, 108–10; plea for additional coach, 158–9, 204
South Wales Association, 166, 168–9, 204–7
Southall toll-gate, 82
Southampton, 230, 251–2; deputy postmaster at, 63
Speed: of early posts, 14, 17; of stage-coaches, 15, 16, 17
Sperink, John (coachman), 269–70
Spittal Beck, 257
Spittal Inn, 243
Splinter-bar, 52
Springs, 43, 46, 210
Staff, of Mail Coach establishment, 49, 59, 84, 88, 92–3, 124, 199; applications for increased salary refused, 105–6, 138–9, 154
Stafford, 237, 238
Stage (distance), 66
Stage-coaches: competition of, 15, 42, 47, 59, 78, 113, 152, 155–6, 196, 200–4, 283–4; accidents to, 43; and

parcels, 54; proprietors of, 61; distance of stage, 62; racing between, 97; proposed as auxiliary mail-coach, 128–9, 232

Staines, 230, 231

Stamford, 114, 118, 142, 242, 243, 244

Stanroyd, Mr (Bristol guard), 75–6, 77, 111

Stark, Mr (of Gloucester Coffee House), 68–9

Statham, Mr (Liverpool postmaster), 174

Steelyard (weighing-machine), 133, 134

Steering-gear, 52

Steyning, 260

Stilton, 100, 114, 242, 244

Stone, 126, 191, 239

Stony Stratford, 94, 236, 238, 239

Strap-bags, 177 n.

Stratford-on-Avon, 235

Stratford St Mary, 110, 111, 113

Sturdy, Anthony, 118

Sudbury, 150

Surveyor and Comptroller of the Inland Office, post of, 36, 39

Surveyor and Comptroller General of the Post Office: Palmer appointed, 21; post modified, 36

Surveyors: Cary's, 3, 37, 65, 67; Allen's, 13; oppose use of mail-coaches, 16, 32; of Highways, 111–12; allowed a guard, 172

Swan with Two Necks (coaching inn), 17, 25, 161, 238

Swansea, 70, 71, 72, 109, 159, 165, 166, 253

Sway-bar, 52

Sweetman, Thomas (guard), 103–4

Tadcaster, 245, 258

Tankerville, Lord, 16

Tarporley, 237

Taunton, 119, 178, 187, 232

Taylor, James (guard), 104

Telegraph (stage-coach), 46, 152, 201

Telegraph spring, 46

Telford, Thomas, 4, 9, 146, 282–3

Terrets, 52

Tetbury, 256, 275

Tewkesbury, 256

Thatcham, 17, 75–6, 94, 109, 110, 232, 233, 234, 285

Thetford, 248

Thomas, Thomas (mail-coach robber), 93–5

Thompson, Mr (Exeter contractor), 119

Thormanby, 245

Thornbury, 159

Time: local and clock, 47, 239, 242; schedule, 48; for changing horses, 53, 234, 263, 278; for meals, 54, 189–90, 230 *et seq.*; Royal Weymouth Mail and, 86–7; punctuality important, 47, 86, 266–7, 278, 288

Time-bills, 48, 53; short, 58, 236–7, 246; falsifying of, 137–8; discovery of, in Bruce Castle, 224–6; list of, 227–61

Time-piece, 47–8, 242; regulation of, 136–7, 225, 239, 250; manufacture of, 175–7; on mail-trains, 286

Tips, 58, 186–7, 198

Todd, Anthony (Secretary of the Post Office), 19, 21, 31, 62, 70, 122

Tokens, motto on, 3

Tolls, 42, 57, 75, 81–2, 112, 145–6, 150

Tools and spares, 208–9

Torrington Diaries, 14 n., 100

Traces, 52

Travelling-post, 14

Trent Bridge, 117, 154

Turnpikes, 9, 14, 15, 42, 57, 66, 82, 112, 146, 150, 267, 282

Tuxford, 242

Tybach, 253

Uniform, 58–9, 68–9, 79, 123, 171–2, 195

Union of Post Office Workers, 222

Uttoxeter, 127, 128

Uxbridge, 235

Vails (tips), 58, 186–7

Valour, awards for, 103–4

Vansittart, Nicholas (later Baron Bexley), 147

Vernon, Henry, 3rd Baron, 127

Vidler, Elizabeth, 284

Vidler, George Moore, 284

Vidler, John (coach-builder), 30, 31, 41, 56, 69, 100–1, 118, 119, 134, 135–6, 138, 171, 180–1, 209, 210, 271, 284–5, 287

Waddell, Mr (of Castle Hotel, Birmingham), 61, 191–7, 214
Wade, General, 11
Waldron, J. (Liverpool guard), 173–4
Walsall, 126, 127, 188
Walsall Mail, 191–7
Walsingham, Thomas de Grey, 2nd Baron (Postmaster-General), 23–4, 25, 26, 28–9, 30–3, 35, 37, 40, 49, 63, 66, 82, 83, 88, 89, 138, 150
Waltham Cross, 244, 246
Ware, 77, 114, 120, 244, 246
Ware, Mr (Bridport contractor), 180, 218, 219
Warmington, Mr (Post Office Packet-agent), 152, 164
Warren, Thomas, 57
Warrington, 127, 173, 239, 240, 259, 280
Waterford, 71, 73, 253
Waterhouse, Mr (contractor), 161, 184, 186, 197–200, 201
Waters, H. (guard), 215
Watson, Mr (Crouse's right-hand man), 197–8, 201, 203–4
Watt, James, 45
Way-bill, 255–6
Weeks, Mr (Salisbury contractor), 65, 84, 87–8, 91, 99, 120, 121, 159, 172, 180
Weighing-machine, 133, 134
Welford, 237
Wells, 187, 232
Welwyn Green, 274
West India Mail, 109–10, 220
West Road, 121
Wetherby, 140–2, 242
Weymouth, 27, 185, 186, 252; Royal Weymouth Mail—see under Mail-coach Services
Wheels, 43–5, 209–10; brakes for, 212, 223; breadth of, on turnpike roads, 267–8

Whetstone, 242
Whitby, 138, 252, 258
White, J. (clerk), 49, 68, 84, 138, 154, 173, 179, 209–10, 216, 218
White, Mr (guard), 190
White, Mr (Staines contractor), 83
Wilkins, S. (Deputy Supt. of Mail-Coaches), 22, 49, 83–4, 88, 91, 104, 105, 108, 110, 114, 130, 159, 178, 179, 189, 215; letters to, 192–7, 215
Willan, John (contractor), 78, 91, 276, 287
Williams, L. (guard), 94
Willoughby, Sir Christopher, 153
Wilson, Mr (of Swan with Two Necks), 17, 25, 26–7, 61, 63, 64, 68, 69, 91, 123, 125, 131–2, 133, 134, 152, 155, 157, 180, 182, 185, 189, 198, 199–201, 203 n.; Hasker's letters to, 161, 179, 184, 190, 220
Wimpole Hall, 244 n.
Winchester, 129
Windsor, 83, 84, 85, 86, 121, 125, 132, 135, 139–40, 181
Wisbeach Mail, 105, 151, 189, 246–7
Witham, 161, 248, 249; Common, 244
Witney, 254
Wolsey Bridge, 237, 239
Wolverhampton, 236, 239
Wood, W. (Blandford contractor), 172, 180
Woodbridge, 133
Woodyeats, 230, 231, 250
Woolmer, W. (Deputy Supt. of Mail-Coaches), 22, 49, 89, 90, 104–6, 108, 145, 170, 183, 215
Worcester, 12, 19, 235, 254, 255–6, 257
Wycombe, 235

Yarmouth, 111, 151, 152–3, 157, 162–4, 203 n.
Yarmouth Mail, 197, 249
Yate, 159
York, 77, 138, 141, 142, 245, 246, 257–8, 259, 265; time-pieces at, 175–6, 177
York Mail, 77–9, 114, 135, 140–2, 175–7, 244, 274, 276
Yoxford, 152, 249